Hitler's Chariots Volume Three

VW Beetle license plate III 43007 on display at Bietigheim, outside the motor city of Stüttgart, headquarters of Daimler-Benz. Note the cut out twin rear windows, the louvres below them, and the light fixture atop the license plate. (VW Museum, Stüttgart.)

Hitler's Chariots

Vol 3

Volkswagen
from Nazi People's Car to New Beetle

Blaine Taylor

Schiffer Military History
Atglen, PA

Dedication

To my father, Raymond Bernard Taylor, and my four stepfathers: "Jack" Seymour Katz; Arthur DiLoreto, Jr.; Burnell David Chronister; and Philip Sgroi, all deceased. Each played a vital role in forming the current product.

Acknowledgments

Stan Piet (Photographic Consultant) of Bel Air, MD/USA, former Director of the Glenn L. Martin Aviation Museum, Middle River, MD.

Book Design by Ian Robertson.

Library of Congress Control Number: 2008943091

Printed in China.
ISBN: 978-0-7643-3753-6

We are interested in hearing from authors with book ideas on related topics.

Published by Schiffer Publishing Ltd.
4880 Lower Valley Road
Atglen, PA 19310
Phone: (610) 593-1777
FAX: (610) 593-2002
E-mail: Info@schifferbooks.com.
Visit our web site at: www.schifferbooks.com
Please write for a free catalog.
This book may be purchased from the publisher.
Please include $5.00 postage.
Try your bookstore first.

In Europe, Schiffer books are distributed by:
Bushwood Books
6 Marksbury Avenue
Kew Gardens
Surrey TW9 4JF, England
Phone: 44 (0) 20 8392-8585
FAX: 44 (0) 20 8392-9876
E-mail: Info@bushwoodbooks.co.uk.
Visit our website at: www.bushwoodbooks.co.uk
Try your bookstore first.

Contents

The original three VW Beetles on display, from left to right: convertible, coupé with collapsible sunroof, and coupé hardtop models. (VW Museum, Stüttgart.)

Introduction

This is my second Volkswagen book, the "prequel" to my first, the critically and popularly well received 2004 work *Volkswagen Military Vehicles of the Third Reich.* I've shown that every single aspect of the Third Reich appears in the VW story.

This current study fills in all that was left out of that prior work, namely, the detailing of the engaging saga of how the famed VW Beetle came to be created and, ultimately, produced. Its spin-off wartime vehicles—the Kübelwagen/Bucket Car and Schwimmwagen/Swimming Car—will be but lightly touched on here, but what will also be explored is how all of these automobiles came to be used by the Nazi regime as tools in the overall motorization of Nazi Germany. This was done in order first, to prepare for the Second World War, and second, to actually wage it.

It was one of Hitler's future goals that the conquered former Soviet Union would be dotted with SS racial settlements administered by the Reichsführer/National Administrator SS Heirrich Himmler. The overall administration of the conquered areas would be run by the new Minister of the Occupied Eastern Territories, Alfred Rosenberg, while Reich Marshal Hermann Göring's Four Year Plan would exploit them economically. Engineer Dr. Fritz Todt's massive autobahn highways would link all of this together, and overtop its concrete ribbons would pass not only the Leadership Corps' Mercedes-Benz limousines so beloved of the top Nazis, but also the Volkswagens for the new colonizers of the mass of the German people, all starting in 1950.

The resurgent Red Army put a stop to all these grandiose visions of a vast Nazi empire—a Germanic version of British India—outside Moscow in 1941, within Stalingrad in 1942, and at Kursk in 1943. The Allied sea-borne invasion of Northwest Europe in 1944 firmly shut the door on German colonization of Europe and Near Asia for good.

But what of those already designed and even built Beetles? They reappeared again after the war. Indeed, on May 17, 1992, *Parade* magazine ran an advertisement commissioned by the world-famous Franklin Mint Precision Models of Pennsylvania, touting the by then beloved Beetle as "The best-selling car of all time!"

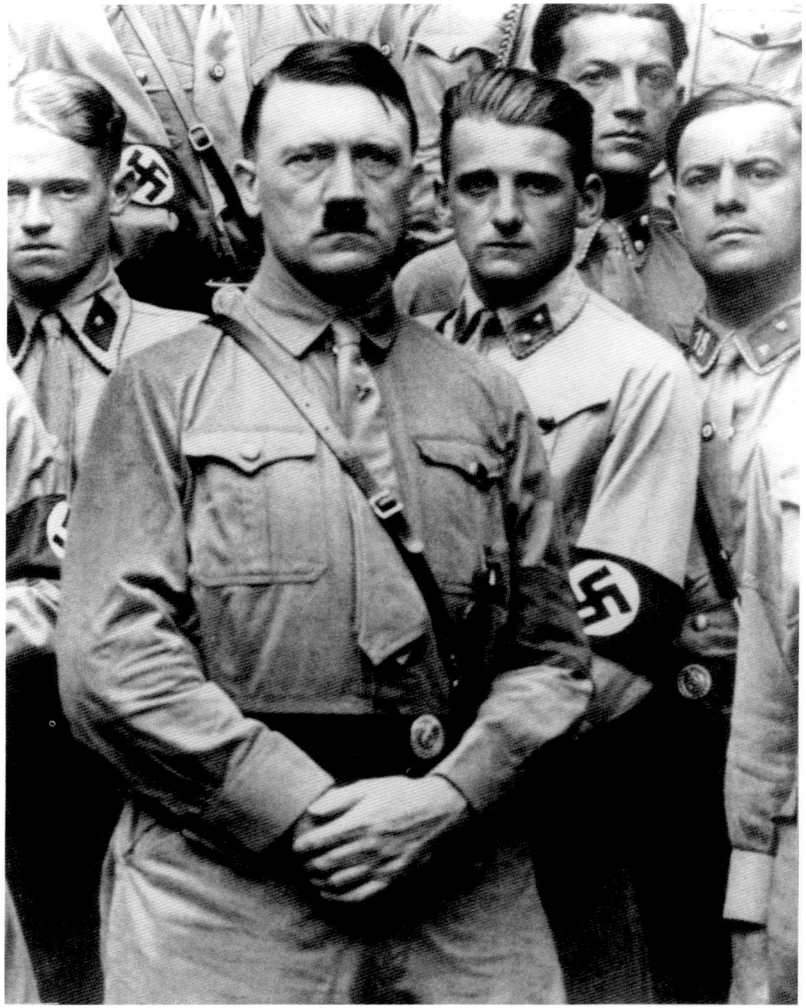

"Gentlemen! There can thus be *only one* Volkswagen in Germany, and not 10!" Adolf Hitler on Feb. 2, 1937, at the annual International Automobile and Motorcycle Exhibition in Berlin. Here, the Führer/Leader is seen with young members of his Brown Battalions, the Nazi Party SA Stormtroops. (Photo from the Heinrich Hoffmann Albums, US National Archives, College Park, MD.)

A German couple and their Porsche-built Beetle before the war, as seen in this promotional photo. (VW Museum)

"Remember when half the cars on the road seemed to be Volkswagens? Well, now you can own one again" (as this author did in 1970, a red convertible). The ad referred to a model of the old Beetle that my generation drove, but later a model of the "New Beetle" also appeared as well, offered by National TV Bargains of Norwalk, CT: "Sure, they retired the old Model T, and yes, they put the GTO out to pasture, but when they tried to give the Beetle its pension, the public outcry broke the sound barrier."

This reflected the massive public interest in the introduction of the 1995 Volkswagen Beetle, and thus I, too, have brought the story up to the present in somewhat abbreviated form for the inclusion of younger readers as well.

Over the years, I have come to employ the investigative style of what I call "the darkened room," in which an investigator walks into it and finds a dead body there without identification. Several questions arise: Whose is it? How did it get there? Was there foul play involved? If so, by whom, with what, and why? The reader may agree that these are the tools of not only a good investigative reporter, but also of a detective, lawyer, and even coroner. That is how I have proceeded with all my books thus far.

In the week of September 20, 1999, the 100th million Volkswagen rolled off the assembly lines. As of August 1, 2009, VW has stated that global deliveries were up by 7%, reflecting the ongoing world economic downturn that began in September 2008. What follows is how this truly remarkable automotive and human saga began.

The Nazi link to the creation of the VW Beetle is here demonstrated by the swastika banner behind it. (VWM)

Blaine Taylor
Berkshires at Town Center
December 2010
Towson, MD

The Beetle
Creating the People's Car

The second born of these two Austrian titans—Adolf Hitler—is well known worldwide, while Dr. Ferdinand Porsche is less so, except perhaps in the global automotive community. Hitler's career will be discussed herein in these pages only in so far as it impacts on the history of the Drs. Porsche—father and son—and the creation of the Volkswagen. When Hitler was born on April 20, 1889, at Braunau-an-der-Inn River, Ferdinand Porsche was already 14 years old.

He was born on September 3, 1875, in the village of Maffersdorf-rechts-dur-Neisse River, the son of a local tinsmith whose father hoped—as he himself would later, successfully—that he would follow him in the family trade. His birthplace is now known as Libarec, in the Czech Republic, founded after the fall of Communism in Eastern Europe.

Initially, he began his pre-professional career as an apprentice in his father's metal smith shop toward achieving this parental goal but, in reality, it was not his own. He began taking classes at the Reichensberg Technical College, and there soon became enthralled by the twin new emerging technologies of the era: home-use electricity and the internal combustion engine, which had been used to help create the automobile in the Imperial Germany of Kaiser Wilhelm I in 1885, when he was 10, and Hitler was yet unborn.

One day young Porsche saw the wonders of having electricity in a local carpet factory, and set about straightaway installing such a lighting system in his own family home. It was his first technical achievement all his own—but it was hardly his last! Although he was a good, practically oriented student who studied hard, like many people, he received the lowest grades in his college class.

Nevertheless, he had already determined that he would not enter the familial trade, and thus his brother Oskar Porsche became its head instead. Young Ferdinand went to Vienna—where Hitler, too, would one day gravitate towards as an unknown, starving artist—and was hired at the famed United Electrical Company at Ferngorngasse headed by Bela Egger, a Hungarian.

He started literally at the ground level sweeping floors, then rose to become maintenance technician, and within four years was the firm's manager of the test department, which enabled him to try out some of his own germinating ideas. After hours he would find his way secretly to the classrooms of the local technical schools, where he could learn more about his chosen profession. He soon began thinking about an all-electric car that would be both noise and pollution free—still a valid concept, especially in this century of climate change.

During this same time—which saw him engaged to Aloisia Kaes, the future mother of their two children, Louise and Ferry Porsche—his initial set of drawings for this project were stolen, but he plunged ahead with the concept of a car with radically new "four wheeled drive" electrical motors in each of the quartets of wheels themselves. He shared his ideas with Viennese carriage builder Jakob Löhner. He was hired in 1898 (when Hitler was nine) as designer-engineer for Löhner & Company, Porsche's first real step into the automotive business that would take him 52 years to greatness and worldwide fame.

His first real car was the Porsche-Löhner Chaise—he got top billing, no less!—an all-electric vehicle with hub drive motors that had a range of 80 km (50 miles) until recharging was necessary. In 1900, Porsche took his car to the prestigious Paris Universal Exposition, where it was awarded the *Grand Prix/Prize*. With this tremendous initial success, Ferdinand Porsche became the darling of the trade media in a single showing.

By the time his career would end in 1950 with his incapacitation from a stroke, his cars "always bore someone else's name: Austro-Daimler, Mercedes-Benz, Steyr, Wanderer, Zundapp, NSU, Auto Union, Cisitalia, and of course, Volkswagen," according to Jonathon Wood in *Great Marques of Germany*. It was his son, Ferry, who would put the stamp of Porsche on the automobiles of his own that are still manufactured today.

At this point in his career, Ferdinand Porsche had built his first electrical generator at age 19, and his first car, from his own blueprints, at 23, and won his first Grand Prize at 25. He was well on his way. The Paris car was a front-wheel drive vehicle only; however, he would help design four-wheel drive cars for the German Army four decades later. In 1905, Porsche won an Austrian prize for another mixed electrical-gas engine onboard car, but Löhner decided not to pursue these designs further, leading to Porsche's resignation.

Hired immediately by Austro-Daimler, he began a 17-year-long association with that firm that was to prove the longest of his life—working for someone else, that is. Named technical director in 1906, from his triumph of the *Mixt* Car for Löhner he went to the *Maja* with a four-cylinder gas engine and four-speed transmission. It was named for the second daughter of the Austrian Consul at Nice, France, Emil Jellinek. His older daughter Mercedes had given her name in 1901 to the famed car of that year at her father's insistence, but this second model did not fare as well in sales.

In 1909, Porsche won a further trio of design awards for his unique hands-on auto engineering work, including a car for the Prince Heinrich Endurance Trials of that year that had been founded by the younger brother of Kaiser Wilhelm II, a race car driver himself and a career sailor who rose to the rank of Grand Admiral in the Imperial German High Seas Navy Battle Fleet.

During this same period before the First World War, Ferdinand Porsche also road tested and raced his own car designs, and then began designing aeronautical engines and tractors to haul mortars for the Imperial Austro-Hungarian Army, as well as dirigibles, in 1913. He recalled later how he was almost killed in one of these tests in the following year to his children:

"I willy-nilly had to make at least one ascent in one of these balloons. It was rather stormy and, in order not to run into a church spire, we were forced to jettison some ballast, a little too much of it!

"As a result the balloon rapidly gained height, and the pressure could not be controlled by the safety valve. I was watching the manometer calculate exactly when it would reach the point at which the fabric of the balloon would burst. We had no parachutes—we hadn't even heard of them! The pressure gauge had long passed the red line, but the ascent stopped just as the pressure had reached its limit. We were able to land.

"Back on firm ground, I said to the balloon crew, 'I have a nice salami sausage which my wife packed for me; that's just what we need after all this excitement.' However, how great was our disappointment when I unpacked the parcel and found that my wife had made a mistake: there was no sausage, but instead a new corset!"

This is how fellow author Walter Henry Nelson described Porsche's career during the First World War:

"In 1913, the Austro-Hungarian Army developed a heavy 305 mm mortar which fired a shell weighing more than 700 pounds, and Porsche designed a 100 hp vehicle to draw this monster, utilizing an adaptation of the *Mixt* car principle. After the war began, Porsche motorized an even bigger 420 mm mortar, similar to Germany's 420 mm Big Bertha. Its barrel alone weighed 26 tons, and its shell another 2,000 pounds. Porsche powered its tractor-like cab with a gasoline engine.

"This was hooked to a generator feeding hubcap motors in the eight trailer wheels. Thus, both cab and trailer were motorized.

"In 1917, Porsche received an honorary doctorate in engineering from Vienna Technical University. Herr Doktor Porsche, General Director of Austro-Daimler, had achieved academic importance, and the proud title never left his calling cards." His son and namesake would repeat this achievement decades later as well.

"Porsche's motorized trailer found other uses. As many as 10 huge troop-carrying trailers were strung behind the gasoline powered cab, separately made mobile by means of hubcap electro-motors. The entire effect was that of an undulating caterpillar, moving troop trains along the French, Italian, and Russian Fronts.

"The troops, however, only moved faster towards defeat. The war's end brought economic ruin, and an end to the empire. Porsche now worked in a minor Republic called Austria. Maffersdorf, in the meantime, had become part of Czechoslovakia, and Porsche found himself to be a citizen of that country."

Of these same years his son would later recall:

"My father (probably the most un-political man who ever lived) received…the Officer's Cross of Franz Josef [the Emperor of Austria-Hungary], the highest distinction that could be conferred on a civilian for 'Magnificent efficiency on military-technical grounds.'…That same year (1916), he also became the managing director of the Austro-Daimler firm…. His technical contributions in Austria had been beyond compare, war or no war.

"They included aircraft engines (one of them an air-cooled flat four that became the distinct forerunner of the Volkswagen power unit), self-propelled, which used his famous electric hub motor, the wagon train…called the 'C-Train,' and even air-cooled engines for small railways.

"Yet all this was, in fact, only the beginning. Seemingly, my father's ingenuity had no limits; his imagination recognized no boundaries. No problem could be dreamed up by one man that was incapable of being solved by another. Of this he was convinced; and if one thinks about it, the argument was hard to refute."

Unknown to them both, a that time a lance corporal in the defeated German Army just across the border in the new Republic of Germany—one Adolf Hitler—was to develop that very same mind set that would get the beaten Reich back on its feet economically, and launch Volkswagen on its road to glory.

In 1919, Porsche built the *Sascha* light-weight sports racer for Austrian filmmaker Count Sascha Kolowrat with a 1.0-liter engine, which recalled to the Herr Doktor that a small, affordable car for the now impoverished masses of Central Europe was what was most needed—and sorely—in the automotive market of the times. Predictably, however—and perhaps even understandably—what almost all European car manufacturers of the day were building was expensive luxury cars for those who could then buy them: the rich and famous. It made economic sense.

But Dr. Porsche was by now an ardent fan of Henry Ford in America, and he stunned his board of directors at Austro-Daimler when he proposed that they, too, now enter this small car market. It was rejected because of financial constraints already in place by the bank that controlled the firm, and the hot-tempered general manager—enraged—threw down boardroom ornaments as he stalked out of the meeting.

He resigned his post in a huff, left Austria for Stüttgart, in Republican Germany, in 1922, and became director of the famed Daimler firm, and the creator and builder of the Mercedes cars that both he and Hitler later came to love. At 47, Dr. Porsche began the next six years of his remarkable career.

Mr. Nelson has left a good physical description of the prickly-tempered "Herr Doktor" at this juncture of his life:

"A prim little man with an amiable moustache and a sharp twinkle that could become a bolt of electricity when he chose. His attire was almost a trademark. He would wear a loose fitting tweed suit with giant patch pockets, and a cloth cap pulled down to his ears.

"At races, a pair of binoculars would dangle from his neck, and a pair of goggles would be perched on his cap. His demeanor was one of intense dignity and concentration."

It was in these six years at Daimler (1922-28) that he would design the famous Mercedes model racers and touring cars that would later catch the eye of Hitler and his Nazi Party: the classic K, S, SS, and SSK models. But still, Dr. Porsche dreamed of one day creating his own, personal fantasy: the *Kleinauto*, or small car.

In 1923, because of rampant inflation in Germany, it cost millions of Reichsmarks just to ride a common streetcar and, noted Nelson:

"Almost to a man, the leaders of European auto companies discounted the general public—and certainly the worker—as a potential customer. The worker in Germany and Austria bicycled to his job if he did not take a bus or a trolley (streetcar). When he saved some money, he bought a motorcycle perhaps, but never a car."

It seemed as if Dr. Porsche was at a permanent roadblock to ever achieving what he knew to be a sound engineering principle that would work with a good business plan, proper manufacture, and efficient promotion. Sometime during 1924-25—at the Solitude Road Race—he met the man who, almost a decade later, would begin to make his dreams come true. At the time Dr. Porsche was 48 years old, and the young Bavarian politician and former World War I veteran, Adolf Hitler, was but 34. The Herr Doktor forgot the meeting, but later the newly appointed Chancellor of the German Reich recalled it to his memory once more, in 1933.

Three years after this fateful initial meeting, in 1926 Daimler merged with its top rival, Benz, to form the corporate entity of Daimler-Benz, with the product line called Mercedes-Benz. Now Dr. Porsche was working for both, neither of which wanted his small car idea, especially since it simply wasn't selling well with the other firms in Germany that had tried such a concept in the 1920s and gone out of business.

Nevertheless, the new firm permitted him to build some of his compact car prototypes, but when their overnight starting capabilities failed in cold weather and Dr. Porsche couldn't start a single one of 15, he characteristically didn't argue the point, but threw down his hat angrily in the snow and again resigned on the spot, just as he'd done before in 1922.

From the ignominious failure of his 38 hp Stüttgart vehicle, Dr. Porsche returned to Austria in 1929 to become director of the Steyr Motorcar Company, while rising politician Hitler was waging electoral campaigns in Germany. These floundered as well until the onset of the global economic Depression during 1929-32 that brought Hitler to office, as well as Franklin D. Roosevelt in the industrial giant of the United States.

At Steyr, Dr. Porsche built the famous *Austria* limousine, but when the firm's bank fell, the Austro-Daimler bank bailed out the company, and he decided to leave employment once more, after barely two years. Thus, in 1930 at age 55, Dr. Porsche embarked on an entirely new career in the depths of the Great Depression, and turned down promising job offers from both the Skoda Company in Czechoslovakia (that Hitler would seize in 1939 anyway) and General Motors in the U.S. to found his own Porsche Design Bureau back at Stüttgart. It was officially called "*Dr Ing. H.c.F Porsche G.m.bH,*" which in time would lead to the creation of the Beetle, and thus make car history.

The new firm served as a consultant to perform work on cars for other firms that would both pay the family bills and also continue his fame in the auto world; by now, his son Ferry was also working in the firm, and father and son collaborated closely for the rest of their lives until the Herr Doktor's death at age 75 on January 30, 1951.

With the sometimes solid financial success of the Bureau, Dr. Porsche could also work in his spare time on his small car projects, fine-tuning what he envisioned and ultimately wanted. In this he was perhaps fortunate, as Hitler later admitted that the decade between 1923-33 had helped the Nazi Party better take over and administer power when the time actually came.

In regards to the VW, one wonders what it would've looked like had it been built in 1928 rather than in 1938 as it, in fact, was.

Dr. Porsche officially opened the new shop in Stüttgart on January 1, 1931, in the very center of the German auto industry, "With many parts plants and machine shops," according to Nelson. His shingle was rather ambitious in English as well as in German: "Doctor, Engineer (honoris causa) Ferdinand Porsche, Construction Bureau for the manufacture of Motors, Motor Vehicles, Aircraft, and Ships."

His first client was the Wanderer Auto Company, during 1931-32. Attested Nelson:

"Porsche developed an auto suspension design which eventually proved to be a radical feature of the Volkswagen...the torsion bar suspension system. After its initial weaknesses had been worked out, it proved a major invention. Until 1950—when his patent ran out—Porsche licensed its use in many other cars, including the Volkswagen. After 1950, it became public property. As a 1965 VW advertisement put it, however, the number of sedans having *both* this system *and* four wheel independent suspension 'can be counted on one finger.' Both VW features were part of the *original* design by Porsche."

Besides his 21-year-old son, Ferry, his staff consisted of the following in the Ullrich Building on Stüttgart's *Kronenstrasse/Crown Street*, stated Nelson:

"Karl Rabe, his chief designer; Karl Frölich (gearboxes); Josef Kales (engines); Josef Zahradnik (axles, springing, and steering); and Erwin Komenda (bodies)...The manager was Adolf Rosenberger, a businessman whose hobby was racing, who owned 15% of the firm.

"Porsche owned 70%, and Dr. Anton Piech—his son-in-law—15%. Rosenberger, however, was Jewish, and had to flee the country after 1933 [because of the Nazi takeover]. He moved to Paris, where he was secretly appointed the Bureau's sales manager abroad, and represented the firm until World War II, selling Porsche designs to foreign countries.

"At the outbreak of war, he made his way to the US," and returned after the war to settle with Dr. Ferry Porsche his financial claims on the firm.

The Nazis did well in the elections of 1931, and that November, Fritz Neumayer of the Zundapp Motorcycle Works near Nürnberg approached Dr. Porsche about the possibility of manufacturing a *kleinauto/small car* together. Dr. Porsche wanted to build a totally new car chassis from the ground up, and put his own money toward a prototype of what he called Project #12.

By borrowing on his own life insurance policy, Dr. Porsche would both meet his Bureau payroll and build the prototype of the #12 concurrently—and this still in the midst of the then on-going Depression!

In order to induce Neumayer to fund the building of the car's mass production, he called it the *Zundapp Volksauto/People's Car.* Noted Nelson:

"The word *Volksauto* had already been used a great deal in the Germany of the 1920s, and, indeed, a car called the Bergmann *Volksauto* had even appeared on the market in 1904. The impetus given the *Volksauto* idea in the 1920s can above all be credited to *Motor Critic* and its editor, Ganz. Neumayer, who thus was planning to give his car a name much in vogue at that time."

He didn't want an air-cooled engine, however, but one that was water-cooled instead. His factory would make the trio of engines and gearboxes for the prototypes, with Stüttgart's Reutter Coachworks building the bodies. Assembly took place at Nürnberg, and road tests began in April 1932. The tests were disastrous for many reasons, one of which was that Porsche needed heavier presses to better stamp out his torsion bars, all of which cracked under the strain.

Neumayer shelved the entire project in favor of continuing to build more and better motorcycles, while the Bureau was paid 85,000 RM for its services, and was provided with one of the trio of prototypes, which survived as a company car in constant use until destroyed in an Allied air raid in 1944.

Next, Fritz von Falkenhayn of the NSU Auto Company of Neckarsulm asked the Bureau to produce another three prototypes. Stated Nelson:

"What emerged in 1933 was a car even more similar to the Volkswagen of today, although it was bulkier, and contained a 1.5-liter engine (at NSU's request).

"Again, the strange cars were built at Stüttgart. This time, engines were constructed at NSU...under Ferry Porsche's supervision. Three prototypes of this direct forerunner of the VW were rolled out of the plant, gassed up, tested, and performed successfully. The three prototypes vanished until December 1950, when one of them unexpectedly reappeared in Stüttgart, driven by a crippled German war veteran who was a former NSU engineer. This ancient forerunner of the VW was parked in front of the Porsche Bureau headquarters and 'ogled with curiosity and awe like a prehistoric fossil.'

"Driven almost daily before the outbreak of World War II, it survived the war and the immediate postwar years in the deserted Friedrichsruh Castle of the Hohenlohes (Dynasty) near Ohringen. There, the NSU veteran found it in 1948, and bought it for next to nothing. He installed new headlights and a new battery, and tested the engines. It worked as though it were brand new."

Thus, the 1934 NSU Type 32 was, in a sense, the first true Volkswagen prototype, and the improved torsion bar suspension was considered to be the ideal such suspension system for a small car. Still, there were small car competitors, and even if they failed, there was the possibility that Dr. Porsche might yet lose the market he had fought so hard to gain, and then fate and history intervened in the person of Jakob Werlin.

Enter Jakob Werlin

Dr. Porsche knew Werlin from their days together at Daimler-Benz, and he had also been a Nazi since 1923, and had even sold Hitler the Führer's very first Mercedes-Benz that he ever owned. There is a telling anecdote about Hitler and Werlin that is here germane to our narrative.

Stated Robert Stuhlemner in *The Coachwork of Erdmann & Rossi*:

"Porsche had his two machines [Type 12 and Type 32] on the road being tested when there occurred an incident involving Adolf Hitler that is a key part of Volkswagen lore. As told by an inspired story in a Münich newspaper, Hitler was on his way to Münich on a raw, wet night in 1933 accompanied by Jakob Werlin—Daimler-Benz director and dealer in Münich—when his car overtook a couple on a motorcycle. The sight of the pair riding along in the rain, drenched and cold, touched Hitler, not best remembered as a humanitarian."

According to Nelson:

"A year earlier, in 1932, he spoke about a small car with Jakob Werlin...and had asked him to suggest to Daimler-Benz that they build one. The directors of the company turned down the idea flatly. Hitler wasn't chancellor yet, and a suggestion by Werlin in 1932 didn't carry the weight it would later."

Then, added Keith Seume:

"A chance meeting with Jakob Werlin...gave him (Porsche) the opportunity to discuss his plans once again. Werlin listened to Porsche with interest, knowing full well that Hitler was anxious to see such a car take to the roads. Porsche had already composed a lengthy paper on the subject, and sent it to the German Transport Ministry, and it is almost certain that Hitler—being such a car enthusiast—would've heard of its existence." (By now, Hitler was the appointed Reich Chancellor.)

The Two Austrians Meet

The first meeting between the Herr Doktor and the now Chancellor had been "in 1924 or 1925," according to Dr. Ferry Porsche in 1976, and he recalled that it happened due to another Mercedes man at the Solitude Road Race: "Hitler...was a close friend of Dr. Richard Voelter, the advertising director of the Daimler Company...Voelter introduced my father to the future Chancellor," when Ferry was but 16.

Their second meeting, according to *After the Battle* in 1976, occurred at the Hotel *Kaiserhof/ Imperial Hotel* on the *Wilhelmsplatz/William's Plaza* in Berlin on May 11, 1933; it is curious to this writer that, since he was Chancellor, Hitler didn't hold the meeting at the Old Reich Chancellery (ORC) across the street. The famous old hotel was destroyed by the war and not rebuilt afterwards.

This was, however, the meeting that cemented the bond between these two men. Recalled Dr. Ferry Porsche, his father, "Was surprised at the Chancellor's memory [of the earlier meeting]." The topic was a new, winning racecar for the Auto Union Company that Hitler wanted Dr. Ferdinand Porsche to design for the Third Reich. A second meeting (their third in all) was held on this same topic at the ORC later, and Hitler gave Dr. Porsche what he wanted to build the famous Auto Union racer after hearing his arguments. The bond deepened between the two men, and the Führer had already the previous February publicly stated his desire for a *kleinauto* at the International Automobile and Motorcycle Exhibition in Berlin. They were discovering that they were, indeed, two kindred spirits on this matter.

After the Battle believed that the matter of the People's Car was also discussed at the May 11, 1933, meeting, and it most likely was. It stated:

"Hitler insisted, however, that the car should not use more than seven liters of petrol (gas) per 100 kms (approximately 40 mpg), one liter less than Dr. Porsche proposed; be a four-seater, able to maintain 100 kph on the new Autobahns being constructed; air-cooled because of the severe winter in parts of Germany, and the scarcity of garages; the final requirement being that it should sell for under 1,000 RM [approximately 50 English pounds]."

Asserted Dr. Ferry Porsche:

"This much must be said of Hitler. When interested in anything, he could grasp both the fundamentals and the details surprisingly quickly."

It therefore didn't take him long to give his nod of assent. "That sounds pretty good to me," he said, adding what was to be an aspect of the deal that would be considered anathema to any American dealership, both then and now: they would simply eliminate the middleman, the German dealer. There would be no showrooms, only the factories. And how would the prospective buyer receive the finished product? He or she would simply go to the site of manufacture, pick up their car, and drive away with it!

Remembered Dr. Ferry Porsche:

"The worst squawk would naturally come from the dealers, which was too bad. The *RDA/Reichsverband der Deutchen Automobileindustrie*/German Automobile Manufacture Association did not seem to be too worried, although I don't think it would have done them much good even if they had been.

"We were now over the two main obstacles: approval from the Führer, and the fact that a totally new firm was responsible for the design of this new car, so on June 22, 1934, a Volkswagen design contract was signed both by my father and the RDA, which set a price target of 990 RM. The basis for this figure was a minimum production figure of 1,000 cars per day (in one shift) to start with.

"There was certainly no shortage of potential buyers...Far more Germans wanted Volkswagens than could possibly be built in the foreseeable future." An initial start-up fund from the RDA was given for 20,000 RM monthly, but "We were compelled to start building and assembling the first three experimental Volkswagens in our own garage at the family villa on Feuerbacher Weg. The trouble now was that we really did not have enough space.

"Somehow, using my personal hobby shop as a base, we moved in two lathes, the milling machine, and a power drill which I already had into there, and also found space for a dozen men to work them! Don't ask me how we did it, but those prototypes known as the VW3 Type were made there, and by really squeezing the budget, we were able to go ahead in 1935 [with testing]."

That same year, Hitler announced the future manufacture of the VW under the direction of the Porsche Design Bureau at the annual Berlin Auto Show. At the Bureau, the staff expanded to 40, with 30 VW prototypes assembled at Daimler-Benz (irony of ironies for the firm) in 1936, but still Dr. Ferdinand Porsche vented his frustration when he blurted out, "It's easier to build a brand new race car than it is to produce a Volkswagen! In terms of price, we are facing a very hard job!"

Hitler's idea of excluding the dealer middlemen had proved to be the right one, however, as he told them once, "I see no need of a sales organization with everyone having a finger in the pie, when the real problem has nothing to do with *selling* Volkswagens, but *building* them!"

For their part, the Drs. Porsche were forced to agree:

"On that basis, the 1,000 mark ceiling suggested for the price tag was much more realistic than appeared at first sight...Hitler never asked stupid or pointless questions. On the contrary, here I thought, was a man who had taken the trouble to study and understand this particular problem of the Volkswagen.

"He asked a surprising number of technical details, all of which made good sense. Obviously, he had made up his mind beforehand that certain things would have to be changed, but nothing he suggested was of major importance. He seemed to combine a surprisingly good understanding of both technical matters and small details, and to help him, also, he had an excellent memory...."

However, the Porsches missed the 10-month completion deadline that the Führer had given them, and hence stalled for time, as road tests went on into 1937 by SS drivers.

Stated *After the Battle*:

"Official road testing of the first three *Volksauto/People's Car* [as the German and U.S. press were calling them] began on Oct. 12, 1936. By Christmas that year, they had completed 30,000 miles. Perhaps the worst fault to emerge from this testing was continual breakage of the cast crankshafts, caused by the adoption of forged shafts which has continued to this day.

"Dr. Porsche was not present at the beginning of the tests, as he had decided it would be necessary to study American mass production techniques if the car was to be produced in sufficient numbers and to Hitler's price. He had arrived in New York on Oct. 8th, and during the following month toured all the major US automobile factories.

"On his way to Germany in the *Queen Mary*, he traveled to Great Britain to visit the Austin factory at Longbridge, near Birmingham. A further US trip followed in 1937 to recruit American workers [of German origin] to form the nucleus of the factory staff that Dr. Porsche considered necessary to produce the car using American production methods.

"In this he was not very successful, and only 20 Americans—mostly of German extraction—signed. Two of the early recruits, Josef Werner from Ford's and Otto Hoehne of ex-International Harvester Company, are still at Volkswagen today (1976.)"

Frustrated that—after his pronouncements at five successive Berlin Auto Shows (1933-37) for the German automobile industry to help build a small car, and that there were now rival models to his sanctioned VW—Chancellor Hitler publicly stated that the government would build the car itself, under the auspices of Dr. Robert Ley's German Labor Front (or DAF) and his hand-picked deputy for the project, Dr. Bodo Lafferentz. This was a gambit that neither of the Drs. Porsche had expected, and that all other German auto makers had dreaded, for it was a step on the road to socialism that they feared, and one espoused by such Nazi left wingers in the Party as Dr. Ley, Dr. Josef Göbbels, and Martin Bormann.

Of Dr. Lafferentz, their new colleague by Hitler's fiat in the VW business, Dr. Ferry Porsche had this to say:

"He was very far from being stupid...I found him bright and pleasant, and always willing to discuss a variety of subjects in a sensible manner. He had a good appreciation of art, but his background remains something of a mystery to me to this day [1976]. He was a very tall and pleasant-looking man who held a doctorate in political science, but obviously his technical knowledge was almost nil. He came into the public eye in Germany as the man responsible for the working of the KdF Movement and for all the artistic pursuits offered to the public.

"...It was Dr. Robert Ley who appointed Lafferentz as a co-director of the Volkswagenwerk, jointly with my father. His responsibility, however, was toward the commercial side of this vast organization and the immense amount of paperwork that went into its structure.

"Dr. Lafferentz was married to Richard Wagner's granddaughter, and that was how he came into close contact with music and the famous Bayreuth Festival [that Hitler attended every year until the start of the war in 1939]. It is likely that important jobs were handed out by Hitler on the strength of old friendships and were, in effect, political rewards of a kind. Hitler's admiration for Wagner may also have had something to do with the appointment of Lafferentz."

Meanwhile, as Ferry himself supervised the SS test drivers on such publicity stunts as climbing the Grossglöckner Mountain in the Alps, fine honing the shape of the vehicle was being worked on by Erwin Komenda. In the final analysis, the shape of the Beetle was determined by its rear-placed engine as much as by aerodynamics. It also happened to be the cheapest place to put a small vehicle's power plant. The designers also struggled with a car that was to cost $142, and $8 additional for a sunroof!

In May 1937—a full year before the cornerstone dedication—it was announced that the new VW company would produce a target figure of 1,500,000 vehicles, and that within a decade there would be no working German who did not own a VW. What this would've done toward the balancing of streetcar, bus, and rail transportation was not stated.

Following the cornerstone dedication, stated *After the Battle*:

"An ingenious stamp saving scheme was inaugurated on Aug. 1, 1938, where—for 5 RM a week—a German could order a VW for delivery when the cars were in production. Some 336,668 people took out savings cards, and eventually saved 280 million marks."

Erwin Komenda was not the only stylist involved with the shape of VW's final look, as Dr. Ferry Porsche recalled:

"The original 30 cars were built by Daimler-Benz under the supervision of a Porsche engineer, but to realize further improvements, we quickly built another 30 with bodywork by Reutter. All were on the road during 1938, which was good going. On these additional cars, we introduced some minor body changes, all of them improvements.

"These were influenced by a sheet metal specialist from the US whom we had persuaded to come back to Germany and work for us. His name was Hans Mayr, and the body changes resulted in a basic shape that has been retained to this day—more than 17 million Beetles later!"

In the June 22, 1934, contract negotiations Heinz Nordhoff represented the Opel Firm, and he considered Dr. Ferdinand Porsche thus:

"This outstanding man was an engineer and designer not by profession, but by heart. Short-tempered and energetic, he was not regarded as being successful in the normal sense of the word," he told Nelson, "but he was a fanatic, and an unusually gifted engineer. He had his own very clear ideas about a small car, and he gripped with all 10 fingers this opportunity to materialize his dreams.

"He had the rare gift of surrounding himself with a team of devoted followers who loved him and were dedicated to his ideas. Among them there was a unity and a determination to accomplish the outstanding, and an unbounded willingness to follow their leader and idol.'"

One of these men was Karl Rabe. Stated Nelson:

"And while the ideas were Porsche's, the designs also owed much to Karl Rabe, who made them work. This brilliant engineer—a first-rate engineer in his own right—with several cars to his personal credit, had served with Porsche ever since 1913, when he met him at Austro-Daimler. Rabe stayed at Austro-Daimler during Porsche's stormy sessions with German Daimler and with Steyr, but when Porsche set himself up in business as a consultant, Karl Rabe could not resist his call.

"He rejoined Porsche in 1931...Says Vorwig, 'Rabe is actually the man responsible for the finished design. Porsche had the grand idea and the concepts, but it was Rabe who designed a mechanism that worked. Porsche could not have performed without Karl Rabe.'

"From 1934-38, says Heinz Nordhoff, Porsche and this team fought against great odds. 'Without question,' he says, 'Porsche led a fight against the entire German auto industry...a secret, underground fight, of course, and one which ended to his and the Volkswagen's benefit only because Hitler stood behind the entire plan.'

"Even Nordhoff was involved, as the Opel man on the RDA. Vorwig remembers him saying at an RDA meeting which discussed Porsche's initial engine design, 'This is an airplane engine. We can't produce that at this price.' 'He was completely disdainful,' says Vorwig. 'He never dreamed he'd one day be the man who'd build this car.'"

The decision had been made to go to a two-stroke engine design, but testing revealed that there was a better way, and Porsche soon adopted it: a four-cylinder, horizontally opposed, four-stroke 985cc unit designed by Franz Reimspeiss. As for the 10-month delay, Wilhelm von Opel thought that the Porsches had snookered the government with a project they knew in advance couldn't be brought in on time, and were being *paid* for it simultaneously. He also believed that—Hitler or no—ordinary German workers should be content to take the bus to work.

As VW30 prototypes continued to be driven by both 200 Army and SS drivers at a maximum speed of 62 mph (100 kmh), the next series was introduced in 1937 of the 44 cars in the VW38 Type, which was virtually identical to the final production model with changes and additions. At last, the VW30 tests were completed by December 23, 1936. Vorwig's official RDA report, given to the Reich Chancellor in January, urged further testing on a larger scale. Although he told Nelson that it was an honest assessment from his viewpoint at the time, he had also asserted in 1949, "It is clear that a privately owned industry (the RDA) had no interest whatever in a Volkswagen with which it would be in competition."

From a strictly capitalist point of view, who can blame the RDA? Hitler did, as he made clear at the very next Auto Show on February 28, 1937:

"Let there be no doubt: so-called private business is either capable of solving this problem or it is not capable of continuing as private business! The National Socialist (Nazi) state will under no circumstances capitulate before either the convenience, the limitations, or the ill will of individual Germans."

Inside that same Exhibition Hall, the Führer was angered when he saw Opel's own rival small car model to the VW, particularly as Opel was then owned by the American firm General

Motors. Heinz Nordhoff was there when von Opel stated to Hitler, "And here, my Führer, is *our* Volkswagen!," leaving an enraged Reich Chancellor to stalk away in a fury. Later, asserted Nelson:

"To demonstrate that he would not brook any last-ditch attempts by private companies to enter the small car field on a competitive basis, Hitler made it difficult for the company to obtain materials necessary for the car. Later, when Opel offered to shave the P-4's price by 200 marks, the company was told unofficially that such price cuts would not be permitted, because no German car would be allowed to approach the price set for the Volkswagen."

As today, it was inescapable that this rift between the Chancellor and his domestic auto industry would eventually leak to the trade media; if not within the Reich press controlled by Dr. Göbbels, then in the world press outside Germany's frontiers.

On April 23, 1937, *The New York Times* sent an Associated Press report from Berlin that was headlined *Hitler's Car Remains a Mystery*:

"Chancellor Adolf Hitler's cheap People's Car, which he promised Germans for three years and with which the Führer dreams of conquering the European market, will remain a myth for at least two years.

"Three models of the mysterious 'Volkswagen' were secretly put on test runs before Hitler proudly exclaimed openly at the 1935 Berlin Auto Show: 'We will solve the problem of the cheap car. Production of this newly designed car, which will be as inexpensive as a middle-priced motorcycle, will be started this year.'

"But Hitler's midget car failed to make the grade, and will have to continue trials 'at least until 1938,' it was learned from the Federation of the German Automobile Industry. Finally, inaugurating the 1937 Auto Exhibition, Hitler banged his fist on the speaker's table as he burst out: 'Either automobile makers produce the cheap car or they go out of business. I will not tolerate the plea, 'It can't be done!'"

The next stalling tactic adopted by the RDA was to ask Hitler to allow each of their individual members to build their own small car model, and have the government subsidize them at 200 marks per vehicle. Calculating the overall cost of this delaying strategy, which might see the Volkswagen *never* built, he decided at length to build the car himself, by having the State construct the plant *and* own it outright.

Nelson was correct when he stated:

"'The auto manufacturers were foolish,' says Dr. Volkmar Kohler, the archivist of today's Volkswagen Company. 'Had they been smart, they would have produced a cheap 'People's Car' for Hitler just as the radio manufacturers produced a 'People's Radio/*Volksempfanger* when he asked for it. Instead, because they thought they could out stall and outfox Hitler, they ended up having the Volkswagen as competition.'"

Not only that, but the loss to the Chancellor in this area of the German economy sent a chilling message throughout the ranks of the rest of the captains and the kings of industry: the Chancellor was not a man to be crossed. Next to find this out would be the diplomats of Europe, and the proud General Staff of the German Army after them.

In May 1937, Dr. Ley announced the formulation of the Volkswagen Development Corporation/ *Gesellschaft zur Vorbereitung des Volkswagen*, which those with a sense of humor nicknamed *Gezuvor!/After you!* for its first syllables. It was an apt metaphor, indeed, for the Nazis at once meant to take the lead away from private industry in this domain that would now be uniquely theirs. The initial, start-up capital was 480,000 marks, and this was boosted to 150 million on July 1, 1939—two months to the day before the Third Reich smashed onto the plains of Poland.

Meanwhile, since Dr. Porsche's January 17, 1934, application to Hitler to build the car had gone ahead after their meeting of the following May, the search for a site for a possible single plant had continued; this accelerated sharply after Hitler's decision of May 1937 that the German State itself would build the car and the plant. When Wolfsburg was chosen by Dr. Lafferentz and approved by the Führer, construction was set to start, with one of Dr. Albert Speer's subordinate architects, Peter Koller, 30, as the town planner.

Not everyone was pleased with the choice of the site—and not only Count Werner von der Schulenburg, who lived in the 14th Century castle nearby, and whose land it was. One who was mystified by its choice was Dr. Ferry Porsche himself, and he records getting into an argument with Dr. Lafferentz about it:

"It was all very well to carry out Hitler's order that the Volkswagenwerk must be built in the middle of Germany, close to an Autobahn/highway, a canal, and a railroad, but the choice of a site required far more justification than that.

"I produced a copy of a book which contained an article about the location of new industrial sites. It stated categorically that such a site would have to be one where raw materials and coal or energy of some sort would be at hand. It would also need to be a place where labor was available.

"'Yet, in Wolfsburg,' I pointed out, 'you have no materials, no energy, no labor, and no coal. How come you chose this place to build a factory? I don't understand it.'...Dr. Lafferentz did not appreciate my comment....'I don't understand you,' he fumed, 'or your negative attitude!'...."

In Dr. Ferry Porsche's view, "the mistake had been made," though, and they must now proceed with the building of the town to support the factory—the first such venture in the Third Reich:

"The construction of the actual building was undertaken by thousands of Italian workmen who, in the meantime, required some sort of living amenities. Besides a temporary camp, the construction of the new town also was begun.

"This was originally planned for 30,000 people, but it, too, had to be expanded rapidly, as more and more hands were hired. Production facilities at the factory at first called for an output of 1,000 cars per day, or a quarter of a million vehicles yearly...

"The main railway in the town ran from Berlin to Hannover. The canal was the Mittelland Kanal, which runs beside the railroad, and connects Berlin with the Ruhr industrial area. Plans were also made to build a new Autobahn from Brunswick, close to the Volkswagenwerk, to Hamburg."

The Nazi paper in Hannover proclaimed:

"A world is being built! The fist of a Cyclops has seized the clear Lower Saxon landscape, but it is a modern Cyclops, one who understands the concept of the beauty of work...One looks from the ceremonial square out over the canal at the softly swaying forested heights. It is there that the German Reich shall bed down the most modern and beautiful workers' city...happy people, who will find their homes here!"

"But," explained Nelson, "the first to move in were not to be Germans, however, but Italians. Mussolini sent Hitler 3,000 of his unemployed construction workers, accompanied by Tuillio Cianetti, Robert Ley's Italian counterpart. They were quartered in wooden barracks clustered about an A-frame community building called Cianetti Hall. 'Chianti bottle and dagger ruled,' *Der Spiegel/The Mirror* wrote years later, 'and the crocodile whip in the watch tower of the SS guards...the first girls pregnant with the babies of Mussolini's unemployed began to appear.'

"German companies in the construction, metals, machine tool, and automobile industries were now ordered to free some of their workforce for the plant and for the construction of the workers' city. These also found themselves in wooden barracks. In requisitioning them, the Nazi Party demonstrated just how ruthlessly it was prepared to operate in furthering this plan in which the Führer had committed himself for so many years.

"Postwar Germany's news magazine *Der Spiegel* comments that such plants tended to keep their best workers and send only expendables to the Volkswagenwerk. This Nazi levy is an example of the regime's arbitrary action towards German private enterprise. Another curious example appears in the Nazi sales brochure for the KdF-Wagen. After citing the fringe benefits enjoyed by workers of the KdF auto plant, it urged other German workers to demand comparable benefits of their employers."

Hitler told his intimates that he "would take care of the problem of the churches after the war," and presumably he might well have included industry in another purge, too.

Work on the plant continued for a brief time after the dedication of the cornerstone, but then ceased during the summer of 1938, as Dr. Fritz Todt built up the West Wall opposite France during the Czech Sudeten Crisis that was at last ended with the four-power Münich Pact of September 30th; thereafter construction resumed at Wolfsburg. On August 3, 1938—two days after a speech at Cologne by Dr. Ley on the savings stamp to buy the car—people began lining up to buy the booklets at KdF offices throughout the Reich.

The forms they filled out revealed a remarkable profile of the prospective buyers, as Nelson described:

"Hitler's analysis of the VW market and his claim that the car would not steal away customers of companies producing other cars proved accurate: questionnaires filled out by the 'KdF savers' [as they came to be called] showed that 70% had never owned a car; of the remainder, 40,000 were motorcyclists [90% of whom did not own a heavy motorcycle comparable in price to the VW]. More than half, says the KdF brochure, earned less than 300 marks monthly."

The 1938 rear-mounted engine, as displayed at Wolfsburg, remained basically the same for the next 20 million cars that were produced after the war. Explained Jonathon Wood in *The New Beetle*:

"Theoretically, a rear-powered car possesses a better drag than a front-engine one, because there is no intrusive vertically positioned radiator to interrupt the air flow. For the same reason, the shape of the hood is not dictated by the presence of an engine. The Volkswagen scored on these fronts and, for the same reasons, the headlamps were faired into the front fenders."

Surprisingly, the first four cars went to Dr. Ley (#1, today in the Wolfsburg VW Museum), Dr. Ferdinand Porsche, Dr. Lafferentz, and Gauleiter/Regional Leader Otto Telchow (1876-1945) of East Hannover from 1923-45, but not to either Hitler himself or to Jakob Werlin. The choice of Gauleiter Telchow may in itself seem an odd one, until one recalls Hitler's lifelong penchant to stay in touch with his Party leaders, the men who led his drive to power. Unlike Stalin, he had but one Blood Purge (in 1934, against the SA), and unlike Mussolini, there was no Fascist Grand Council to vote him out of office in the dark days of the lost war.

A Type 64 Model for a possible Rome-Berlin Race was never built due to the end of European racing caused by the war, but its drawings hinted at the future postwar race cars that Dr. Ferry Porsche would one day design and manufacture on his own.

By 1939 210 Type 60s had been built, and by September 1st—the day Hitler invaded Poland—a VW Beetle was selling for about $343, a figure $17 below what Hitler had pressured the Drs. Porsche to produce (from an initial cost-per-unit of $560.)

By August 15, 1940—following the fall of Poland, Denmark, Norway, and all of Western Europe to the *Wehrmacht/Armed Forces*—the first salable VW Kafer rolled off the assembly line, followed by the initial mass-produced "series" run in 1941. In all, 630 wartime KdF-Wagens were manufactured, until Dr. Speer convinced Hitler to convert the Reich to a wartime economy after his appointment to succeed Dr. Todt as Armaments Minister in 1942.

The mass production for civilian consumption that was to have been started in October 1939 just after the fall of Poland was wisely postponed by Hitler "until after the war" (when, in fact, it *did* occur, but under the Occupation auspices of the British Army, as we shall see).

Noted Dr. Ferry Porsche:

"The reason why I knew that we had a winner was the fact that just before the war broke out, more than 200,000 Germans had paid for their cars in full, and were awaiting their turns for deliveries which never took place. Thousands more had also begun monthly payments, so our detractors were talking through their hats."

There was more, too: "As far back as 1939, we had already begun work for the first time on a turbo-charger for the Volkswagen engine. A skilled engineer named Specht was assigned specially to this project, but it was unfortunately interrupted by the outbreak of the war. Still, it is interesting to recall that the principle of the VW turbo-charger was the same as that which we use today on the special Carerra and the Porsche 917 racer."

He was not incorrect in stating the popularity of the KdF-Wagen among the people on the eve of the war, as a secret report of April 1939 from police informants revealed from Rhineland-Westphalia:

"For a large number of Germans, the announcement of the People's Car came as a pleasant surprise. There developed a real KdF-Car psychosis. For a long time, the KdF-Car was a big talking point among all classes of the population...With the KdF-Car, the leadership of the Third Reich has killed several birds with one stone.

"In the first place, it removes for a period of several years money from the German consumer which he would otherwise spend on goods which cannot be supplied. Secondly—and that is the most important thing—they have achieved a clever diversionary tactic in the sphere of domestic politics. This car psychosis—which has been cleverly induced by the Propaganda Ministry—keeps the masses from becoming preoccupied with a depressing situation.

"Hitler has acquired domestic political credit with the 'car-savers' until the delivery of the car, for it is well-known that, while they are saving up for a particular commodity, people are prepared to make quite a lot of sacrifices. Another aspect must not be overlooked.

"Despite all the export subsidies paid by other countries for their cars, the KdF-Car will be at least half the price of an equivalent car from the other exporting countries. In all the countries of Northern and Southern Europe, Asia, South and Central America, everywhere the market is open, the KdF-Car will beat all the other mass produced cars...."

On September 1, 1939, the Drs. Porsche had a private discussion, as Ferry recalled in 1976. Speaking of his father, Dr. Ferry Porsche related:

"I don't think he ever forgot what I told him the day we heard over the radio that war had been declared. 'Hitler simply cannot win this war with the so-called help of all the people around him,' I said at the time, 'so there can only be one end to this....'"

He was proven right by events. In the midst of the first production for propaganda purposes of the Beetle, "Hitler received the first convertible model as a gift," with Bormann's Gauleiters getting the remaining 49 production cars. Ultimately, this so-called "Berghof VW"—which made its way to Führer Headquarters in East Prussia during the war as well—was bought back in 1956, and is today in the Volkswagen Museum at Wolfsburg.

Noted Graham Robson in *Volkswagen Chronicle*, "In 1959, the cornerstone (from 1938) was buried in the foundation of a bridge at the nearby Mittelland Canal," but that is *not* the end of that particular mini-saga, as we shall see.

Author Chris Barber's excellent 2003 study *Birth of the Beetle: The Development of the Volkswagen by Ferdinand Porsche*, has as an appendix the complete text of what has become known as *Porsche's Expose*, the Herr Doktor's basic position paper on why he felt a German small car was necessary, what it should contain, and how he thought it should be designed and built. I do not include it herein because it was later modified, both by his tinkering and, more importantly, by Hitler's demands on what *he* wanted.

Barber also provided some new details of the all-important initial Werlin-Porsche and Porsche-Hitler meetings that helped launch the VW Beetle, and I here include a synopsis:

"There are differing views as to the date when the Berlin *Hotel Kaiserhof/Imperial* meeting between Reich Chancellor Hitler and Ferdinand Porsche actually took place. The meeting was organized by Jakob Werlin, who told Porsche about it on the telephone—there was no written evidence.

"Even the two recent definitive works about this period do not agree on whether this meeting took place on or after Jan. 17, 1934, the date on *Porsche's Expose!* Did Porsche actually have his first designs in his pocket on that occasion (indicating a meeting during spring 1934?), or did he go back to Stüttgart and produce them later (indicating that the meeting really took place during late summer of 1933? As Ferdinand Porsche is quoted as once saying, 'Only God knows who is really right, and who wrong!'"

Barber feels that Dr. Porsche met with Werlin in his office in Crown Street at Stüttgart at the end of March 1934:

"Porsche knew Werlin, and knew that he worked in Münich for Daimler-Benz and had—in fact—sold Hitler his first Mercedes-Benz car [on credit!] in 1923."

Initially, Dr. Porsche viewed Daimler man Werlin as a spy concerning the new Auto Union Type 22 racing car, but changed his mind, apparently, during their meeting:

"It was a week or so after Jakob Werlin's visit to Stüttgart that Porsche received a telephone call from him in Münich, telling Porsche to travel the next day to Berlin...in early April 1934. Werlin would meet him in the *Hotel Kaiserhof* the following afternoon—it was very important, but he could say nothing on the phone...In the middle of the (Berlin) discussion, Adolf Hitler walked in. Then it was Hitler who did most of the talking.

"He had quite definite ideas about what he wanted—four-wheel-drive and 30 bhp. He also told Porsche that a three-cylinder, air-cooled diesel engine would be suitable, light, hard wearing, and robust—in fact, suitable for the military. And it must have been at that point when the oft quoted 'Price? Any price, Dr. Porsche, any price below 1,000 RM!' comment was made by Hitler...

"The first mention of the Volkswagen being used for military purposes was right back in the *Expose* of Jan. 17, 1934."

Hitler dedicates the VW plat at Wolfsburg, May 26, 1938: German workmen muscle into place the VW Werks cornerstone in preparation for Reich Chancellor Adolf Hitler's momentous speech in the factory grounds at Wolfsburg, Germany, which the Führer that day named *KdF Stadt/City of the KdF Car*. According to Hitler speech archivist Max Domarus, "The Volkswagen factory had built its production halls, administrative buildings, and living quarters for its workers on a huge terrain; 28 separate communities were founded, the aggregate of which later formed the city of Wolfsburg. The construction of the Volkswagen factory was accompanied by the establishment of a savings association. For a weekly contribution of five marks, members acquired the right to buy a Volkswagen, the commercial value of which was 990 marks." (Photo from the Heinrich Hoffmann Albums, U.S. National Archives, College Park, MD)

A trio of KdF Wagens are covered with drop cloths to heighten the excitement of the cornerstone dedication event, when the Führer himself would present them to an expectant and curious world. Continued Domarus, "The whole [payment] scheme was doomed, however. While the worker continued to make his weekly payments, he never obtained the car he coveted. The Second World War soon prohibited civilian driving anyway. The Volkswagenwerk was refitted to accommodate the production needs of the *Wehrmacht/Armed Forces*. The military started producing its famous cross-country *Kübelwagen/Bucket Car* there. This vehicle was to be of enormous value to the troops in Africa and Russia, since its motor did not require water-cooling." (HHA)

The frontal view of the dedication scene, with Dr. Bodo Lafferentz at the speaker's podium and the cornerstone in front of it. Note the Hitler Youth drummers in the bleachers high above and behind him, and the Führer's personal standard at left, indicating that he is present. Noted Domarus, "Lafferentz was the *Reichsamtsleiter/National Office Leader* of the DAF, and head of the society for the advancement of the Volkswagen." (HHA)

A side view of the same scene, showing at center, from left to right: two unknown General SS men; Porsche engineer Herbert Kaes and his brother, Ghislaine Kaes (hat), Dr. Ferdinand Porsche's personal secretary; another SS man; and an SA officer. Note the band at far left. The two were first cousins of Dr. Ferry Porsche. After the war, Herbert became a race car driver, while Ghislaine started the Porsche Company archives that exist to this day. (HHA)

A view of the assembled dedication crowd from the tribune's stand, from behind the trio of VW models in front. Afterwards, the trio of cars was driven to Hamburg, according to Chris Barber. (HHA)

The picture that is still published around the world: Hitler giving the cornerstone dedication speech on May 26, 1938, at Wolfsburg behind the first trio of VW Series 38 KdF Wagens: sedan, sedan sunroof, and (seen here) convertible. According to the 1939 Nazi-published sales brochure *Your KdF Wagen*, "The DAF worked so fast that, by the end of 1939, Germany had the most modern and advanced automobile plant in the world." Added Dr. Richard Barth of Hamburg, "Porsche's design of an automobile accommodating four persons—with rear-wheel drive, air-cooled engine, top speed of 100km/hr (about 60mph), and eight liter (2.11-gallon) gas tank, at a price of 1,000 RM, was presented as early as January 1934. Prototypes of the sedan, coupe, and convertible were ready by 1936," but the German automobile manufacturers resisted going into production, so Hitler took matters into his own hands. (HHA)

What happened to the cornerstone? Here it is seen being cemented by the German builders dressed in the traditional top hats of their craft for the occasion, as Hitler solemnly looks on at center. According to the British magazine *After the Battle* in 1976, "The box should have contained plans for the building, but these arrived too late to be included." The box was disinterred after the war, when its eagle and swastika on the lid could be plainly seen in 1976. On the front of the stone there is the Nazi swastika emblem, surrounded by the spinning cogwheel of the DAF. (HHA)

Hitler dedicates the cornerstone with a slight tap of a small hammer as Dr. Ferdinand Porsche (second from right) and Werlin (far right) look on. It was Werlin who reintroduced Hitler and Dr. Porsche in 1933 after a hiatus of a decade to discuss a project that interested them both: a *Volksauto/People Car* that the mass of the German people could actually afford. The Führer's 1938 name for the car, *KdF-Wagen*, caused its sales staff to groan, however, at the prospect of selling such a car thus named domestically, much less to foreigners! (HHA)

Another view of the same scene, showing at far left German Regular Police Chief Gen. Kurt Daluege, later Reinhard Heydrich's successor in 1942 as Acting Reich Protector of Bohemia and Moravia in Prague. Note the Nazi DAF swastika-and-gear logo on the front of the cornerstone at left. Added *The Volkswagen Story* in 1976, "When the new administration building was erected in 1959, the stone was removed and broken up," thus having a lifespan of but 21 years. The empty bronze box—complete with Nazi eagle and swastika—was still existent in the Volkswagen Museum at Wolfsburg in 1976. (HHA)

A frontal view of the sedan Beetle at Wolfsburg as Nazis cluster front and center to watch the cornerstone cementing. Noted the 1939 sales brochure *Your KdF-Wagen*, "For years the workers have constantly worked on new improvements in the drafting department." (HHA)

Stated *After the Battle*, "The foundation stone of the Volkswagen plant at Wolfsburg—laid by Hitler in 1938—vanished for over 40 years, only to be unearthed in 1998. Now it is displayed in the factory's museum." According to Beetlemania, "The Auto Museum opened in Wolfsburg on Apr. 26, 1985, providing a full display of the tradition that is Volkswagen. Among its prized displays are the third oldest VW, which sports over 300,000 miles on its original engine, and the sole surviving VW-Wagen Cabriolet," which was given to Hitler as a 50th birthday present on April 20, 1939. (VWM)

A side view of the dedication ceremony at Wolfsburg. Hitler is seen at the far right with Dr. Philip Bouhler in SS black inspecting the sedan with sunroof (beyond the lens.) In his introduction to the 1939 sales brochure *Your KdF-Wagen*, Dr. Robert Ley wrote, "Maintenance, the question of storage and obtaining spare parts, will be solved in such a way as to enable a broad mass of people to own the KdF car." (HHA)

Taking a closer look at the prototypes are, from left to right: NSKK *Korpsführer/Corps Leader* Adolf Hühnlein, Party philosopher Alfred Rosenberg, Dr. Ley (with gloves in hand), two unknown officials, Hitler, and Dr. Ferdinand Porsche. Noted Dr. Ley in his introduction to the 1939 sales brochure, "No hassle in getting to the workplace, rest and recuperation on weekends and on vacation. Participation in the inventions of technically oriented fields: all of these will bring the KdF car to the German worker." According to the US Army Ordnance Museum at Aberdeen, MD, "Photo obtained in May 1945 at the plant by Maj. F.G. Wilson of the Ordnance Technical Intelligence Team, OTIT-9," courtesy of the late Museum Specialist Armando Framarini, Sr. (HHA)

VW passenger Hitler seems delighted as he tries out the back seat of this prototype convertible at the Wolfsburg cornerstone dedication on May 26, 1938. Just opposite him in the brown Nazi Party uniform is Dr. Robert Ley. The others are, from left to right: Jakob Werlin (in black SS uniform), a top level Mercedes-Benz official; VW designer Dr. Ferdinand Porsche; Hitler's adjutant SS Gen. Julius Schaub; SA (Stormtroop) Chief of Staff Viktor Lütze (killed in a mysterious auto accident in 1943, incidentally); Hitler aide Albert Bormann (brother of Martin Bormann, and here attired in his official Nazi NSKK uniform); NSKK *Korpsführer* Adolf Hühnlein; and Alfred Rosenberg. (HHA)

Hitler and Dr. Ferdinand Porsche (center) inspect the inside of a VW. Noted one account, "At the end of the war, the Russians confiscated the 280 million marks in installment funds from a Berlin bank, but the newly constituted Volkswagen Company honored the old savings stamps, and in 1946 the People's Car began cruising on the Autobahn at last." (HHA)

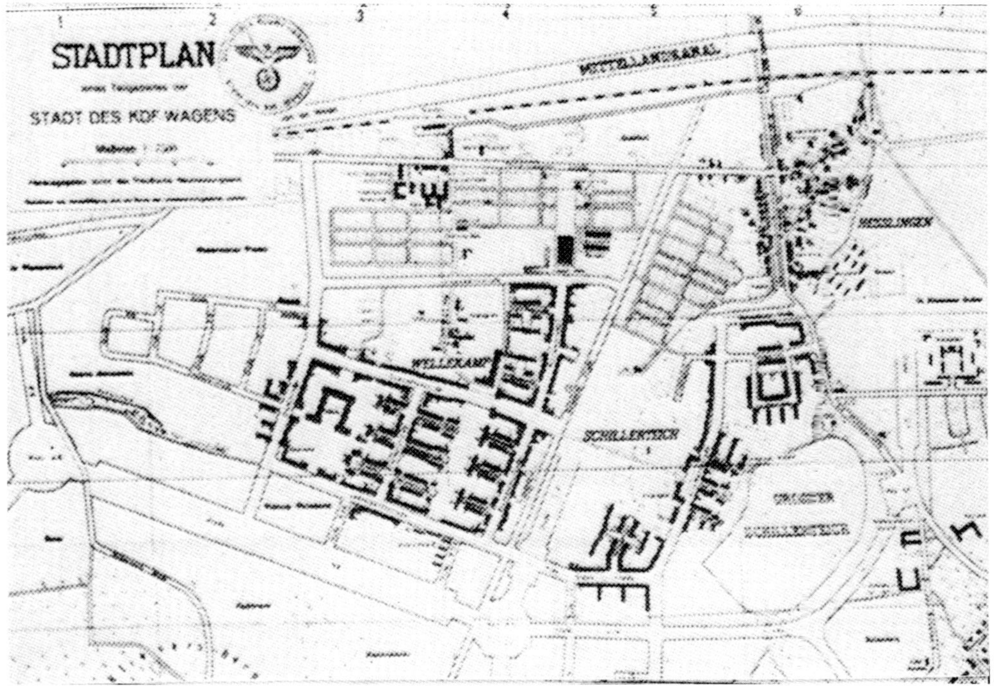

The May 26, 1938, KDF Stadt (City) plan that wasn't in the cornerstone box. Stated the authoritative magazine *After the Battle* in 1976, "The empty bronze box should've contained plans of the building, but these arrived too late to be included." This is how they looked. (Robert Gilmore Collection, LC.)

With Dr. Ferry Porsche at the wheel, and Dr. Ferdinand Porsche and Dr. Lafferentz in the rear seats, Hitler gives the Nazi salute, as the VW Beetle convertible license plate # IIIA 42803 is driven away from the dedication to the Fallersleben railway station. (HHA)

The May 26, 1938, cornerstone document at Fallersleben (Wolfsburg). It read: "The Führer and Chancellor of the German Reich Adolf Hitler in 1937, the fifth year of the National Socialist ascent to power, ordered the leader of the German Workers' Front, Reich Organization Leader Dr. Robert Ley, to implement all measures necessary to build the German People's Car. The cornerstone for the People's Car factory—the largest automobile factory in Europe—was laid today, the 26th of May 1938. In the year of the homecoming of Austria, the Führer and Chancellor of the Greater German Reich Adolf Hitler. His goal is the well-being of his people." From *Your KdF Car*, the VW sales brochure published in 1939. (VWM)

According to *The Volkswagen Story* in *After the Battle* issue #12, 1976: By 1938, "unofficially, the car had been called the Volkswagen, and this had already led to an engine designer at Dr. Porsche's office, Francis Reimspiess, to design the now famous VW emblem, originally surrounded by a spinning swastika, without ever being asked to do so. [When Dr. Porsche saw the emblem, he rewarded Reimspiess with a 100 mark bonus]." This is confirmed by Dr. Ferry Porsche in *We at Porsche*, when—writing of the postwar period 1949-50—he recalled, "There was also Franz Xaver Reimspiess, who had not only designed the Volkswagen engine to my father's specifications and concepts, but had also conceived the VW sign which became famous throughout the world and remains, to this day, unchanged. He was a former Austro-Daimler man." Added Nelson, the original VW design was concocted by Reimspiess in 1937-38, but "in subsequent years, (his) original design was embroidered with gear teeth and other decorative elements; after the war, it was again used as originally designed." The spinning swastika of the DAF thus almost became the symbol of the VW early on, but gave way in the end to the better-known VW symbol encircled and known around the globe today. (LC)

The von der Schulenburgs, and How Their Land was Appropriated for VW

The German Labor Front was searching for a site upon which to build the projected plant. According to Nelson:

"Under consideration were several possible locations: the Weser River Valley, the Mannheim industrial area, the Furstenwalde region near Berlin, a site near Regensburg, and another near Stendal on the Elbe River. All were rejected for reasons of congestion or distance from raw materials."

Dr. Bodo Lafferentz embarked in a light plane to inspect all the regions under consideration, and eventually settled—from the air—on the *Luneberger Heide/Luneberg Heath* that runs from north of Hannover and Brunswick:

"To the moor and marsh country beyond the Autobahn from Bremen to Hamburg…From the plane, it seemed perfect for the purpose he had in mind; perhaps he was not aware that below lay a mosquito-infested swamp" (as was also the case for Hitler's 1941-44 FHQ site selection at Rastenburg, in East Prussia.)

"Below also lay *Schloss* Wolfsburg, the 14th Century castle belonging to Count Werner von der Schulenburg, built on lands granted his ancestor *Ritter/Knight* von Bartensleben by Emperor Lothar II in 1135. The grant rewarded his defense of the area against the Slavs, and the lands had in succeeding generations been held successfully against all comers.

"Of these landlords it was written in 1584, 'In particular the von Schulenburgs and the von Bartenslebens were the true captains of men… the noble Lord Otho took the field against the proud Junkers…nor was any of them strong enough to confront the proud young lion, but he routed them again and again…' Ironically, his lands were fated to fall before the assaults of such a one as Robert Ley.

"The von der Schulenburgs—forced to surrender to the Nazis in 1937—were to prove themselves 'proud lions' in later years. Count Friederich Werner v.d. S., whom (William L.) Shirer terms 'an honest, decent, German of the old school,' served as Ambassador to Russia from 1934-41. He had honestly worked to improve Russo-German relations, was respected in Moscow, and was never informed of German plans to invade the USSR, an event which caught him completely by surprise.

"He later joined the July 20, 1944 plot to kill Adolf Hitler. Count Freiderich Dietloff v.d. S. joined the Nazis in 1932 and became Deputy Police President of Berlin in 1937 [and thus served under Himmler, who was Chief of the German Police nationwide]. However, he soon became an active anti-Nazi, and joined Gen. (Franz) Halder's stillborn plot to overthrow Hitler in September 1938.

"He resigned from the Nazi Party in 1940 [a brave thing to do at that juncture when Hitler the Führer was riding high] and also became involved in the 1944 conspiracy to assassinate Hitler. Both men—the former 69 and the latter 42 years of age—were murdered by the Gestapo in late 1944. The wife of Count Werner v/d. S, who was resident in the castle in 1937, met an ironic end: driving a Volkswagen near the VW plant in 1951, she died after crashing into a gas station on the very land her family had surrendered in 1937.

"Her castle is today [1965] being restored and transformed into a municipal art center. Count Werner, still living, no longer occupies it. His son Rudolf spent five months employed by Volkswagen of America before taking up studies for a doctorate at Harvard."

A car carrying a mysterious stranger on the morning of September 15, 1937, was spotted by several people surveying the land of the Count. A woman who was a neighbor of his approached the car and told the men in the Maybach that they were trespassing on private property, to which Dr. Laffarentz responded, "My dear lady, *I* am allowed to drive anywhere my car is able to carry me!"

Initially, it was thought they were looking for new Autobahn right-of-ways, but at lunch at the local inn, the men were overheard discussing plans to locate an entire new city there, and at length official payment was offered to the Count from Berlin. The Count wasn't interested in selling lands that had been in his family domain for five centuries, and prepared to fight back officially by contacting a boyhood friend who had grown up in nearby Fallersleben, the Führer's Minister for Church Affairs, Hans Kerrl, who also led the Bureau of Planning that reported to Hitler directly.

"The Count reached Kerrl immediately, but Kerrl was unable or unwilling to help his old friend. He tried to comfort him by saying that he was being asked to surrender only 7,600 morgen (approximately 5,000 acres) of the required 15,000 morgen. The rest would be commandeered from Herr/Mr. Gebhard von der Wense, who would give up another 2,500 morgen, and from 26 other, smaller landowners, who would make up the balance.

"Von der Wense was ruined by these and subsequent events. He bought land in Mecklenburg with the money received for his land in the Fallersleben area, but this was lost to the Russians at the end of the war. Back home, the only land he owned was the family graveyard. He took a job with the postwar Volkswagenwerk as a guide, touring visitors around the plant. His younger son works for VW's service department."

Nevertheless, Count von der Schulenburg fought on:

"His arguments convinced the Ministry of Transport. It reported to the government that the site would overload existing railway facilities and would prove too much of a burden for the important Mittelland Canal which flowed through the area. The Count convinced the Forestry Department that the ancient oaks on the property were worth preserving [Hermann Göring had been appointed by Hitler as Chief of the German Forests.]

"He even convinced the Luftwaffe/Air Force [which Göring also ran] that the planned site would prove a ridiculously easy target for enemy planes, and that the open countryside, the industrial complex to be erected, the railway lines, and the canal would prove irresistible to bombers [All these things came to pass as well in World War II].

"Finally, he rallied the aid of the mosquitoes, and made it known that the proposed location was an insect paradise, unfit for human habitation.

"Joseph Werner recalls his first sight of the proposed factory area towards the end of 1937, a few months after he had arrived from the US to work with Porsche in Stüttgart: 'It was a sandy field, and didn't look like it would support a factory,' he recalls. 'No private company would've wasted money building there.'"

Despite all of this, Drs. Ley and Lafferentz got their site:

"There reportedly was a meeting in Berlin to argue all positions. After heated discussion…Kerrl produced a paper containing the news that Hitler himself had decided in favor of Fallersleben…The delegation from the Forestry Administration, which objected to the destruction of centuries' old oaks, left the room muttering, 'You could've notified us of *that* on a postcard!'

"As for the mosquitoes, an appropriate specialist was sent to Fallersleben from the Reich Institute for Soil, Water, and Air Pollution to inspect the area and offer recommendations. The man examined the region carefully, then reported, 'Under no circumstances must you drain the water meadows of the stream valleys, because this would destroy the breeding grounds.

"A unique opportunity to study about 70 of the most interesting gnat species would be lost!' This scholarly gentleman's misplaced scientific curiosity was throttled. He was permitted to select and mount the more interesting species, and then the Third Reich moved exterminators into the insect paradise.

"Finally, in January 1938, all opposition ceased. Papers transferring the land to the State were drawn up and signed. Albert Speer...was charged with construction of the plant. Speer himself was busy with grandiose plans for rebuilding Berlin into a city called *Germania*, a magnificent center of the expanding Nazi empire.

"He looked around for an architect to whom he could entrust the job of planning not only the factory near Fallersleben, but also an Autostadt (Auto City) to house the 90,000 people who would be brought (from where no one knew) to the site [Plans called for 12,000 workers in each of two shifts. The families of these 24,000 would bring the population to 90,000.].

"Speer recalled a young Austrian architect, Peter Koller, an international prizewinner whom he had met lecturing in Berlin. He found him working in obscurity in the Augsburg regional planning office, and offered him at 30 a chance to be top man at Fallersleben.

"Koller threw himself into the task enthusiastically, evolving elaborate plans. The mile-long factory and a tall administration building would lie along one bank of the Mittelland Canal, while the city itself would reach out from the other shore. Vast blocks of apartments and two-family houses would shelter the Kleinauto workers and their families; parks, hotels, marketplaces, and broad boulevards to rival Berlin's would beautify the site.

"At the center would be a cultural core, the site of theaters, public halls, palaces of culture, government and Nazi Party buildings. It was to be, as Ley put it, 'A materialization in stone and iron' of Hitler's grandiose visions, 'proof' of what National Socialism could produce."

The plans were unveiled at the 1938 Berlin International Automobile and Motorcycle Exhibition, at which both the Führer and Dr. Göbbels spoke. The latter "Reviewed the gains made by motorists under Nazism. In 1932, he said, Germany had 548,000 passenger cars; by 1937, there were 1,108,500. Before Hitler, there had been only one car per 40 inhabitants; after Hitler, one for every 24." (Göbbels was exaggerating. As late as 1939 there was only one automobile for every 49 Germans.)

When Hitler entered Vienna the following month to conclude the *Anschluss/Union* of Germany with Austria, he told the enraptured Viennese crowd that the VW "Will also make a wish come true, a wish harbored by so many hard-working, underpaid Austrian people."

Two months later, on May 26, 1938, Hitler was ready to dedicate the plant cornerstone at Wolfsburg.

From left: Göring (second) and Hitler (third) visit one of the annual Berlin Auto Shows. Regarding the shape of the new Beetle, Hitler noted, "It should look like a beetle (Maifaker); one needs only to observe nature to realize how it produces a streamlined form." Noted British Führer biographer Ian Kershaw in his work *Hitler: Nemesis 1936-45*, "336,000 German civilians bought the new German civilian car, but none got it, either in part or in full." (Previously unpublished photo from the Hermann Göring Albums, Library of Congress, Washington, DC)

Count Werner Friedrich von der Schulenburg (1875-1944), uncle of the original owner of the Wolfsburg property near Fallersleben. Born at Kemberg in Saxony on November 20, 1875, this future German Foreign Office career diplomat studied law and political science before entering the diplomatic service of Kaiser Wilhelm II in 1901. After serving as an officer in World War I, the Count was named German Ambassador to Tehran under the Weimar Republic in 1923, then Ambassador to Bucharest in the service of the last years of the von Hindenburg Presidency, 1931-34. That same year he was sent to Moscow as Ambassador in the first year of the new Third Reich by Foreign Minister Konstantin von Neurath. Despite the political hostility of the two regimes between 1933-39, von der Schulenburg maintained friendly relations with both the Soviet Foreign Commissars of his time in office, Maxim Litvinov and Vyacheslav Molotov, leading Hitler's hand-picked successor to von Neurath (Joachim von Ribbentrop) to retain him from 1938-41. Von der Schulenburg was present with Stalin, Molotov, and von Ribbentrop when the Nazi-Soviet Non-Aggression Pact of August 23, 1939, was signed in Moscow, and later believed—as did von Ribbentrop—that the Führer's decision to negate the Pact by attacking the USSR on June 22, 1941, was an unmitigated disaster for the Third Reich. Recalled to Germany, in 1942 he nevertheless backed Stalin's secret calls for a separate peace, but this was rejected out of hand by Hitler, and von Ribbentrop went along, or else. According to Mathias Forster of Hamburg:

"Schulenburg offered his services to the (German) opposition circle around Karl Friedrich Gördeler [former Mayor of Leipzig], and went so far as to suggest that he be slipped through the front lines by (Col.) Henning von Tresckow. The conspirators of the [anti-Hitler] July 20, 1944 [plot] planned to make Schulenburg Foreign Minister. After the coup d'état failed he was sentenced to death by the People's Court, and was hanged at Berlin-Plötsenzee Prison with piano wire suspended from a meat hook." "I shall hang them like cattle!" Hitler had raged about the caught conspirators, and was as good as his word in this case. According to the Führer's valet, Heinz Linge, in his 1955 memoir *With Hitler to the End*, the Führer added, "Pity that Schulenberg, a man with so much backbone, was not on my side." It was the Count's land that formed the basis for KdF Wagen Stadt/Strength Through Joy Car City in 1938 that since May 1945 has been known as Wolfsburg under Volkswagen. Here the Count, as German Ambassador to the USSR (left), leaves the Embassy Chancery in Moscow with an aide in a typical Russian fur cap and fur-collared overcoat before the war. (CER)

From left to right: Architect Peter Koller was chosen to build what was to be known as KdF-Wagen Stadt at Wolfsburg; unknown aide; Dr. Ley; SS Gen. Julius Schaub; Hitler; Dr. Ferdinand Porsche; and Dr. Bodo Lafferentz (tallest man) seen examining a model of the proposed factory site. Continued Dr. Ferry Porsche, "The 'action' he [Hitler] had taken or made up his mind to take was quite simple. The RDA was to hand over the entire Volkswagen project to the German Labor Front (DAF) as a gesture of 'goodwill,' without any repayment. 'That will give the government a free hand,' Hitler said, 'and I think it will be a much better investment to build our own factory. You see?' What he meant was that by absorbing the cost of building the factory and equipment, the government would make it possible to sell the car for RM 990, ex works. My father and I looked at each other, finding it a little difficult to hide a smile, which Hitler was quick to spot." (HHA)

A broader view of the same scene, with a better grasp of the VW new town as a whole. The tall tower at left is at the heart of the plant site, the administration building. The man in SS black at far right is the Führer's future deputy for all things automotive in Nazi Germany, Jakob Werlin. Continued Dr. Ferry Porsche, "'I see we're in agreement,' he [Hitler] nodded, 'but we will have to go ahead with the major decision I spoke of a moment ago—and incidentally, just where is this factory going to be built? Have you given that any thought?' We had no chance to say anything before Hitler rattled on with the speed of a machine gun, each word brimful of enthusiasm." (HHA)

Hitler as a Car Driver

This seems to be a good place to discuss whether or not Hitler ever learned to drive a car himself. This is what he said on two different occasions to his intimates at Führer Headquarters. The first instance was on the night of February 3-4, 1942:

"The first thing I did on leaving the prison at Landsberg on December 20, 1924, was to buy my supercharged Mercedes. Although I've never driven myself, I've always been passionately keen on cars… [Nazi Gauleiter of Münich] Adolf Müller had taught me to drive all right, but I knew that, at the slightest accident, my conditional liberty would be withdrawn, and I also knew that nothing would've been more agreeable to the government."

On the 10th he added:

"Adolf Müller's the man to whom I owe the fact that I understand the art of driving a car…Since he was going to Wurzburg to buy a rotary press, Müller suggested that I should come with him… When he told me he would himself drive his car, my first reaction was to inform him that I wouldn't come with him. 'Get in,' he told me, 'and you'll learn what it is to drive a car.' I must honestly confess that the journey was a revelation to me! Unlike most people, I'm always ready to learn…Müller opened my eyes to an infinite number of small details that escape most drivers. Every pedestrian who is installed behind a wheel at once loses his sense of consideration to which he is convinced he is entitled whilst he is a pedestrian! Now Müller never stopped thinking of the people on the road. He drove very carefully through built-up areas. He believes that anyone who runs over a child should be put into prison at once. He didn't skirt the edge of the road—as many people do—but instead he stuck rather to the top of the camber, always mindful of the child who might unexpectedly emerge. When he wanted to pass a car, he first of all made sure that the driver in the car in front of him had taken cognizance of his intention. He took his curves cleverly, without making his rear wheels skid, and without sudden spurts of acceleration—all gently and flexibly. I realized that driving was something quite different from what I'd hitherto supposed, and I was a little ashamed at the comparisons that forced themselves into my mind. During that journey I made two decisions: I'd buy a Benz, and I'd teach my drivers to drive."

There you have it, "straight from the horse's mouth," so to speak. (HHA)

The Führer arrives for a surprise visit to inspect the nearly completed VW factory. At the wheel of his Mercedes-Benz Grosser/Grand parade car is longtime (and final) chauffeur SS Col. Erich Kempka. Martin Bormann's face is visible just beyond the white sleeve of Hitler's raincoat. Standing below the car, left to right are an unknown man, Dr. Ley doffing his cap, unknown man, Dr. Ferdinand Porsche, and Hitler's SS valet in black, Heinz Linge. It was he who, in 1945, wrapped his Führer's dead body in a brown Army blanket, carried it out of the Führer Bunker and into the Reich Chancellery park, and then aided in dousing it with gasoline from the Reich Chancellery garage. It was then burned according to the late dictator's orders. As for this June 9, 1939, visit to VW, Max Domarus noted, "Ferdinand Porsche, Robert Ley, and the factory director Werlin briefed Hitler on the progress being made there." (HHA)

The official party pauses for a photo. At center is Dr. Ley, then (from left to right) Martin Bormann, Hitler with arms crossed, Jakob Werlin, and Dr. Ferdinand Porsche, in profile. According to *The Encyclopedia of the Third Reich*, "Porsche's design of an automobile accommodating four persons, with rear-wheel drive, air-cooled engine, top speed of 100 km/hr (about 60 mph), and 8-liter (2.11-gallon) gas tank, at a price of 1,000 RM, was presented as early as January 1934. Prototypes of the sedan, coupe, and convertible models were ready by 1936." (HHA)

A very rare photo of Hitler's Grosser/Grand Mercedes Open Touring Car (right) and a KdF-Wagen (left) being prepared as a 50th birthday surprise for Hitler on April 20, 1939, with SS men. (Hermann Ahrens)

US EIGHTH AIR FORCE ATTACKS ON THE VOLKSWAGEN FACTORY IN 1944

Date & Time of Attack	Number & Type of Aircraft	Bombs Dropped				Height Dropped in Feet	Number of Hits Approx.	Un-Ex. Bombs	Wounded	Killed
		Type	Number	Size lbs.	Tons					
April 8, 1944 1415-1419	56	High Explosive M-47 100lb Petrol	251 1651	500 100	63 83	19,700- 21,000	950	None Reported	40	13
June 20, 1944 0904-0909	137 B-17	High Explosive " M-17 110 lb. x 4 lb. Magnesium	130 372 330	2000 500 500	130 93 83	24,000- 26,000	582	32	93	27
June 29, 1944 0939	41	High Explosive Incendiary	306 520	500 100	77 18		350	28	None	8
August 5, 1944 1336-1337	85 B-24	High Explosive	548	1000	274	22,000- 23,500	300	24	27	7

Bombing raids over Wolfsburg in 1944 destroyed about 60 % of the factory. Noted *The Volkswagen Story* in *After the Battle* (Issue #12, 1976): "The first recorded [wartime] bombing of the factory occurred in the summer of 1943, but no damage was sustained. As the factory was selected at the end of the war by the United States Strategic Bombing Survey team, accurate records are available on the four major raids on the plant... Two other incidents occurred. The first of these—on Apr. 18, 1944—when a single unknown aircraft dropped incendiary bombs, destroyed part of the front of the building. Then, on Apr. 29th at 11:19 in the morning, a US 8th Air Force aircraft believed to be a [B-17] Fortress returning from a raid on Berlin was hit by anti-aircraft fire. An engine was set on fire, and the crew bailed out, but the un-piloted bomber flew on to the factory where—after circling—it crashed into the corner of Hall One." A visual mock-up model of the damage of Hall One indicates that 50 % destruction was achieved—at least to the physical buildings, at any rate—but nonetheless production continued. (USSBS Chart)

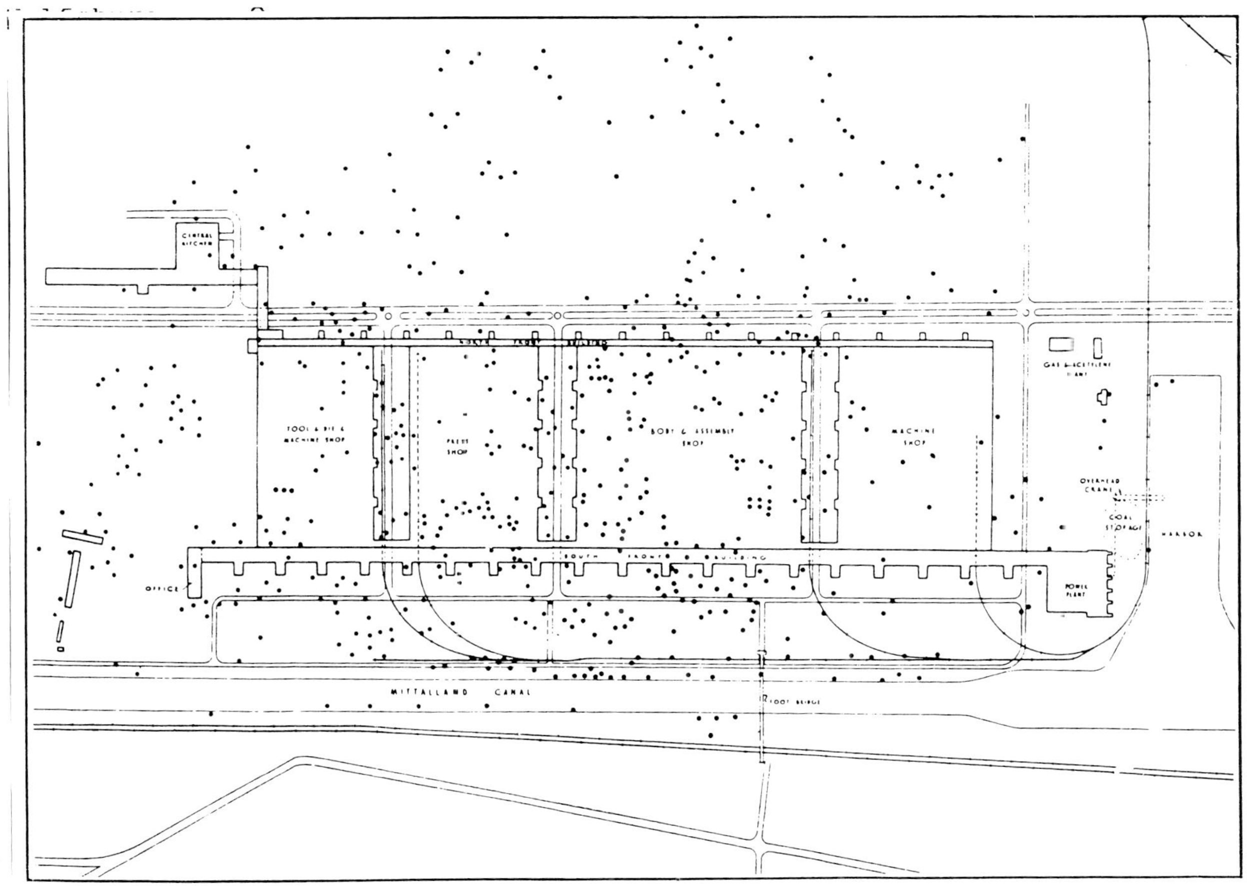

The Master Bomb Plot as produced by and for the US Strategic Bombing Survey as to where and how many bombs landed at VW Werks during the various air raids. (USSBS Chart)

A damaged American 8th US Army Air Force Boeing B-17 four-engine bomber over Germany. By the summer of 1942, the B-17 and the B-24 Liberator were the two strategic bombers attacking targets in the Reich, protected by Mustang fighter escort aircraft. (US Army Signal Corps photo, USNA, College Park, MD)

The nose of *Briefing Time*, a fully restored vintage Consolidated B-24 Liberator at Martin State Airport, Middle River, MD, in May 1990. According to Editor Wayne Laufert of *The Dundalk Eagle* of Dundalk, MD, "The B-24 Liberator was produced more than any other plane in American military history [May 3, 1990]." This was the major Allied aircraft that attacked the VW Werks at Wolfsburg in 1944. (Previously unpublished photo by Blaine Taylor, Towson, MD)

The start of the August 5, 1944, raid by the 93rd Bomb Group B-24s from Hardwick, Norfolk, England, attacking the VW Werks plant (marked off) "from high level." The Mittelland Canal is dissecting the aerial photo from right to left at the top of the photo, moving upwards. (USAAC photo.)

A B-24 bomber with a badly damaged right wing over Germany. According to Stan Pie[illegible] of the Glenn L. Martin Aviation Museum of Middle River, MD, "This is probably a J model." According to author George Sullivan in his 1985 work *Famous Air Force Bombers*, "Like the B-17 Flying Fortress, the four engine B-24 Liberator was a workhorse bomber of World War II. More B-24s were built and used during the war than any other airplane, a total of 19,251 in all versions…." (US Army Air Corps photo, USNA, College Park, MD)

A postwar company-built model of the factory to show part of the damage sustained during the Allied bombing raids. Asserted *After the Battle*, "By May 1945, 58% of the factory lay in ruins, and as the war came to an end, orders were given to evacuate the remaining undamaged machinery to the west, away from the advancing Russians; 200 machines were shipped to mineshafts at Longwy, other equipment being scattered throughout the surrounding countryside." (CER)

At right and following: Ground-level bomb damage. Stated *The Volkswagen Story* in 1945, "An advance unit of the 405th Regimental Combat Team of the US 102nd Infantry Division reached Fallersleben, four miles from the factory, on Apr. 10th, but the Americans did not come to KdF Stadt, as it was not marked on their maps. The SS guarding the forced laborers fled, leaving the prisoners unguarded. Overnight, they broke free of their camp and—after looting the few executives' houses south of the canal—turned their attentions to the factory. Telephones were ripped out, files overturned and burned, and typewriters smashed. Others captured freight trains at the railway station, and the exhilarated looters soon threatened to burn the town." (CER)

Bülow Street in Berlin in July 1944 after an Allied air raid. A KdF-Wagen VW Type 60 is seen here driving past a damaged elevated railway line. One prewar VW sales slogan had been, "Save 5 marks a week if you want to drive your own car!" According to *The Encyclopedia of the Third Reich*, "It was offered at affordable prices and was intended to introduce mass motorization to Germany. In the VW's creation, an industrial investment program was united with a sociopolitical goal: the automobile lost its character as a status symbol for wealthy people." (CER)

Another ground level view of the bombing destruction wrought by the Americans in 1944. Continued *After the Battle*, "When the priests returned, they were preceded by an armored car and a jeep. The children were found safe, but at the hutted camps, the intoxicated looters seemed to have lost their senses. Three bursts into the air didn't succeed in serving its purpose as a warning; two further bursts along the road, leaving several bodies lying motionless, soon restored sanity. The following morning, 200 US troops with Sherman tanks occupied the factory and town. On May 25, 1945, the name of KdF Stadt was changed by the town officials to Wolfsburg, after the nearby castle. The Americans were persuaded to keep the factory power station operative, as it supplied (as it still does) electricity for the townspeople, and Rudolf Brormann, the factory's former chief inspector, was put in temporary charge." (CER)

Yet another ground-level angle view of the bombing damage at VW Werks Wolfsburg. When production ground to a halt, the freed slave laborers looted, and the cowed German staffers waited in fear for the Allies—hopefully not the Russians—to arrive. Continued *The Volkswagen Story*, "Although captured by the Americans, Wolfsburg and nearby Fallersleben came within the [previously agreed upon at Yalta] British Zone of Occupation. On May 26 [1945], the British 52nd Division started assuming responsibility for the area occupied by the 406th Regimental Combat Team, and a few days later, the changeover was complete. Repatriation was begun for the foreign workers, although no arrangements existed for the return of the Russians and the other East Europeans. The British soldiers guarding the camp frequently had to break up disturbances amongst these displaced persons." (CER)

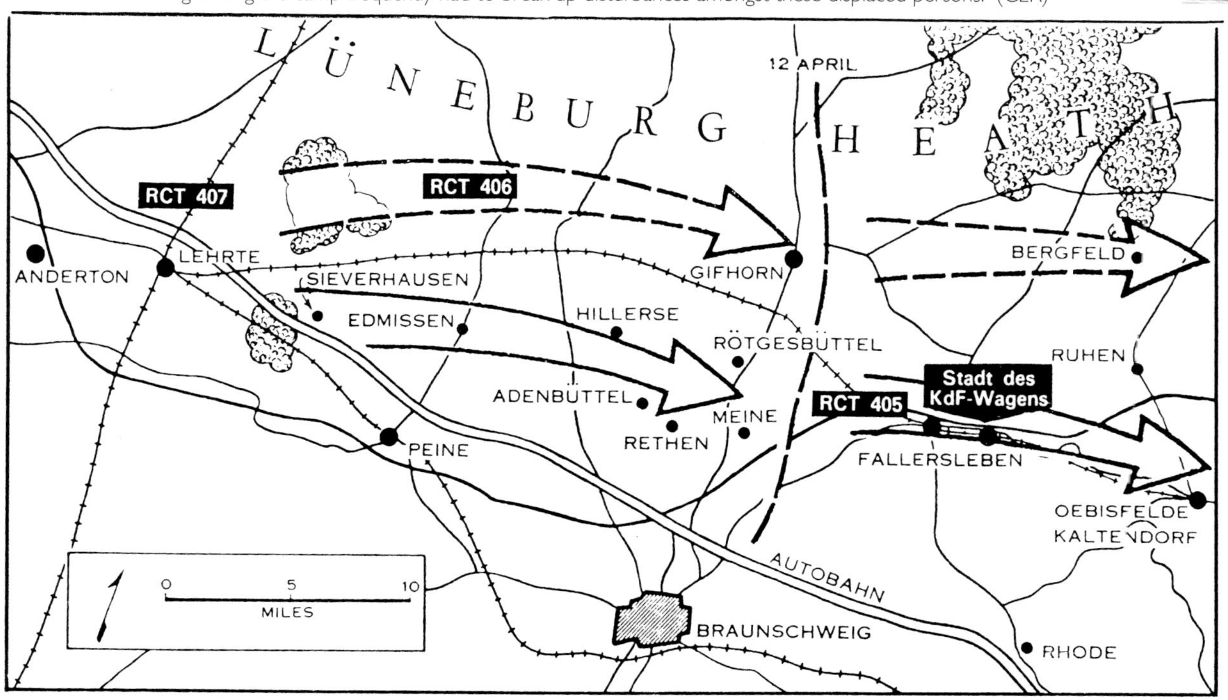

The unexpected American Army drive on KdF Statdt (or, officially, as shown here, City of the KdF Car) in April 1945, as a trio of US Regimental Combat Teams push forward. Although this map shows both the nearby railway line and Autobahn, KdF Stadt didn't appear at all in US Army maps, explaining why, originally, they stopped short of it, and took it only when asked to by the townspeople!" US Army engineers occupied the factory after its capture on April 11, 1945. The factory had made flying bombs, aircraft wings, and Teller mines, as well as assembling vehicles," concluded *After the Battle*. (Map from *After the Battle*.)

The first general surrender of the war in Northwest Europe took place in British Army Field Marshal Bernard Law Montgomery's command post tent on the Lüneberg Heath in North Germany that covered that area as well as Denmark, Holland, the Frisian Islands, Heligoland, all other German islands, and Schleswig-Holstein on May 4, 1945—including both Wolfsburg and Fallersleben. Here, famed British military writer Chester Wilmot is just to the right of the left hand tent pole. From right to left the others are an unknown British Army officer, German Army Field Marshal Ernst Busch (back to lens), Field Marshal Montgomery, unknown aide looking over his shoulder, German Navy Adm. Hans-Georg von Friedeburg, unknown German Army officer (back to camera), and unknown German Navy admiral. Ironically, a British caption to this photo read, "The end of the Anglo-German war." (LC)

The factory rebuilt, "Stretching nearly a mile from one end to the other," according to Nelson, "Volkswagen's 'home plant' in Wolfsburg rates as one of the world's largest factories. There are five other VW factories in Germany," he noted in 1965. After being handed back from the British to the West Germans by 1949, VW was the Federal Republic's major manufacturer, with 45% of the country's total industrial exports—and changes made to the basic product only after two decades of production. The first VW franchise was founded in the US in 1953 with Max Hoffmann representing both VW and Porsche—until VW chief Heinz Nordhoff decided instead to found Volkswagen of America. He also believed in staying the course once set of "no radical changes" that put the company on first a sound, and then a wildly profitable, financial footing. (VWM)

The VW plant at Wolfsburg in 1965. (VWM)

This is the "body drop" on one of the eight circa-1965 final assembly lines at Wolfsburg, which combined completed body shells to their respective platform chassis. In 1965, asserted Nelson, " A car was built by then at the rate of five per minute, and the plant employed 55,000 workers. Virtually all of the new cars leave the factory on double deck trains, each carrying 250 vehicles." Student graduates of construction schools went to work at the same plants where their parents worked, such as used to be the case at plants across the United States during the period 1930-80, like Bethlehem Steel Corporation at Dundalk, MD, and the Martin Aerospace Company at Middle River, MD. For the last three decades both have operated on a reduced manpower shift basis. The one millionth Beetle was made in 1955—a decade after the catastrophic end of World War II, just as Hitler predicted—and today's VW banners are blue-on-white, similar to the Nazi swastika banners of yesteryear. In 1956, the second VW plant was opened at Hannover, West Germany. For the million car celebrations, Dr. Ferry Porsche and Heinz Nordhoff were each given a car painted in green and gold, with a bouquet of flowers also being presented to Nordhoff. Even greater production and sales were ahead, however, as "the love Bug" became the automotive symbol of the "flower power" generation of the "baby boomers" of the Sixties and Seventies, who today are buying the latest incarnation of the New Beetle, along with their children. (VWM)

Postwar mass-produced Beetles. According to *Beetlemania*, "Sales had plummeted from 90,000 in 1975 to less than 20,000 in just three years. The last German Beetle was completed on Jan. 19, 1978. Only the Beetle cabriolet convertible remained in production, and actually maintained its popularity until it was replaced by the Karmann-built Rabbit convertible in 1980. The idea to build a cabriolet version of the Beetle began after the war," by famed coachbuilder Wilhelm Karmann. (VWM)

VW of America executive Will van de Kamp came to the US in 1955, and convinced Americans to become "pioneers" in the VW organization, noted Nelson. This shot was taken in 1957, with J. Stuart Perkins (left) running after his boss. (VW of America)

VW of America executive Carl H. Kahn replaced van de Kamp in 1959 "and set the basic pattern and tone of the American marketing program," stated Nelson. (VW of America)

VW of America executive J. Stuart Perkins in 1962 led the VW organization in becoming the envy of many major US companies. (VW of America)

May 26, 1938: Hitler as passenger is driven in a VW Beetle convertible by young Dr. Ferry Porsche (left) after the Führer's dedicatory speech at the Wolfsburg plant. On June 22, 1942, Hitler said at a table at Rastenburg—on the first anniversary of the German invasion of the USSR—"Rommel's victories, moreover, have been made possible by our timely recognition that desert warfare is a battle of machines. The enemy, on the other hand, had a completely wrong conception of desert warfare, because they had arrived at completely wrong conclusions about the capabilities of motor vehicles in the desert. How often in the history of war has some General Staff officer or other—unhindered by any practical experience—developed the thesis that motor vehicles in the desert can operate only along the highways—and how often has this thesis been hailed as axiomatic! It has always been my wont to insist that theoretical theses of this sort must be tested practically, and it was on these grounds that I ordered the construction of the Volkswagen, which is now giving so magnificent an account of itself in the desert, that convinced me of the futility of this particular thesis. The Volkswagen—and I think our war experiences justify us in saying so—is the car of the future! One had only to see the way in which these Volkswagen roaring up the Obersalzberg overtook and skipped like mountain goats round my great Mercedes, to be tremendously impressed. After the war—when all the modifications dictated by war experience have been incorporated in it—the Volkswagen will become the car par excellence for the whole of Europe, particularly in view of the fact that it is air-cooled, and so unaffected by any winter conditions. I should not be surprised to see the annual output reach anything from a million to a million-and-a-half." (HHA)

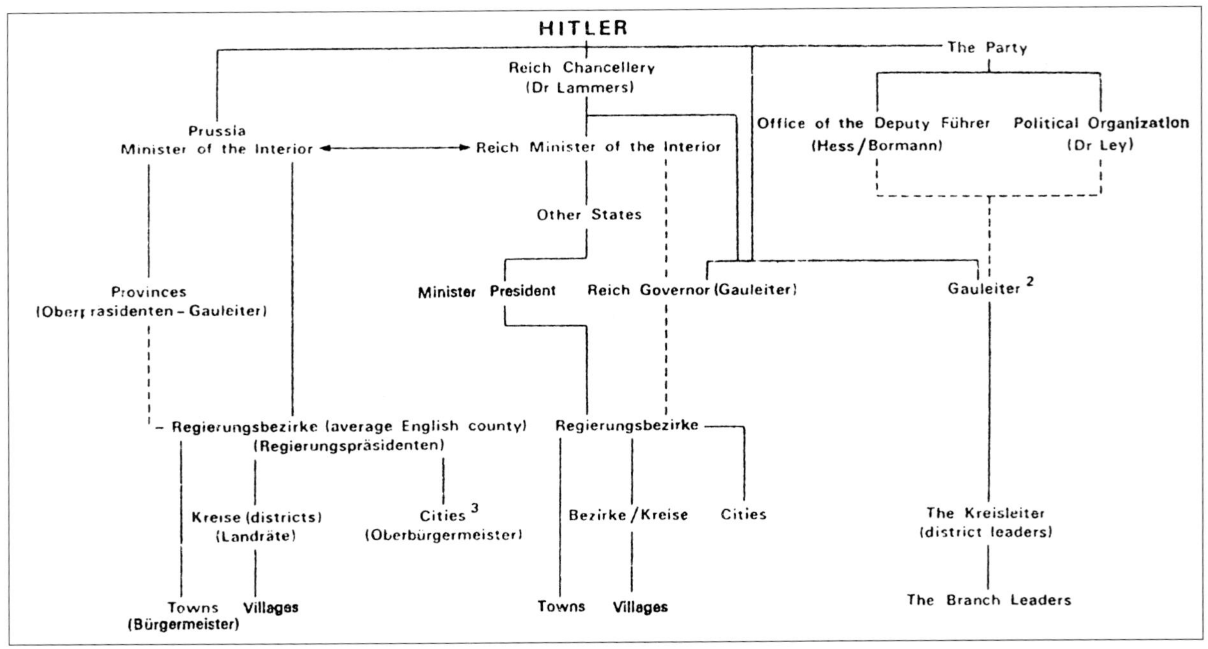

Nazi Party/State relations in the Third Reich after the death of President von Hindenburg, who would've stood above Chancellor Hitler in this chart. At his death in August 1934, the Nazi Führer/Leader merged the two offices of President and Chancellor into one, with his new title being Führer and Reich Chancellor. Thus, they would remain until his own death on April 30, 1945, when his Last Will and Political Testament named Navy Grand Adm. Karl Dönitz as the next Reich President, and Dr. Josef Göbbels as his Reich Chancellor. (LC)

An impassioned Chancellor Hitler speaks in the German *Reichstag*/Parliament. On the left is Dr. Hans Heinrich Lammers, and at right Dr. Walther Funk, who took over the Reichsbank Presidency from Dr. Hjalmar Schacht in January 1939. Behind them all—in the President's chair above and at left—is Hermann Göring. According to German editor Max Domarus, Hitler typically only spoke to those who wanted to hear him: Nazi Party regulars, cleverly manipulated by Dr. Göbbels to appear as if the entire country embraced Nazism. Before he had been named Reich Chancellor, on April 7, 1932, Hitler gave a campaign speech at Darmstadt in which he asserted, "When I prophesied six million unemployed one year ago, I was laughed at, and made out to be an irresponsible agitator. I have been proven right in my theory that the loss of liberty leads to loss of work." In this "liberty," Hitler meant the loss of German freedom of action under the Treaty of Versailles that had taken away German national self-determination in 1919. Like the much larger United States of America, tiny Germany (about the size of the American state of Wisconsin) had been particularly hard-hit by the worldwide Great Depression. (HHA)

Hitler and the Nazis tackle the unemployment issue head-on, 1933-39: Chancellor Hitler (center) addresses Nazi Party faithful in the Berlin Lustgarten/Pleasure Park with a balding Rudolf Hess (left, center) and Baldur von Schirach at right rear (Previously unpublished photo from the Heinrich Hoffmann Albums, USNA, College Park, MD)

An election poster from what the Nazis called, "The Time of Struggle" to gain political power in the Reich, "die Kampfzeit." This one screams, "Workers. Elect the frontline soldier Hitler!" By the time Hitler became Reich Chancellor on January 30, 1933, it was estimated that unemployment numbered 6,013,612 people, or about 19% of the total available work force nationally, an increase from 1932, when the average was 5.5 million, just as candidate Hitler had said. According to Dr. Bernd Wegner of Freiburg in 1985, "Employees in commerce, unskilled workers, laborers in the iron and other metal industries, and also skilled construction workers suffered in particular from the crisis"—people who in the U.S. would be referred to as "blue collar" workers, and who in Europe made up the membership of the Socialist and Communist Parties. For them the word "Socialist" was embedded in the overall designation of National Socialist (Nazi) Party by the astute politician Hitler. It was they who had led the Revolution of 1918-19, and their class he would need to win over by ending unemployment and, in the future, to build both the Autobahns and the Volkswagens, as well as his future war machine. (HHA)

"Wives! Vote for Adolf Hitler!" asserted this Nazi election poster depicting the plight of the unemployed husband, father, and head-of-household unable to provide for his family. As with John F. Kennedy in 1960, Robert F. Kennedy in 1968, and Bill Clinton in 1996, the female vote was an important Hitlerite constituency in Germany. After Hitler took office in 1933, "Unemployment fell rapidly in Germany," attested Dr. Wegner, "due to the Party's Work Creation measures—alá Franklin Roosevelt in the USA—and rearmament. The yearly average of unemployment in 1933 was 4.8 million, and within his first year in office, was down 2.7 million"—something the Party naturally enough took credit for and of which the German people at large credited Hitler as well. One of the major Nazi programs during 1933-34 was Work Creation, reflecting Hitler's 1930-32 campaign promises of "Work and bread for everyone" and "A husband for every German girl" to boot. Hitler abolished all other political parties in the *Reichstag* in March 1933, and enacted his first Law to Decrease Unemployment on June 1st, followed by a second on September 21st, concurrently with the start-up of the Autobahn road-building program and town reconstruction projects as well. Noted Dr. Wegner, "The total budget for Work Creation efforts may have amounted to some 5.5 billion Reichsmarks." These, rearmament, and an improving global market all combined to give the impression that the Nazis, and primarily Adolf Hitler, had worked an economic miracle. In the end, he would work the Volkswagen miracle twice: during 1938-44, and again in the decade after his death, in the mid-1950s. (HHA)

Having been unemployed myself in the early Nineties, I can testify first-hand that when one's benefits run out, that doesn't mean you're not still unemployed! The only thing that's changed is that the numbers change, and you then become one of the "invisible" unemployed, i.e., you no longer appear on the official rolls of unemployed persons. The same was true in Weimar Republican Germany as well, noted Dr. Wegner, "The statistics reflected only those unemployed persons seeking employment who were registered with the employment and welfare offices, so that the real numbers were far higher. Because the chance of finding work was slight, fewer and fewer of the unemployed registered during the course of the crisis. The 'invisible' unemployed were primarily women, young people, and older workers. If they were counted, then unemployment in the spring of 1933 would have been around 7.8 million." This led to millions of these people joining the Nazi Party (such as the young man shown here) as the only political group other than the Communists showing a way out of the ever-worsening morass. A country whose young people no longer believe in it is headed for disaster. (HHA)

In the U.S., FDR had enacted through the American Congress his Civilian Conservation Corps (CCC) measure to help put millions of young American men back to work, and they built my own Federal Post Office Building at Towson, MD, in 1938. Meanwhile, Hitler was doing virtually the same thing in Nazi Germany with his SA, SS, RAD, Hitler Youth, NSKK, and other like paramilitary formations with the identical original design: get men off the streets and doing something useful, as here, peeling potatoes. A key Nazi credo was that all young men were equal—there were to be no classes in the New Germany—and all work, particularly manual work, was dignified. This put everyone on the same level, working toward a common goal: economic recovery and rearmament. The same spirit would later underlay the creation of Volkswagen. How successful was Hitler in dealing with unemployment? According to Dr. Wegner, "Unemployment sank by 1937 to a yearly average of 0.9 million," putting teeth into the Führer's 1933 boast, "Give me four years, and you won't recognize Germany anymore!" Truly, it was an economic miracle by any standards, and paved the way for the phenomenal success of Volkswagen later. (HHA)

Auto Show 1933-34

Top Nazis at the annual International Automobile and Motorcycle Exhibition on the Kaiserdamm in Berlin, 1933-39. Noted German editor Max Domarus in his ground-breaking series, *Hitler: Speeches and Proclamations, 1932-45*:

"On Feb. 11, 1933, Hitler made an appearance of a completely different nature. Festively attired in a cutaway coat, he inaugurated the opening of the International Automobile and Motorcycle Exhibition on the Kaiserdamm/Imperial Roadway in Berlin. It was the first time a Reich Chancellor had opened an exhibition of this sort, and the magnates of the automobile industry were flattered by the honor [as well they might be, considering the fact that this was but his 11th day in office!]. Their satisfaction increased when Hitler presented himself not only as a respectable and responsible statesman, but also as a knowledgeable expert on motorization as well."

The years spent fostering the growth of the NSKK and crisscrossing the country in his Mercedes-Benz Grossers had not been wasted:

"His speech commenced with a lengthy perspective on the evolution of the various means of transportation in general and Germany's outstanding contribution to this field in particular."

It also was his first public step in inserting both himself and the Nazi Party into things automotive on a governmental scale, and thus also preparing the way for the creation and production of the Volkswagen. He stated:

Here, Reich Chancellor Hitler (left), surrounded by the silken, top hat magnates of the car industry and wearing formal morning coat attire, peers pensively into a Mercedes chassis. (HHA)

"As I am today given the honor of speaking to you at the request of the Reich President (von Hindenburg), my dear gentlemen of the (automobile) industry, I would not want to neglect conveying to you my opinion regarding what I believe to be necessary toward promoting what is probably today's most important industry. 1) Separation of the State motor traffic syndicate from the present realm of transportation. The automobile—by its very nature—is more closely affiliated with the airplane than with the railroad [and he had campaigned over and across Germany via both by this time]. Automobiles and airplanes have a common basis in the motor industry. Without the development of, for instance, the diesel engine for motor traffic, it would've been practically impossible to lay the necessary groundwork for its utilization in aviation. 2) Gradual reduction of the tax burden. 3) Institution and implementation of a large-scale road-building program. 4) Promotion of sports events. Just as the horse and cart once burned their trails, and the railroad built its required track network, so must motorized traffic be supplied with the requisite roads. In the past, one attempted to measure a people's standard of living in terms of track kilometers; in the future, road kilometers for motorized traffic will replace this yardstick. These are momentous tasks that are also part of the program for the reconstruction of the German economy! Now I would like to thank you on behalf of the Reich President and the Reich Government for everything you have accomplished in the meantime on your own initiative. We are able to view this attractive exhibition today thanks to three factors which I would like to recall here: You businessmen and leaders of industry and commerce have possessed the boldness not to abandon the struggle even in these troubled times, but to take up the fight against the foreign automobile industry, which is in part, so much better situated, but I would also like to thank the countless German designers and technicians whose genius is creating wondrous works of human invention. It is regrettable that our people are rarely given the opportunity to become acquainted with these nameless men who—by designing our cars—not only make hundreds of thousands of individuals happy, but have also opened up new and comfortable means of transportation for millions across the board of motorized traffic. I would also like to take this opportunity to pay tribute to that great army of German workers, whose industriousness and ability and tremendous conscientiousness in their work makes it possible to transform technological ideas into machines that can be described as real masterpieces of precision, as well as aesthetic beauty. Lastly, I wish to commemorate the German people. May it, as well, fully appreciate the work, industriousness, and genius of so many efforts. May it here, as well, revere its German masters of brains and brawn, and may it never forget that many tens of thousands of our people are without work, and have the right to expect that the entire people remember these comrades and—out of solidarity with their need—recognize their brotherhood with German workers. With this hope, I hereby, with proud confidence, declare this Automobile Exhibition on behalf of the Reich President open to the public."

Hitler had thus accomplished a number of things with this talk: he had identified himself publicly with the revered Reich President, the esteemed Field Marshal of the Great War; he had told his listeners what they wanted to hear (and they were among his top financial backers during the just concluded *Kampfzeit*, or Time of Struggle); and, most importantly, he had not mentioned a word about Volkswagen—a concept that they would have uniformly opposed outright, with the sole exceptions being the Porsches. That would come later, when he eliminated all other opposition to him within the Third Reich.

This time appearing in Nazi Party Leadership Corps brown uniform, Hitler opens the auto show of March 7, 1934, viewing an Opel car. (HHA)

According to Max Domarus:

"In his speech on the [1934] occasion, he proclaimed that Germany's fuel supply would be secured in the future on a national [i.e., synthetic] basis, and also announced the creation of a Volkswagen. The German automobile industry was reluctant to take on this project, for it had hitherto adhered to the principle of manufacturing distinctive, high-quality vehicles, and was disinclined to turn to mass production. Hitler cured them of these individualistic ideas, declaring, 'The Government will be persistent and rigorous in continuing the program announced last year. It will give to the entire automotive sector the strong impulse it needs to overcome the general preconceptions on the one hand, and the lethargy on the other. It will attempt to continue to directly and indirectly decrease taxes for the automobile owner. In addition to extending the tremendous Autobahn road network, the Reich is determined to devote practical attention to improving the existing motor roads. The Reich Government will provide every possible support to the development of the automobile to establish a close and profitable link between this most recent means of transportation, and the large existing transportation institution on the Reichsbahn/Reich Railway. The problem of securing and producing fuel on a national basis will be solved! Gentlemen, I do not need to paint a picture for you of the consequences of the existing attitude and the measures that have resulted from it. There is no clearer proof of the effectiveness of our actions in the past year than the International Automobile Exhibition of 1934 in Berlin, which was organized literally as fast as lightning, and which has become such a wonderful success. Above all, it gives me the indestructible confidence that the commercial adroitness of our plans, the ingenuity of our technicians, and the miraculous productivity of our German manual laborers and precision workers will doubtless succeed in accomplishing the great tasks which still lie before us—and these tasks are not small! Gentlemen, if we really want to increase the automobile owners in Germany to figure in the millions, this is only possible if we adapt the price to the financial capabilities of the mass of millions of potential buyers in question. The German Government desires that the German people take an animated interest in motorized vehicles, and it follows that the economy must design and build the right vehicle for the German people. Only a few months ago, German industry succeeded, by fabricating a new people's radio, in introducing and selling an enormous number of radio sets on the market. I would cite the most significant task of the German automotive industry as that of increasing production of the one car which will necessarily open up a class of buyers numbering millions, for only if we are able to win over the broadest possible masses for this new means of transportation with its economic and social advantages be indisputable. What German industry has accomplished in the years behind us is admirable. There is no country in the world showing greater progress in the construction of new automobiles than Germany. All the way from small models to the most modern racing cars, from trucks with diesel engines to motorcycles: everywhere we see new paths being taken and truly ingenuous ideas becoming reality. It should be noted that this Automobile Show is not the product of long planning, but shows a random sample of our industry's products…March 17th is the 100th anniversary of the day upon which the builder of the first automobile first glimpsed the light of day… who can doubt that we will succeed in carrying on this wonderful development for the benefit of our entire German people?…Thus, I am happy and proud to declare the International Automobile Exhibition of 1934 in Berlin open to the public."

The address was significant for a number of reasons: he made no mention of "our Reich President," but opened the Show on his own; he made mention of the concept of the VW, if not its name, and the economic underpinnings for it; and he issued the first veiled threat to his former backers that those who had ridden the back of the Nazi tiger in the days when they could control it would wind up inside the belly of the beast if they didn't now obey its declared wishes. Thus, Volkswagen had taken another important step forward.

Hitler (center) at a Berlin Auto Show. (HHA)

Two VWs at center in a garage yard before the war. Note the two different rear configurations. (VWM)

Reich Chancellor Hitler (center, wearing swastika on his brown uniform jacket's left sleeve) inspects a Borgward bus at a Berlin International Automobile and Motorcycle Show before the war. Seen in the military cap just to the left of Hitler is NSKK Führer Adolf Hühnlein. (HHA)

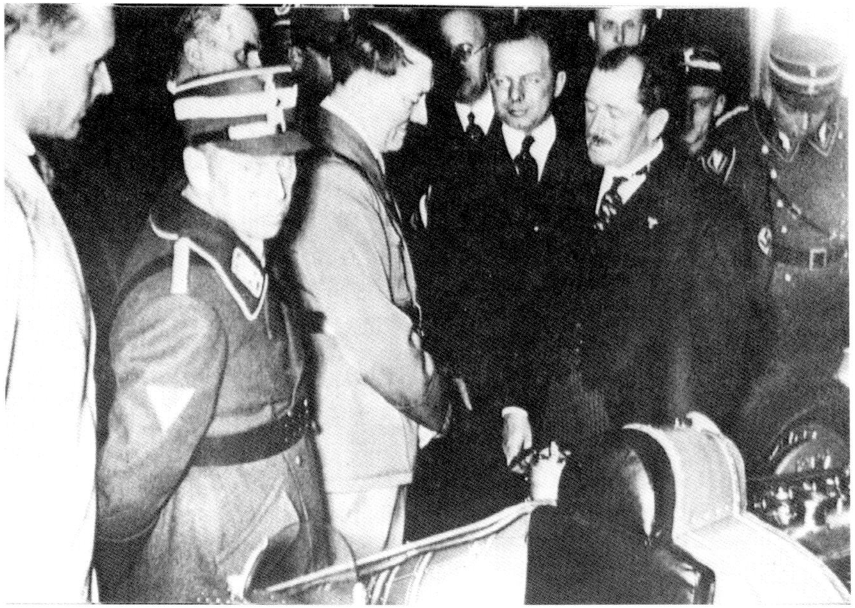

According to Dr. Ferry Porsche in *We at Porsche*, this photo caption reads, "1934: Professor (Ferdinand) Porsche (winged collar) explains the technical points of the first completed Auto Union (car) to Adolf Hitler. The car was brought especially to the Chancellery in Berlin. At left is Hans Stuck von Villiez, the team's number one driver. In full uniform, between Stuck and Hitler, is Korpsführer Konrad (sic) Hühnlein, head of the National Socialist Automobile Korps (NSKK). Facing camera, between Hitler and the professor, is Herr von Oertzen, manager of the Auto Union Firm." Actually, Hühnlein's first name was Adolf, not Konrad, and the year is 1935, as seen in a series of pictures in the Hermann Göring Albums for the opening of the Auto Show itself (where this photograph was, therefore, taken) on February 17, 1935. Despite Dr. Ferry Porsche's recollection, I am inclined to go with that of Göring's personal photographer, who took the pictures and entered them in the albums. However, Domarus gives the date for the actual opening as February 14th, adding, "As in previous years, he discussed general aspects of transportation, and then focused his attention on government measures promoting motorized traffic. In respect to the Autobahn and Volkswagen projects, he stated, 'When the Reich Autobahn network is finished, Germany will be able to call its own the most modern system of roads in the world by far. Tremendous evidence of peaceful progress! These measures are to be complemented by the task of creating a car for the people at large. I am happy to say that a brilliant designer has succeeded, with the cooperation of his staff, in completing preliminary plans for the German Volkswagen, and will finally be able to test the first models beginning in mid-year.' Hitler closed his speech by pointing out that the possibilities of producing synthetic rubber and synthetic gasoline were now theoretically given." (HHA)

Auto Show 1936-37

Noted Max Domarus, at his opening of the Automobile Show on February 15, 1936, Hitler asserted that, "The government of the Weimar Republic had not done much for traffic concerns, doing more to impose restraints upon it than to seek its advance." In Hitler's eyes this was the obvious outcome, which the misbegotten conception of the equality of all men had led to. In the end, all it had brought about was an equally low standard of living for all. As Hitler maintained, the percentage of cars per person in Germany had been so low in 1932 that only the Russians possessed even fewer automobiles. He regarded the low level of motorization in the Soviet Union as proof of the primitive nature of Bolshevism. Imagine his surprise when in World War II the supposedly primitive Russians threw row after row of motorized vehicles and tanks at the German lines." Unlike his previous trio of speeches before this same audience, Hitler's opening speech today was critical:

"I believe it is particularly fitting on a day such as this, if merely to counter the forgetfulness of mankind, to stress those factors that have been psychologically responsible for the sorry decline of our automobile industry, and thus of our transportation industry as a whole, that is to say of that industry which can currently be described as the single most powerful industry, and which is thus called upon to put its unique and characteristic stamp on today's age…Fiscal authorities and police headquarters [under the deposed Weimar Republic] cooperated to choke off and stamp out the development of German road traffic, and with it the transportation industry as thoroughly as possible, and—this is one complement which must be made to the Marxist-Centrist governments—they succeeded brilliantly in their joint attack. Whereas, in America, approximately 23 million automobiles were on the roads and three-four million were being manufactured annually, the combined efforts of the leadership of people and State succeeded in limiting the number of automobiles in Germany to barely 450,000 and in reducing the number produced in the year 1932 to 46,000. It was bad enough that the leadership of people and State—under the influence of such ideas—had no comprehension of the development of motorization; it is as least as bad as that of the German economy itself, albeit perhaps unconsciously, gave in nonetheless to quite similar thoughts. Thus, the economy was likewise incapable of understanding that the automobile must become a tool for the general public, for otherwise the broad potential for development slumbering therein will not be realized. The automobile is either a costly luxury object for very few and thus of no particular consequence in the long term for the economy as a whole, or, it should truly give the economy the enormous impetus of which it is intrinsically capable, and then it must evolve from a luxury object for very few to an object of use for all. And this is where the German automobile industry—and I fear this is still a general view—was not yet fully aware of the fact that the development of German automobile production as a whole can only truly be successful if its pricing is commensurate with the incomes of the customer groups it is to reach. The question as to the number of automobiles Germany can bear is very easy to answer. The desire for automobiles in our people is at least as lively as in any other country. I would almost like to say that the yearning for automobiles is so strongly in evidence here because our people have been deprived of them, and, gentlemen, you can see the best proof of this in the enormous, incomparable number of visitors, particularly at these exhibitions. They are the most pointed disproof of the view held by those who believed, only a few years ago, that they could completely dispense with these exhibitions as being merely insignificant and uninteresting. The German people have exactly the same need to use automobiles as, for instance, the American people. It is superficial to regard a quantity of 23 or 24 million automobiles in America as natural and understandable, and 500,000 or 600,000 as such in Germany, although in terms of numbers, the German people makes up somewhat more than half of the population of the North American Union. No, the people's requirement is given in Germany, too. The prerequisite for the fulfillment of this desire can, however, be no different from the rest of the world. That means that the price of an automobile must correspond to the income of its potential buyer, and that means that there will be people who are in the position to sacrifice 20,000 Marks and more for an automobile because their income is proportionate, but the number of these people will not be large. Lowering the cost to 10,000 Marks will result in a much greater number of respective able buyers, and lowering the cost of a car to 5,000 Marks will mobilize an even greater group with corresponding incomes. All this means: if I hope to achieve a volume of three or four million automobiles in Germany, then the price and maintenance costs for these automobiles must be graded to correspond to the incomes of the three or four million potential buyers. I advise the German automobile industry to proceed on the basis of these ideas, and gather information on the income situation of the four or five million best-situated Germans, and you will then understand why I am so ruthlessly determined to have the preliminary work for producing the German Volkswagen carried on and brought to a conclusion, and, gentlemen, I am talking about a successful conclusion."

With the words "ruthlessly determined," Hitler left no doubt what he meant, since he had murdered his own SA chiefs in June-July 1934, and—after Hindenburg's death that August—was now undisputed dictator of Nazi Germany.

"I do not doubt the genius of the constructor (Ferdinand Porsche) entrusted with the task, as well as the subsequent manufacturers, in connection with the highest insights into national economy on the part of all those involved, will succeed in putting the costs of acquisition, operation, and maintenance for this car in a ratio accessible to the income of this broad mass of our people, as we can see has successfully been accomplished in the brilliant example of America. It is a regrettable error for anyone to believe in this context that such a development will move the buyers of better and more expensive cars to drop down to the Volkswagen. No, gentlemen, this car will act to mobilize millions, of whom hundreds of thousands will all the more easily find their way to better and more attractive cars as a result of their continuously rising standard of living. The Ford car did not displace better and more expensive American automobiles; on the contrary, it served initially to loosen up and mobilize the enormous masses of American buyers, from whom particularly the more expensive models later profited. Hence, in finding two or three million buyers for a new German Volkswagen, there will be some who, in the course of their lives, will quite naturally switch to better and thus more expensive cars of their own accord. A great number will never be in a position to purchase an expensive car, not because these people have no desire to do Mr. Manufacturer Whoever a favor, but because they are unable to do so because of their modest income. Yet to simply exclude these millions from the pleasure of this modern means of transport because one is unwilling to run the risk that, of the two or 300,000 better situated people, perhaps, a few could buy the cheaper car, would be not only humanly unprincipled, but also economically unwise. For this would mean nothing but artificially bringing to a halt the most tremendous economical development for our people and our country out of both selfish and shortsighted considerations. I know that I am thus assigning an extremely large task to the German economy, but I also know that Germans are no less capable than anyone else in the world, and matters which have been solved in one corner of the globe can and must be solved in Germany as well...The crisis of Germany's fuel supply, whose paramount significance we can gauge particularly at the present time, in political terms, can be considered overcome. Our chemists and inventors have truly accomplished wonders, particularly in this sector as a whole, and trust in our determination to put this theoretical solution [This was a precursor announcement of Göring's future role as head of the new Four Year Plan that fall.]! In this exhibition, you will find for the first time tires made of German synthetic rubber, and it is my pleasure to inform you and the German people at this time that the performance tests which have been conducted by the *Wehrmacht*/Armed Forces for nearly a year now, have shown that this synthetic rubber surpasses natural crude rubber in terms of life and durability by 10-30%."

On February 27, 1936, the Führer and Reich Chancellor visited the Auto Show for a second time that year from 11 AM-1 PM, and told a conference of automobile executives, "Now the German automobile industry is back in shape!" Apparently, someone had communicated to him their collective decision to go along with his stated plans for VW. According to Domarus:

"On Feb. 20, 1937, Hitler presided over the opening of the International Automobile and Motorcycle Exhibition in Berlin. His welcoming address commenced with a lengthy and highly detailed account of efforts connected with the motorization process in the previous four years. Turning to the 'tasks of the future,' he stated that the production of the new Volkswagen was a major priority. Evidently, the industry continued to be wary of this project, and its opposition to it had yet to be overcome. One more time Hitler had to argue in favor of his brainchild. 'I would like to add here that it would be a capital error to believe the production of the cheapest People's Car might in any way reduce the numbers of those who purchase more expensive automobiles. As I have stated, that makes no sense. People do not refrain from buying more expensive and hence better quality automobiles because they basically want inexpensive ones, but because they are not in a position to afford the more expensive ones! And to the extent to which total production figures increase, there will necessarily be a corresponding progressive increase in price production. This reflects the constellation of our assets and income! It has, however, invariably been the case in the past that just as the cheaper product aroused and cultivated the attention and interest of the buyers—and consequent owners—in a certain direction, it was from these same classes that buyers for the better products later issued. Gentlemen! There can thus be only *one* Volkswagen in Germany, and *not 10!* Yet in the gap between the forthcoming Volkswagen and the top luxury automobile, there must be a large group of other classes of automobiles corresponding to the economic climb of the buyers.' Hitler employed a markedly sharper tone in his opening address than he had in earlier years. Germany's leading industrialists were ill at ease with Hitler's new Four Year Plan, which was tailored to suit the exigencies of a wartime economy. For them, much was at risk under the Four Year Plan: they did not have 'everything to win' (as allegedly did the politicians), but rather there was much to be lost, indeed. Nevertheless, Hitler reminded them that nothing would keep him from 'Putting plans once conceived into practice, no matter how.' This was also his attitude with Volkswagen, which he was now pursuing with 'ruthless determination.' Here for the first time he spoke of his 'unalterable decision'—a term that he would employ with increasing frequency, in particular during the years of the Second World War. As time passed, the meaning of this expression would become equivalent to 'mad decision.' Yet Hitler was confident that a man such as he—who had 'Succeeded in rising from an unknown soldier of the World War to the leader of the nation'—would be capable of dealing with whatever the future would bring. 'I have no desire to concern myself with those who know only the one well-worn objection to all major decisions: 'It won't work.' For 18 years, I have grown accustomed to hearing this remark as the logical and simple justification for fighting every single new idea, every single new decision, and every single new action... Thus, it is my unalterable decision to make the German automobile industry—which is one of our people's greatest industries—independent of the insecurities of international imports, and to place it on its own solid and secure foundation. In one to two years, we will be independent of other countries as regards our needs for fuel and rubber...Nor let there be any doubt: either the so-called free economy is capable of solving these problems, or it is not capable of surviving as a free economy! Under no circumstances wil the National Socialist (Nazi) State capitulate to the idleness, the narrow mindedness, or the ill will of any individual German. Employees and employers both represent contracting parties in the German economic process, and neither has the right to do damage to the interests of the body of the people by pursuing one-sided aims.'"

Thus, in ramming through the Volkswagen project roughshod over their combined objections, dictator Hitler was at last showing his true socialistic colors to the very captains of industry who had bankrolled him through the decade of the Time of Struggle of 1922-32. The threat—indeed, the promise—was clear and well stated: if they would not comply, they would simply disappear, and their plants and firms would be taken over en masse by the Nazis, as with Stalin and the Bolsheviks in the USSR. Indeed, the lambs had brought themselves to the Nazi slaughterhouse by backing Hitler as Chancellor in 1933.

Air Force Col. Gen. Hermann Göring (fifth from right) visits the Berlin Auto Show on February 28, 1936, and inspects a new motorcycle. (Previously unpublished photo from the Hermann Göring Albums, Library of Congress, Washington, DC)

Auto Show 1938

Field Marshal Göring and his Führer touring the Exhibition: (left) Hitler inspects a Krupp engine, while Dr. Ferdinand Porsche can be seen in the distance at center, and Göring (holding baton) is visible fourth from left.

(Right photo) An auto official makes a point to car enthusiasts Göring and Hitler. (Previously unpublished photographs from the Hermann Göring Albums, LC)

Noted *Germany*:

"The International Automobile and Motorcycle Exhibition to be held from Feb. 18th-March 6, 1938 will demonstrate in all its aspects the successful development of the German motor industry. In 10 large halls of the Berlin Exhibition Grounds, more than 1,200 stands will be occupied by German and foreign manufacturers of motor vehicles and accessories. The German Army, the Reich Post, the NSKK, and the German Automobile Club, as well as the Motor Mechanics, will have special exhibits. As the Berlin Automobile Exhibition will be followed immediately by the Leipzig State Fair, our foreign friends will have an opportunity of attending both events."

These events are typically called "trade shows" in all countries and economic climates, and, in the United States, as Public Relations Director for the former Emery Advertising Corporation of Hunt Valley, MD, during 1984-86, the current author either helped stage or covered many of them for our clients in Atlanta and Chicago, one being American Hoechst, the U.S. firm of the German-based chemical giant. Stated Domarus:

"On Feb. 18th, Hitler delivered an address at the opening of the International Automobile and Motorcycle Exhibition in Berlin...Hitler repeated his arguments of previous years in favor of the Volkswagen, which in essence was, 'To make the automobile accessible to millions of new buyers from the lower income ranks.' Further, he stated: 'Let us therefore ensure that—by providing a tremendous number of inexpensive German Volkswagens in the future—the wishes of those will be satisfied who are willing, out of their love for, and pleasure in, automobiles, to invest a part of their income for that purpose. This will above all result in the fact that the automobile will no longer be the symbol of a certain class of those with higher incomes; it will instead increasingly become the general means of transportation for everyone in Germany, and then all this tremendous propaganda work we are accomplishing toward the motorization of our people in a both material and non-material sense will not have been in vain. In a material sense, by virtue of building the best roads in the world; and in a non-material sense, by virtue of a sporting activity that has regained for our German production of engines, automobiles, and motorcycles its good reputation throughout the world.'...Thereafter, Hitler announced the foundation of a 'German Motor Sports Badge' and predicted that—within a short time period—Germany would produce not only 'The best, but also the most inexpensive, cars in the world. This is the reason why I have decided to create the German Motor Sports Badge... Above all, this most prestigious Award shall be an incentive for German youth interested in motor sports. Korpsführer Hühnlein, the head of automobile sports, will issue the conditions governing the conferral of the Award. As ever, I am filled this time, too, with sincere gratitude to all those whose work we will once more be able to admire in a few minutes' time. There is no doubt: we owe the best cars in the world to our directors, engineers, foremen, workers, and merchants. Today I am certain: within a short time, we will also produce the most inexpensive car, yet at the same time I believe that it is the duty of every single German to profess his faith in work of his *Volksgenossen/People's Comrades*. With this request, I hereby declare the 1938 International Automobile and Motorcycle Exhibition in Berlin to be open.' After delivering his speech, Hitler went on a three hour tour of the Exhibition halls."

Two views of the last Berlin International Automobile and Motorcycle Exhibition, February 17-March 6, 1939, at Berlin-Charlottenburg. (Webb and Ziegelhofer)

Auto Show 1939

Continues Max Domarus:

"These new insights imparted by Hitler to the audience in his appeal for economy were intended to challenge the automobile industry to construct new car models, weighing no more than 2,000 kilograms instead of the customary 3,000...Hitler further argued that the Autobahn highways had not been built for 'Speeds from 120-140 kilometers per hour, but rather for average speeds, let us say, of 80 kilometers.' This speed limit soon became law. Ironically, after the National Socialists' rise to power in 1933, one of the first pieces of legislation enacted had been a repeal of earlier speed restrictions that allegedly had inhibited the development of motorization. At the time, the Nazis had claimed that high speeds even reduced the number of accidents on the road! A change of heart on this subject now turned speeding into the 'un-National Socialist behavior [After the war, all speed limits were abolished, and remain so in Germany today.]. Hitler began his speech...with the following remarks: 'For the seventh time, I have the pleasure of opening an Exhibition which affords us insight not only in to the workings of one of the most important branches of industry in our country, but also of a large part of the world...The automobile is not a luxury article, it is an article of general use... Within the framework of the Four Year Plan, we sought to free motorization in Germany from dependence on factors abroad, and to establish our own independent raw material base. After only a few years, the results of this effort may today already be called gigantic...In an overview of these facts, which in themselves reveal to us the greatness of the results attained, we note the striking evidence of the gigantic increase in production, the extraordinary rise in exports, the lowering of prices for certain models of automobiles and motorcycles and, above all, the excellent work in detail... There remain great tasks yet to be accomplished: it was understandable that, in times of grave concern for sales, each individual firm, more or less nervously, tried to scan the market and its requirements. Hence...each firm seized that model which apparently held the greatest promise, without considering how many other factories were already involved with this particular model, or the potential size of the series already in production at any rate in one factory. The resulting competition precluded a potential decrease in prices for certain models...A relentless competition for customers ensued, which led to an exaggeration of the mechanical element. This meant the incorporation of any type of innovation in the car, no matter how insignificant its practical application, simply because of the belief that one had to oblige a highly sensitive customer. The conditions that led to this technically and economically undesirable phenomenon no longer exist today. It is less the task of today's German automobile industry to seek potential customers than to satisfy the demands of existing customers. *The demand for automobiles is overwhelming!* The following are necessary in order to satisfy this demand: 1) Lower prices. This is possible in the long run only if one instills order in the types of models produced. This means that individual firms must achieve a consensus on the types of models to be produced and restrict the overall number of models. Indeed, there must be a simplification of the production program to very few models. It is crucial to augment the total production of automobiles instead of increasing the number of models offered. The multitude of these would ultimately lead to splintering off into an affinity of models, encumbering the production process, and possibly lowering total output...Two cars in a heavyweight class [i.e., at 3,000 kgs or above] simply rob us of the materials needed to produce a third one. I do understand that, in the end, the industry was not capable of arriving at such an ordering of its production on its own. Therefore, I appointed Col. (Adolf) von Schell as Plenipotentiary to see to these tasks being carried out. He is presently issuing binding directives to all appropriate offices within the framework of the Four Year Plan. His activities have

Dr. Ferdinand Porsche (fourth from right) makes a point to an intense Hitler (center) as Dr. Ley (fourth from left) looks on at the February 17-March 6, 1939, Auto Show in Berlin on its opening day—its final one, alas. (HHA)

already resulted in exceptional results, and hold great promise. He will be in a position to account for his activities for the first time at the 1940 Exhibition [which was never held]. The resulting further decline in prices for our automobile industry will undoubtedly have a positive effect on exports. [Von Schell, born in 1893 in Magdeburg, was Plenipotentiary for Motor Vehicles in the Reich Ministry of Transportation as of November 1, 1938, a major general in 1940, lieutenant general in 1942, and commander of the 25th Panzer/Armored Division in 1943, who retired in 1944.] Let the new Volkswagen represent an enormous, real avowal of these principles. All those concerned are called on to devote the greatest energy to press forward the construction of its factory! I sincerely rejoice in being able to afford you a glance at the car for the first time in the Exhibition! The Volkswagen's ingenious designer has bestowed an object of extraordinary value on the German people and the German economy. It is up to us now to persevere in our efforts to shortly begin mass production of this car. The pending increase in the flow of motorized traffic due to the Volkswagen and the introduction of a series of low-price trucks, now forces us to take steps necessary to ensure traffic safety. In a period of six years, the German people sacrifices nearly as many men to automobile-related accidents as it did in the Franco-Prussian War of 1870-71! This cannot be tolerated. Though the beneficial cooperation of State and Party offices—and the deployment of traffic police and NSKK patrols—has already brought some relief, these results can neither be regarded as satisfactory, nor can the situation be regarded as tolerable. Above all, there are certain principles and duties all those who participate in traffic on German roads must be aware of: When someone causes an accident today, whether he be the engineer or the switchman, then the responsible party will be regarded as an unscrupulous criminal who is indifferent to the life of his contemporaries, and he will be punished accordingly. The driver of a private vehicle bears similar responsibility, not only regarding his own life, to which he may be indifferent, or which may be of little value, but for that of other participants in traffic. Whoever nonchalantly endangers these lives acts in a criminal manner and without any scruples. Those who cause the nation to lose 7,000 annually, in addition, to imparting to it the care of 30-40,000 injured, are parasites on the people. They act irresponsibly. They shall be punished as a matter of course, provided they do not escape the *Volksgemeinshaft's/People's Community* wrath by dying themselves. It is truly not an art to drive fast and to endanger the lives of others! Rather, it is a great art to drive safely, i.e., carefully. Lack of caution coupled with high speed is the most common cause of automobile crashes, and it is discouraging to realize that the majority of those driving could easily spare the extra 10, 20, or even 30 minutes that, at best, they can hope to save by their insane, reckless driving, even on long stretches…I wish to take advantage of today's occasion to thank all those who have not only contributed to the domestic significance of the German automobile and motorcycle industry, but also to its renown worldwide; the businessmen for their enterprising spirit; inventors, engineers and technicians for their ingenuity; and masters of their trade, and laborers for their astounding achievements. The German people today can justly be proud of the marvels of an industry that once took its first gingerly steps toward practical application in this country. In this spirit, I hereby declare the 1939 International Automobile and Motorcycle Exhibition in Berlin open to the public!"

Thus, after six years, the Führer and Reich Chancellor at last had his prototype Volkswagens produced at Wolfsburg on display for the car trade and general public alike. It was an automotive triumph of the first order. (HHA)

VW Beetle Cabriolet model with roof tarp rolled back. (VWM)

Noted Chris Barber, "Car 43003 was used on a series of publicity runs during the winter months, usually with a set of skis on the roof rack. Many pictures of this car appeared in the KdF-Wagen brochure issued during 1939." (VWM)

The VW steering wheel center with its Wolfsburg Castle logo. (VWM)

Dr. Ferdinand Porsche (September 8, 1875-January 30, 1951), world famous automotive genius and Volkswagen creator—the "Herr Doktor" seen here framed within a car steering wheel. The center of the Beetle steering wheel of 1962 featured its famous Wolfsburg Castle logo. At age 19 in 1894, Porsche installed a generator in his father's home. Papa Porsche wanted his son to follow him as a tinsmith, but young Ferdinand's own interests were in the fields of electricity and engineering. Initially trained as a plumber, through at-home self-study he progressed to becoming an engineer, and got a job with the Löhner Automobile Factory in Vienna—the scene of the young Adolf Hitler's early, failed artistic ambitions, and also in March 1938, two months before the dedication of the VW plant at Wolfsburg, the scene of his triumphant return to occupied Austria. This would not be the last time that the two men's paths would cross. In 1934, Nazi Propaganda Minister Dr. Göbbels awarded him "citizenship of the Reich" by mail on orders of the Führer. Prof. Porsche, asserted Nelson, "was not elated. 'I'm afraid there's nothing much we can do about it,' he shrugged." (Porsche Museum, Stüttgart, Germany)

The 1900 Porsche-Löhner Chaise, a car powered by what would still today be considered a most unusual power train: twin electric motors in the front wheels! Since he himself hailed from a working class background, Porsche's ideas always tended to favor that class, as opposed to plant bosses and their financial backers, despite his meteoric later rise in the top echelons of both the Austrian and German car manufacturers. (PM)

In 1906, Dr. Ferdinand Porsche's brother-in-law, Otto Kaes, drives a trackless electric streetcar provided to the City of Aberdare in Wales that employed the patented Porsche wheel-mounted motors. It was built in Wiener Neustadt by Oesterreiche Daimler Motoren Gesellschaft/Austrian Daimler, GmbH. Author Graham Robson asserted that Jakob Löhner—the Vienna coachbuilder—hired Ferdinand Porsche in 1898, when he was 23. Porsche car #1, seen here, was introduced at the Paris Auto Salon in 1900, and it was this show that changed his life, converting his initial interest in electricity to a deeper one for automotive engineering. From that moment on, car history worldwide was about to be made. In 1906 Porsche left Löhner to become an engineer with Austro-Daimler, where in 1916—during the First World War—he created a "train" of connected wheeled wagons used by the Imperial Austrian Army. It had a power train of a Porsche "Mixte" petrol electric system. Noted Dr. Ferry Porsche, this was, "A generator driven by an internal combustion engine (that) supplied current to electric motors mounted on all wheels. This military train consisted of 10 detachable cars that could also be used on rails, and proved invaluable in transporting war material during World War I." Thus, this was his father's first wartime vehicle; there would be more a generation later. (PM)

Inventor Ferdinand Porsche, 19 (1894), with the generator he installed for his father's home. (PM)

In 1909, this London fire brigade hook-and-ladder truck also used Porsche-patented front wheel-mounted motors. (PM)

Two Austrians. During 1938, Hitler speaks at the lectern at left. Behind him, fourth from left sitting down, is Dr. Ferdinand Porsche in dark overcoat and holding his trademark Homburg hat. Past the blurred figure next to him (left to right) is SS Hitler Escort Physician Dr. Karl Brandt, another blurred man, and then Austrian Chancellor Dr. Artur von Seyss-Inquart. Underneath the wall-mounted, wreathed swastika to the right of Dr. Brandt's head can be seen Jakob Werlin. (HHA)

A tall SS man (center) with a pair of early VW Beetles lacking rear view mirrors. (VWM)

Dr. Ferdinand Porsche (center) with some colleagues. (PM)

Dr. Ferdinand Porsche, behind steering wheel at right, and wearing hat and suit, poses with a chassis and some of his workers before the war. (PM)

Dr. Ferdinand Porsche (second from right) poses in November 1940 with Schimmwagen Car 128/3 at the Wünsdorf military training ground in Germany outside Berlin. (VWM)

ICH VERLEIHE HIERMIT
FERDINAND PORSCHE
DEN DEUTSCHEN NATIONALPREIS
FÜR KUNST UND WISSENSCHAFT

NÜRNBERG-DEN 6. SEPTEMBER 1938.

The document awarding Dr. Ferdinand Porsche the German National Prize at the September 1938 Nazi Party Congress at Nürnberg, its last, signed at bottom by Hitler. (PM)

VW Car #11 (license plate IIIA-37011) seen here driving out of the driveway of the offices of Dr. Ferdinand Porsche and a VW Branch Office as well, as noted by the two signs at left. (VWM)

A transparent VW Beetle model at the 1939 Berlin Auto Show. (VWM)

In the summer of 1944, the Type 276 Kübelwagen was developed with a strong bar installed at the rear to tow a light artillery PAK 3.7 gun. Here, Dr. Ferdinand Porsche sits on the tow bar, with the covered piece at right. (WVM)

Dr. Ferdinand Porsche in Vienna with a VW "Saloon car without a sunroof, NOT the 'radio car,'" as it is labeled here, according to Barber. Note, too, the wartime issue headlamp covers. (VWM)

At a Stüttgart gas pump are seen (left) a BMW Dixi small car model, and also driver Herbert Kaes emerging from the VW at right. Noted Barber, Kaes began working for Porsche on February 5, 1936. (VWM)

Hitler's personal VW convertible Beetle, equipped with headlamp covers, and also a Notek nighttime driving lamp mounted in the center of the hood. According to Chris Barber, this VW 60 was given to Hitler by Dr. Porsche on his 50th birthday on April 30, 1939, along with a midnight blue Mercedes 770K, and *not* canary yellow, as stated by writer Griffith Borgerson in *Automotive Quarterly*. Barber asserts that Eva Braun was at the wheel in this photo on the road on the Obersalzberg outside Berchtesgaden. (VWM)

Eva Braun (left) poses for a snapshot with her friend, and Hitler's architect, Dr. Albert Speer. (EBH Albums)

Hitler's official photographer, Reich Photo Reporter Prof. Heinrich Hoffmann (1885-1957, left), and a colleague on the driveway of the Berghof, Hitler's mountain home on the Obersalzberg. (HHA)

Hitler, Stalin, and Porsche

A tale of two dictators: Hitler, Stalin, and Dr. Ferdinand Porsche. As it turned out, Adolf Hitler (left) wasn't the only dictator who wanted the services of Dr. Ferdinand Porsche; so did Soviet ruler Josef Stalin (right), when, in 1932, he invited Herr Doktor "To become chief Soviet industrial designer," according to Nelson:

"A Soviet delegation had come to Porsches' Stüttgart office, listened attentively, said little, and taken careful note of everything being done. It was not long afterward that Porsche received an invitation to the USSR. He left on July 20, 1932, and after three weeks in a Moscow bed—nursing a foot he'd hurt alighting from his train—Porsche toured much of the country. His hosts were eager to impress him with their technological growth and hospitality. Once, when Porsche complained of the vodka that was endlessly served to him, and expressed a wish for some beer, a case of Pilsner awaited him at the next stop. Negotiations began. Porsche was offered a luxurious Crimean villa for his family and entire staff, as well as a blank check...He would never again have to concern himself with personal or developmental expenses. The Russians were even interested in small car designs, and had shown Porsche some preliminary designs of their own"—and this was six months before Hitler unexpectedly took office in Weimar Republican Germany.

"When Porsche returned home, he confessed he was tempted—and impressed. 'Well, one isn't supposed to say it, but what I saw was wonderful!' he said to Ghislaine Kaes, his nephew, and by then his secretary."

(Left photo HHA, right photo LC)

At that time, the Soviet Union of "bloody Stalin and his barbarous Bolsheviks" was still considered a pariah among "civilized" nations because of the killing of the Tsar and his entire family in 1918, and the Russian Civil War of 1918-21, especially by such right wing leaders as Hitler and Benito Mussolini in Fascist Italy. "Still, he declined the offer. It required him to break all ties with his homeland. Porsche felt he was too old to make the change...." He was 57 in 1932. In *We at Porsche*, his son Ferry provided some more fascinating insights into this intriguing aspect of his father's career. When the invitation was made to him over dinner at Boppard, Germany, Dr. Porsche asked why the Soviet government wanted him to come, and was told, "Because, sir, you're obviously the greatest automotive engineer in Germany today, the most imaginative, and the least inhibited." He was told he could see whatever he wanted to.

"The Soviet government was as good as its word. The moment my father reached Moscow... he was immediately taken on a visit to the Central Drawing office. This was the heart of Russia's entire automotive industry, such as it then existed. From there, he was rushed to a large tractor factory in Stalingrad [the site of the fiercest fighting in that city during the later battle of 1942-43] and had to admit himself (he later told me) that it was an impressive occasion. Things were not nearly so backward as people in the West [such as Hitler until late 1941] had been led to believe. The interpreter proved very useful. My father recalled one particular evening when the interpreter took him for a walk in Stalingrad along the banks of the Volga River. This Russian sat down beside the river and began a relaxed conversation just as some Russian workmen came strolling by. The whole thing was so perfectly timed that it made my father wonder, yet he was encouraged to ask questions, and got some seemingly unrehearsed answers to a number of them that the interpreter could hardly have foreseen. What seemed especially convincing was the real interest these workmen took in their jobs at the factory, and their willingness to talk openly about the latest tractors and their capabilities...." Later, the key question was asked: "Would he be interested in accepting the post of chief of the *entire* automotive industry in the Soviet Union. His area, would, of course, be the vital one of design and development. But one of the basic reasons that made him decline in the end was the language barrier. 'Hopeless,' my father shrugged. 'Not even a dozen interpreters could really solve the communications problem. It's one thing to translate an ordinary conversation, but quite another when you try to put over some highly abstract technical ideas in a totally strange language. It just could not work.'"

When Hitler took office, he wasn't about to make the mistake that Stalin had made when he had Dr. Porsche (if not yet his family and staff) in his grasp. While he had them all within the borders of the Third Reich, the Führer compelled the former Austrian subject and later Czech citizen to become a German citizen, in 1934. Thus, it also came about that, during 1941-45, Dr. Ferdinand Porsche built weapons of war to conquer Stalingrad and the Soviet Union, rather than building those same implements for Stalin instead of Hitler. What would have happened if he had become a Red Army POW in 1945 instead of the French is an interesting point to consider; would Stalin have shot him as a war criminal, or compelled him to work for the USSR instead? My own guess is that the latter is the more likely possibility, and that the Porsches and their organizations would've done so gladly without missing a heartbeat—and who could've blamed them in the circumstances? The Cold War might have turned out somewhat differently.

Left: Stated one VW account, "The VW Beetle with normal body was built again in December 1945 in very meager form, as can be seen: no chrome, matte military paint, uniform Wehrmacht headlights (leftover supplies) in the front, also used in the Kübelwagen and trucks (Opel Blitz/Lightning, Ford 3000 S, Mercedes 4.5 ton). The hubcaps and right windshield wiper were also eliminated. The British occupation forces painted white identification numbers on the front and rear hoods." (WPM) Right: "VW/Porsche Type 98 Kabrio-Limousine with four wheel drive, seen here. Widened fenders and running boards for the military off-road wheels, October 1943." (WPM)

Non-Hitlerian famous personages and Dr. Ferdinand Porsche: the Archduke Franz Ferdinand of Austria-Hungary (right), Heir to the Imperial Throne of Kaiser Franz Josef and his wife, the Duchess Sophie (left), in Sarajevo in June 28, 1914, shortly before their joint assassinations by Serbian patriot/terrorist Gavrilo Princip. The uproar that it caused helped launch the First World War. On November 8, 1902, the Archduke had sent Ferdinand Porsche (not yet a doctor) the following note: "His Imperial and Royal Highness deigns to transmit to your honorable person a memento of this year's maneuvers in West Hungary. The performance of your automobile—as well as your sure and exact guidance of it—have satisfied His Imperial and Royal Highness in every particular." Ferdinand Porsche was but 27 years old at the time. (Imperial War Museum, Vienna; LC)

Josip Broz Tito—Marshal and President of formerly Communist Yugoslavia—reviews an all-military Service Honor Guard on the lawn of the White House (right) with U.S. President John F. Kennedy (left) and the Guard's commanding officer on October 17, 1963. "In 1912," Tito told one of his biographers (Vladimir Dedijer, in *Tito*) "I got a job in the Daimler factory in Wiener Neustadt...The work here interested me more than in any other factory. I even became a test driver, running the big powerful cars with their heavy brass work, rubber-bulb horns, and outside hand brakes, to put them through their paces." (Photo from the JFK Library, Columbia Point, Boston)

German Kaiser Wilhelm II (left) and his younger brother, Navy Grand Adm. Prince Heinrich of Hohenzollern, nicknamed "the Sailor Prince." An auto enthusiast who became partial to Daimler-Benz products, the prince had both a race and a trophy named after him, and he was also a race car driver himself of some renown—complete with old-time motoring cap and goggles. Ferdinand Porsche raced in the 1909 and 1910 events, and his daughter, six-year-old "Louisi," posed at the wheel of her father's designed "Prince Henry Car" in the latter year. Prince Heinrich remained a car enthusiast after World War I, and died in 1929; the Kaiser passed away in 1941. (LC)

The VW's traction demonstrated uphill, and in mud. Note the windmill. (WPM)

Dr. Ferdinand Porsche wins the September 16, 1938, German National Prize for Art and Science; top Nazis await the awarding of the 1938 Prizes, from left to right: Dr. Walther Funk, Hitler, SS Gen. Julius Schaub (behind the Führer), Baldur von Schirach, Alfred Rosenberg, and Hermann Göring; with the exception of Schaub—all had played, or would play, a role in affairs VW. The Prize—established by the Reich Chancellor on January 30, 1937—was designed as a substitute for the Nobel Peace Prize, which Hitler forbade Germans to accept henceforth "for all time." According to Reinhardt Beck, "Specifically, the institution of the Prize was a reaction to the 'shameful events' connected with the bestowal of the Nobel Peace Prize on Carl von Ossietzsky. Every year at the Reich Party Congress, two 'worthy Germans' were to receive such a Prize of 100,000 RM each [the prize was divided if there were more than two], as well as a medal." In 1937 Hitler and Rosenberg received four such winners: surgeon Dr. Ferdinand Sauerbruch, Frau Dr. Gerdy Troost (for her late husband, Dr. Ludwig Troost), August Bier, and Wilhelm Filchner. (HHA)

Hitler's personal pilot, Col. Hans Baur (1897-1993). In December 1941 at the Führer's order, Dr. Ferdinand Porsche went to the German-occupied area of the USSR in his capacity as head of the Panzer/Armored Commission to inspect and evaluate captured Red Army T-34 tanks, the best medium tank built by either side in the war. He was flown by Hitler's own pilot in the Führer's personal aircraft, a four-engine Kondor. Dr. Porsche had designed both the PzKpfw Panther and the PzKpfw Tiger, two of the best heavier tanks of the war constructed by either side, so he was well qualified to judge the T-34. Baur and Dr. Porsche, technicians both, quickly took a liking to each other, and gave each other mementoes of their flights together. Baur gave Dr. Porsche this photo, inscribed, "Prof. Porsche, head of the Panzer Commission, in remembrance of the flight to the front Smolensk-Orel, December 1941. Most heartily, Hans Baur, Colonel and Flight Captain." For his part—according to my professional colleague and fellow author C.G. Sweeting in his epic 2001 biography *Hitler's Personal Pilot: The Life and Times of Hans Baur*, "When Baur had flown Hitler to Berlin [weeks later], Dr. Porsche invited him to his office and presented him with a painting by the well known artist Claus Bergen, showing Hitler's Kondor flying over Smolensk and the Dnieper River. This beautiful painting still hangs in Baur's home in Bavaria." (LC)

Stated one VW account, "An original VW was used in goodly numbers by the (West German) *Bundeswehr/Federal Armed Forces* and, for example, also by the armies of Holland, Belgium, and Switzerland. The Beetle shown here is a VW 1200 of 1977, used by a Luftwaffe (!) communications unit in Karlsruhe, Germany." (VWM)

The Famed Porsche Logo

Origins of the Porsche logo, colors, and company crest:

According to Klaus Parr of Porsche in Stüttgart on October 22, 1992, in a letter to the author:

"The Porsche logotype is another symbol that represents Porsche quality products worldwide This symbol has the great advantage that it actually spells out the corporate name, and is thus recognized instantly. There is only one officially recognized Porsche logotype. Through its history, the Porsche logotype has appeared in several variations. The letters have been of different lengths and thickness. The spacing between the letters has varied as well. The variation included in these guidelines is the only authorized Porsche logotype. The logotype must not be used in any other variation.... Traditionally, in regard to color, Porsche AG has been identified by the burgundy color, and also by the combination of the three colors of the Porsche crest: yellow, red, and black. Everyone will be familiar with the characteristic expanded Porsche logo. The crest with rampant horse and the claret color used for our stationery are familiar Porsche features, too, yet their origins are not so well known. Internal telephone directories, car owners' handbooks, and the Porsche inscription have been produced in claret for as long as most Porsche staff can recall. When the company's own printing shop in Plant 3 was completed back in 1963, this particular shade of red was already standard for a wide range of printed documents. Even our architects latched onto this color in 1978; after much thought, the production Building (Plant 2) was painted in a harmonious scale of shades, the darkest of which was this selfsame claret. In 1980, our 'environmental specialist' Daniel Marracini adopted color columns following the same scale of shades for our new high-bay store in such a way as to overcome the 'box' effect, and create the impression of a hill instead. All Porsche's production premises in Züfferhausen, with the exception of the clinker-finished Plant 1 and the Sales Center in Ludwigsburg, have since received a similar graduated color finish. One particularly bold example, whose very audacity is the secret of its success (as architects tend to say), is the style in which the new paint shop is treated. The exterior strongly implies this building's association with paint and color. The claret—together with the series of colors derived from it, is becoming more and more a symbol of Porsche—a good reason to wonder who came across this color in the first place. Erich Strenger, a freelance graphic designer who has carried out commissions on Porsche's behalf for more than 30 years, supplies the answer: 'After the Second World war, colored inks were in short supply, and we had to economize. When Porsche ordered the first owners' handbook for the 356 back in 1951 from Glauner, a small family firm of printers, I had to discuss the layout with the printer. This was about the time when colored paper was just appearing again, and since we could only print in one color, we decided to adopt a colored envelope. The printer happened to have claret paper in stock, which is why we used that color. Nobody had any idea that it would establish itself as Porsche's company color.' The Porsche crest—reflecting the car manufacturer's Swabian roots [in Germany], was probably adopted at the suggestion of Porsche's American importers. Company chief Dr. Ferry Porsche went on to propose evoking a little heraldry and devising a coat of arms. The coat of arms of Stüttgart, with its prancing horse, is superimposed on the antlers and red-and-black stripes of Württemburg, with the Porsche inscription emblazoned along the top edge. This coat of arms has been used both on and inside Porsche cars since 1952: first of all at the center of the steering wheel, then on the hood, and wheel caps. The Porsche inscription, too, has quite a history. Erich Strenger conceived the broad, streamlined letters as a matrix. All letters in the name 'Porsche' can be represented with the aid of the three horizontal bars, but letters with diagonals, such as the double R in Carrera, or the 'Y' in Spyder, were difficult to represent using this style. As a result, new typefaces had to be devised for these types. 'Back in those days, nobody had thought of the numbers 924 and 994 either,' explains Erich Strenger. 'It's difficult to work the number '4' into this matrix. The designers over at the 'Style Porsche' department at Weissach sometimes find themselves confronted with quite a few problems by the established logo and the new model designations. When we came up with the original idea, we had other things to think about, and little did we suspect that this logo would have such an influence on Porsche's identity. This provisional design became a fundamental aspect of the Porsche identity, but a company consists of more than an inscription and coat of arms! The products are naturally of far greater importance.' Anatole Lapin, head of 'Style Porsche,' expressed a similar opinion: 'More than any emblem or logo, Prof. Porsche himself represents the bond between tradition and progressive technology that makes Porsche such a unique company.'"

Incidentally, the Mayor of Stüttgart for many years—as when the current author corresponded with him in 1977—was none other than Manfred Rommel, only son of Field Marshal Erwin Rommel, and co-editor of *The Rommel Papers* after the war. (From *Carrera #9*, a publication for the employees of Dr. Ing. h.c. F. Porsche AG.) According to an e-mail sent to this author on February 28, 2003, from Jorg Thilow of the Porsche Museum at Stüttgart, "You asked for the symbols shown in the Porsche crest. The center of the Porsche emblem—the small black horse—stands for the name of the foundation of Stüttgart. The city name comes from the word 'Stütengarten,' that means farm for mares. A member of the Royal family founded the farm, and close to it, a lot of people settled down. That was not the birth of the settlement—the Romans were there before that—but the birth of the city's name. So the horse as a kind of coat of arms became a part of the Porsche logo. You can also see red and black stripes. Germany is a Federal Republic; one of the states is Baden-Württemburg, with the capital city being Stüttgart. As you can see in the name of Baden-Württemburg, the state is also a union, a composition of three states: Baden, Württemburg, and Württemburg-Hohenzollern. There were a lot of monarchs and wars in history of those three. Then, in 1952, they were united, but there was a strong movement against the union; the idea of separation is still alive today. The 'Schwaben' on the one hand are joking about the 'Badener' on the other hand, and vice versa. So the Badener were called 'Gelbflusser,' that means 'yellow feet,' they've got another dialect, they like to party, they've got carnival. The 'Schwaben' are stingy, they work their whole lives, and don't laugh, the Badenser say, but they are united, and this is what you see in the Porsche emblem, and that is similar to the Baden-Württemburg crest. The colors of Baden are red and yellow. The colors of Württemburg are black and yellow. The result is red and black. You can also see the horn of a stag. That is the symbol of one of the most important monarch families. It was their coat of arms during the Middle Ages."

Finally, there was also this material sent from the firm to me:

"Historical origins of the Porsche crest. The crest design is derived from two historical crests. The larger—in the background—is the crest of the German State of Württemburg. The smaller—applied to the center of the larger—is the historical crest of the City of Stüttgart. Legend has it that the concept for the Porsche crest—including the curved word 'Porsche' across the top of the crest—was sketched by Prof. Ferdinand Porsche personally. Colors of the crest: in heraldry, crests of the nobility, or of the states and cities, are represented in colors combined with metals, such as gold and silver. At times when the actual metals cannot be used, they are represented by particular colors. Yellow normally represents gold. Thus, in addition to representing the Porsche crest in colors and gold metal, as on the cars, there are applications where the crest is represented in yellow, red, and black, the original colors of the Württemburg and Stüttgart State and City crests." (PM)

According to Barber, "The Daimler-Benz version (Type 230/4) was also built, probably only as a single prototype. It is seen here during 1943, looking a bit the worse for wear." (VWM)

Brother and sister, baby Ferry and Louisi, 1910. She grew up to be the mother of future VW Chairman Anton Piech, and the child with the cherubic face became his father's successor on January 30, 1951, when Dr. Ferdinand Porsche died at age 75. (PM)

According to Barber, "Car V3/3 had two accidents…including one when a huge stag got hit on the Autobahn at about 85 kph. It didn't do too much good to the front of the car, but it got back to Stüttgart under its own power. Yet another advantage of a rear engine!" (VWM)

(Left) The Villa Porsche on Pottendorferstrasse at Wiener Neustadt, in Imperial Austria-Hungary, where Ferry Porsche was born on Sept.ember 19, 1909; thus, both like his father and Hitler (who was 20 years old at this time), Ferry began life as a subject of the Habsburg Empire. After its fall in 1918 and the creation of the new Republic of Czechoslovakia, he, unlike his father, retained his Austrian citizenship. (Right) Father, 37, and son, three, when Porsche, Sr. was already famous as a car designer in 1912, two years before the outbreak of the First World War. Three years later, in 1915, his father patented the all-electric Austro-Daimler town coupé in which he and his sister "Louisi" daily were driven to school at Wiener Neustadt. Its power train consisted of rear-wheel, hub-mounted electric motors. (Porsche Museum, Stüttgart.)

Nazi Beetles lined up, with a Nazi Party banner at left and a DAF banner at right. The slogan reads, "The first in the Volkswagen factory produced KdF cars." Asked *Beetlemania*, "What do you call your Beetle? In Germany, it's a *Kafer*, in Japan, the Kabuto-mushi. It's the Bobia in Norway, and the Bubian in Sweden. In Italy, it's the Maggiolino; the Escarabajo in Spain. The French call it the Coccinelle, and in the Philippines, it's the Pagong." (VWM)

Left: Ferrry Porsche at age 20 in 1929 in Vienna, when he was studying automotive engineering on the path to one day succeeding his famous father. The year before he'd met 17-year-old Dorothea ("Dodo") Reitz—his future bride—who gave him the cold shoulder at first, however. That same year (1928), his sister Louise married Anton Piech, and they were the parents of a future Volkswagen Chairman of the Board, also named Anton Piech after his father. As for Ferry and Dodo, they were married in January 1935, and at length had the following children: Ferdinand Alexander ("Butzi"), born on December 11, 1935; Gerhard Anton ("Gerd"), born June 5, 1938; Hans-Peter ("Peter") on October 29, 1940; and Wolfgang Heinz ("Wolfi") on May 10, 1943. (PM)

Left: In July 1929, father and son (left) pose with a Type 30 Steyr car designed by Dr. Ferdinand Porsche in front of the family home at Feuerbacherweg, in Stüttgart. Next to Ferry at right is his Aunt Anna, his father's sister. Ferry officially joined the Porsche Design Bureau in 1933, the same year that Adolf Hitler was named to office as Reich Chancellor by President Paul von Hindenburg. (PM)

The slogan on the sign reads, "The first Volkswagen built in the war year 1941." Noted *Beetlemania*, "The Volkswagen Beetle is the world's most beloved icon, second only to the Coca Cola bottle in recognition around the globe. It seems as if everyone had a VW 'Bug'—or had a friend who had one—and the very mention of its name elicits a smile. No wonder it is the best-selling car ever produced, with over 20 million sold worldwide." (VWM)

In July 1930, father (left) and son camp out at Nürbürgring during the annual German Grand Prix race. Since money was short in the Great Depression they slept this way, much like Bonnie and Clyde in the United States during the same period, but for different reasons! In 1932, the Porsche-built Type 12 designed for the Zundapp Motorcycle Co. by Dr. Ferdinand Porsche was "Just short of production when Zundapp backed off to cash in on motorcycle revival." "This advanced prototype featured a central backbone-type chassis, independent suspension, and a 1.2-liter, five-cylinder, liquid-cooled radial engine," as noted in *We at Porsche*. "The prototype was unfortunately destroyed during a 1944 bombing of Stüttgart." It was another forerunner of the eventual VW Beetle. (PM)

Note that the car at right has a Michigan license plate on the return trip from the Ford Motor Company at Detroit in 1937. This is a stop in Rochester, NY, with Dr. Ferdinand Porsche at far right, and Ferry in the center at left wearing a snappy, white, wide-brimmed Panama hat. The other two men are Gleason Works officials from Rochester, a firm that manufactured "Machinery for producing ring gears and pinions," recalled Dr. Ferry Porsche in *We at Porsche* 39 years later. The car is a new "small" Ford V8 bought by his father on their joint U.S. tour. (PM)

"A Single Great Man, Ford"
Hitler, Ford, & the Porsches, 1923-48

On page 639 of the still-in-print American edition of Hitler's *Mein Kampf* is this statement:

"While England sweats to maintain her position in the world, the Jew organizes his attack for its conquest. He already sees the present day European states as will-less tools in his fist, whether indirectly through a so-called Western democracy, or in the form of direct domination by Jewish Bolshevism, but it is not only the old world that he holds thus enmeshed, the same fate menaces the new.

"It is Jews who govern the stock exchange forces of the American Union. Every year makes them more and more the controlling masters of the production in a nation of 120 millions; only a single great man, Ford, to their fury, still maintains full independence."

As the editor added in a footnote to this 1943 second edition, "only very few" had been substituted for "A single great man, Ford" from the original published in 1925. Hitler had dedicated the book on October 16, 1924, at Landsberg-am-Lech Fortress Prison to the 16 men who fell on November 9, 1923, in a hail of police gunfire during his failed Beer Hall Putsch in Münich.

During his time spent incarcerated at Landsberg, Hitler read American automaker Henry Ford's autobiography, as well as conceived his ideas for the future People's Car and the Autobahn upon which it would travel. The interaction between Hitler and Ford—and later Ford and the Porsches—forms a central core to the current work.

To Americans Henry Ford was one man, but to the Nazis, that same man plus one other; let us examine both herein.

Ford was born on a farm in Dearborn, MI, on July 30, 1863, the same month as the pivotal Battle of Gettysburg in Pennsylvania, and like the young Ferdinand Porsche a generation later, was immediately enthralled by all things mechanical. When of age, and with his parent's blessing, young Henry left the family farm to take up a machine shop apprenticeship, first working as a wandering repairman for a farm machinery company, then a sawmill operator, and later as chief engineer for the new Edison Illuminating Company in Detroit, "Tending and maintaining the generators," according to author Alan Axelrod, PhD.

He soon became interested in the car that had been jointly invented by Karl Benz and Gottleib Daimler in 1885, when he was 22. On June 4, 1896, at age 33, he built his own first car, and later a racing car for the famed American driver Barney Oldfield, a contemporary of driver Eddie Rickenbacker.

He founded the Ford Motor Company in 1903, when he was 40, "And the company turned a profit from day one," stated Axelrod. As in Europe, Ford as an auto maker built cars only for the wealthy, until he realized in 1908 (when he was 45) that there was a vast new market on the horizon as yet untapped; "the common man," who, as in Europe and elsewhere, walked, biked, or rode the streetcar. He simply could not afford the expensive cars of the day, as in Hitler's early era later. He established the Model T:

"Ford understood that the main cost of manufacturing a car was in labor, not parts. If you could reduce the amount of time it took to build a car, you could lower the price of the car. Ford introduced a new manufacturing technique: the assembly line. Instead of a few specialist craftsmen working on one car, each car would pass through a larger number of semi-skilled (and lower-paid) workers, each one trained to do some specific aspect of assembly. The result was a car that sold for $ 850, significantly cheaper than a custom-made vehicle.

"In 1908, $850 was still well beyond the reach of the average American. Ford introduced further modifications to his assembly line, further subdividing procedures and making each one simpler and more efficient, reducing the price to $ 360 by 1916," just before America entered the First World War on the side of the Allies and against the Central Powers of Germany, Austria-Hungary, Turkey, and Bulgaria.

Ford once asserted that, "The idea for the assembly line came in a general way from the overhead trolley that the Chicago (meat) packers use in dressing beef."

As for his innovative car that has since become world famous:

"Sturdy, reliable, homely and humble, the Model T changed the world in many ways. It fostered a society driven (the pun is intended) by consumerism as never before. It leveled economic classes to an unprecedented degree: rich and poor alike were now mobile. It furthered the unification of the nation by triggering construction of what would become a vast network of roads."

Reading about all this in Landsberg, Hitler conceived his vision of the new Germany that he wanted to create. At home, he would build both the car and the roads, as well as the classless society encompassed by his new Hitler Youth. In foreign affairs, he would first bring all ethnic Germans back "home" to Germany, and then set off on a series of conquests that would result in the end in a "German India of the East," the conquered USSR, all based on the model of what he most admired in the world: the British Empire.

Not for nothing did he model himself on both Frederick the Great and Bismarck, and the Nazis concocted the catch-all slogan *"Ein Führer, Ein Volk, Ein Reich"/One Leader, one people, one nation*. That was his entire political program in a nutshell; all the rest was mere window dressing.

Continues Dr. Axelrod of the Model T, "It changed the face of the nation. Once divided between cities and farms, America saw the rise of suburbs, satellites of the city made accessible by automobile." Since Germany would in the end lack such "*lebensraum/living space*," Hitler resolved on the conquest of Eastern lands in Russia, just as he had read of the Americans doing in their "Manifest Destiny" drive (westward to the Pacific Ocean during 1830-1910). As a young student at Linz, Austria, and later in Vienna as a starving artist, Hitler later became the nascent pre- and post-World War politician in Münich. The VWs and Autobahn would serve his ultimate purposes here as well.

Continues Dr. Axelrod:

"The Model T and the methods used to produce it also dramatically changed the relation of labor and management. At first, this was to the benefit of labor. Ford—interested in efficiency and quality—paid his workers well for the times. Then, in the interest of maximizing profits, he started to demand higher levels of production from his workers. This profoundly changed the nature of labor itself.

"No longer were products the creation of individual craftspeople; they were the collective result of an anonymous assembly line. No longer did human beings control the nature and tempo of production. They performed the same tasks repetitively, without variation, without creativity. They did this in time with the moving machinery of the assembly line, not at any human pace."

This has been satirized by both English actor Charlie Chaplin in the 1936 film *Modern Times* and American actresses Lucille Ball and Vivian Vance in a famous episode of the *I Love Lucy* television show of the 1950s, and later still condemned in the hit song *Take This Job and Shove It* by singer Johnny Paycheck in the 1970s, just as—paradoxically—both Ford and VW sales were leveling off.

In the U.S., the auto industry came to be dominated by such figures I knew, or knew of, in the 1980s as James W. Jeffcoat, J. Bruce Innes, Eugene Arbaugh, and A. Samuel Penn of Petersen, Howell, and Heather of Hunt Valley, MD—the world's largest leaser of fleets of cars, vans, and trucks where I once worked briefly—as epitomized by the "golden parachutes" for top corporate executives and the "pink slip" for the workers, as they were either fired outright or laid off with little notice.

As plants nationally downsized or closed in the U.S., my stepfather, the late Philip J. Sgroi, Sr., was one of the lucky ones; he took early retirement after 43 years as a forklift operator at Bethlehem Steel Corporations' Sparrows Point, MD, plant.

The workers began being replaced altogether in the early Eighties by robotics, as well as by foreign buyouts, a process that continues to this day more than two decades later. Ford most likely foresaw this development, and maybe Hitler and the Porsches as well, but they planned on a different scheme of things had Nazi Germany won World War II; German masters of slave labor across the Russian steppes and on into Asia.

In the end, a look at Ford sales statistics between 1908-27 is in order here: he manufactured 10,607 units at $850 in 1908, and 730,041 at $360 eight years later, with 15 million Model Ts by 1927, nine years after America had been a victor in World War I and 24 years since the establishment of the historic Ford Motor Company. He was 64 years old.

In films, Ford has been portrayed by British thespian Sir Laurence Olivier in *The Betsy*, and by American actor Cliff Robertson in a made-for-TV miniseries.

Now for the Nazi side of the ledger on Henry Ford. Asserted authors Adam LeBor and Roger Boyes in *Seduced by Hitler: The Choices of a Nation and the Ethics of Survival*, "Like his friend, Adolf Hitler, Henry Ford—founder of the Ford Motor Company—believed in plain food, a puritanical lifestyle, and virulent anti-Semitism. Finding a kindred spirit, Henry Ford was one of the Nazi leader's earliest admirers. The feeling was mutual; during the 1920s, a large portrait of Henry Ford hung behind Hitler in his office at Nazi Party Headquarters in Münich [the current author found no evidence of this in my own 2007 work *Hitler's Headquarters from Beer Hall to Bunker, 1920-45*, however].

"When Hitler was put on trial after the failed Münich *Putsch/Revolt* of 1923, a member of the Bavarian parliament testified that Henry Ford had given Hitler money. Ford's book, *The International Jew*, published in 1927, is full of anti-Jewish conspiracy theories, and he was also the proud recipient of the Nazi Grand Cross of the German Eagle.

"There is evidence that links between the Ford Motor Company and the Nazis continued after the United States entered the war, through Ford's German subsidiary, Ford Werke/Works AG, set up in the 1920s. Ford Werke was an enthusiastic supporter of the 'Aryanization' of the German economy, that is, the forced purchase at extremely low prices of Jewish-owned businesses. As early as 1935, Ford Werke used Nazi criteria for deciding who could be employed at the company.

"General Manager Erich Diestel carried out many of the dismissals, until he was sacked (fired) himself a year later for having a Jewish ancestor. By September 1939, Ford Werke was the second largest producer of trucks in Nazi Germany. The company manufactured light trucks and spare parts throughout the war for the Nazi war machine. German troops drove into Poland on Ford trucks.

"The trucks were also used in the concentration camps. Declassified US intelligence documents record that 'Of the 350,000 trucks which the motorized German Army possessed in 1942, 100-120,000 were Ford-built.' The Ford truck plant at Cologne was supplied with forced labor from the concentration camp at Buchenwald, and Russian POWs were also used for war production work, in breach of the Geneva Convention.

"In wartime Washington, DC, there was anger that the German subsidiary of perhaps the most famous American company was churning out motor vehicles for the enemy. In spring 1943 [the Nazis were trying to overcome their defeat at Stalingrad and gearing up to fight the Red Army again that summer] the Treasury Department carried out an investigation into the files of the Ford Company and its relationship with its subsidiaries in Nazi-occupied Europe, such as France, Germany, and the Netherlands. It discovered that the Ford factories in Nazi-occupied Europe were still producing for the Nazis.

"There were strong ties of friendship and business between the Ford family and the Nazi economic elite, dating back to before 1939, with sinister implications for the American war effort. In 1925, Ford sold 40% of its German subsidiary's shares in IG Farben and other German companies. Henry Ford's son, Edsel—one of the directors of Ford Werke—was close friends with Hermann Schmitz, head of IG Farben.

"They were also among the founders of the American branch of IG Farben, known as American IG/Chemical Corporation. In turn, American IG owned the General Aniline and Film (GAF) Company, which supplied khaki and blue dyes for Army and Navy uniforms. US branches of German businesses were natural targets for espionage by pro-Nazi German expatriates and immigrants in the United States.

"'Ford subsidiaries in Nazi-occupied countries were not run directly from US headquarters in Detroit during the war,' recorded Christopher Simpson in his study of big business and genocide, *The Splendid Blonde Beast*, nor did they repatriate profits and report directly to Ford headquarters. But, as with IG Farben, key individuals who had managed the firms during the Third Reich found their Nazi past no hindrance to a successful business career in postwar Germany.

"In fact, it positively helped. After 1945, Ford Werke director Heinrich Albert, leader of the company's effort to fire Jewish employees during the Third Reich, was appointed custodian of United States and British corporate properties in Berlin."

Ironically, in 1925 the Ford Model T had actually begun assembly in Weimar, Germany, itself in a plant at Berlin's Westhafen district, and this gave way three years later to the Model A, which was then far cheaper than any German domestic product by comparison; both Hitler and Porsche recognized that they might well lose their own home small car market to the gigantic American firm across the Atlantic, and the Führer's admiration for Henry Ford in this arena stopped at the water's edge.

In 1937, Hitler had named Dr. Ferdinand Porsche Reich Auto Designer, and a top-level car conference was planned in Detroit with the man they both admired: Henry Ford, whom the Führer had also just presented with the Grand Cross of the German Eagle for "Giving autos to the masses." Dr. Porsche's initial visit to the United States had consisted only of him and his secretary, but this time there was to be a larger and more formal automotive entourage: Ferry, the first Dr. Anton Piech (his son-in-law); Hitler's eyes and ears, Jakob Werlin; Ley's man Dr. Bodo Lafferentz; Ghislaine Kaes; and production/design expert Otto Dyckhoff.

Walter Henry Nelson describes this momentous auto summit conference that would have a lasting impact on the future of car history up to the present day:

"Porsche regarded this meeting as the high court of his visit. He idolized Ford as a genius who had materialized Porsche's own personal dream in another country. They conversed through interpreters and Porsche poured out all his plans for the Volkswagen. Did they worry the elder Ford? Not in the least. 'If anyone can build a car better or cheaper than I can, that serves me right,' he said.

"Ferry Porsche, in his mid-twenties, was present at this meeting, and Henry Ford asked him to talk about the car of the future, not necessarily the Volkswagen, but the ideal European car of the next decade. 'Let *him* tell *me*,' Ford said. 'The young are the ones who will build that car.'

"Ferry spoke of independent suspension, streamlining, and low gas consumption—actually enumerating the VW's specifications. Would Ford care to visit Germany? Asked Ferdinand Porsche. Would he like to see what they were building? That would be impossible, said Henry Ford, because there would be a war in the near future. Porsche was astounded. He and his colleagues looked at each other with the naivete of those who read only the technical press.

"'No!' said Porsche. 'We cannot believe that! We live in an era of economic improvement, in which many problems take time to solve. Why should there be war?' Ford murmured that he hoped that they were right, but he had his doubts. Then he excused himself; 400 orphans were waiting to see him." Returning back to New York, they bought a Ford V-8. "En route, they stopped at various manufacturers to buy machinery for the factory in Germany. From the US, Porsche also shot back a cablegram ordering a further change in the design of his car.

"All the Volksautos so far had doors which opened from the front (as had many other German cars); Porsche ordered these changed, to open from the rear. In the US he had learned that this was the trend now, and also safer."

In *We at Porsche*, Dr. Ferry Porsche recalled the trip thusly:

"Our visit to the US lasted four weeks and was very instructive and interesting in many ways. The American firms we visited included the Cincinnati Milling Machine Co., Reading, OH; the Fisher Body Corporation, Lansing, MI; and Ambi-Budd in Philadelphia, spot-welding specialists—an operation with which we were still not too familiar in Europe.

"In fact, we became so fascinated by what we saw at Fisher we actually timed the production it took of some parts by stopwatch to see, for example, just how long it took to stamp out a fender, or a door, or some other component, and get it ready for rustproof dipping. The factory officials didn't seem to mind at all, and didn't hold back answers to any of our questions, which were many....

"We also wanted to know whether we might be able to recruit Americans of German origin to come back with us to Germany and help build up the Volkswagenwerk. Ford, General Motors, and Chrysler each had numbers of German-American engineers, and we made a particular point of asking them whether they would be interested in returning to Germany to help with the mass production planning of the new Volkswagen.

"In the end, we persuaded several Americans of German descent to come to work for Volkswagen, little dreaming of the holocaust [the war] that was only then two years away. Prominent among these specialists was Frederick Kuntze, a US citizen who had built the gigantic River Rouge Plant for Ford, and was in charge of it....

"Later we visited the Ford Research Center at Dearborn, and this was my first opportunity to have an extended conversation with the great Henry Ford [after the joint meeting with the overall Porsche delegation already described] ...Here was a man who had really put automobile mass production on the map, and I know that my father—in fact, all our group—would have liked to do business with him. Perhaps something like mass-producing the Volkswagen in the United States, and turning it into a world project.

"...I was also privileged to meet Henry Ford's son Edsel, and so became acquainted with more than one generation of the family...As for the Ford factory, everything was thrown wide open to us. If we wanted anything at all, we had only to ask a question..."

One anecdote of this trip recalled when they asked where Henry Ford's office was, only to be told, "Mr. Ford has no office. Since he owns the entire plant, Mr. Ford sits where he wants." The

Porsches were also amazed when they carried their own lunch trays in the cafeteria.

Continued Dr. Ferry Porsche:

"On our return, my father was rewarded with quite an honor. The 1937 National Prize of the Third Reich went to only three people... My father received his award for outstanding work on the Auto Union racer and the Volkswagen. Automatically, along with this award, the recipient was also given the title of 'Professor honoris causa.'...My father's reaction was simply, 'Do I look that old to be addressed as 'Herr Professor?' Naturally, he was pleased to receive this award."

In 1948, when Edsel Ford was offered the entire Volkswagenwerk by the British REME, he was told by one of his top aides, "Frankly, Mr. Ford, I don't think that what you're being offered here is worth a damn!," but on February 17, 1972, Beetle sales surpassed the overall global record held by Ford's Model T as the most popular car ever made, with 15,007,034 units produced. Two years later the Beetle would suffer its first serious losses as the Golf succeeded it. The last German-built Beetle rolled off the assembly lines on January 19, 1978, but the Cabriolet model was built by Karmann until January 10, 1980, ending 40 years of Beetles in Germany, with Wolfsburg being the world's largest car factory under a single roof—*just as Hilter had predicted it would be.*

In 1981 a Silver Beetle was produced, followed six years later by a 50th anniversary model; 1987 was also the year when Ford and VW merged their operations in Brazil, and thus Dr. Ferdinand Porsche's goal of joint production five decades before had at last been realized as well.

Ford and the Führer

Excerpts from *Ford and the Führer: new Documents Reveal the Close Ties Between Dearborn and the Nazis* by Ken Silverstein, *The Nation*, January 24, 2000.

A pro-Hitler poem "Ran in an in-house magazine published by the Ford Motor Company's German subsidiary in April 1940, titled *Führer.*

"Ford argues that company headquarters in Dearborn, MI lost control of its German plant after the US entered the war in 1941. Hence, Ford is not responsible for any actions taken by its German subsidiary during World War II. 'We did not do business in Germany during the war...says...a Ford spokeswoman. 'The Nazis confiscated the plant there, and we lost all contact.' She added that Ford played 'A pivotal role in the American war effort. After the US entered the war, Ford threw its entire backing to the war effort.'"

Writer Silverstein disputed this, asserting that:

"The new materials—most of which were found at the (US) National Archives—show, among other things, that up until Pearl Harbor, Dearborn made huge revenues by producing war materials for the Reich...Ford's cooperation with the Nazis continued until at least August 1942, eight months after the US entered the war, through its properties in Vichy France....

"Ford's director of global operations...said in a statement, 'Because Ford did not do business in Germany during the war—our Cologne plant was confiscated by the Nazi government....

"Ford Motor set up shop in Germany in 1925...Ford of Germany prospered during the Nazi years...Sales increased by more than half between 1938-43...Ford eagerly cooperated with the Nazis...German Ford began producing vehicles of a strictly military nature for the Reich even before the war began...Following Hitler's invasion of Poland...German Ford became one of the largest suppliers of vehicles to the Wehrmacht...By 1941, Ford of Germany had stopped manufacturing passenger vehicles and was devoting its entire production capacity to military trucks....

"Ford vehicles were crucial to the revolutionary strategy of *blitzkrieg/lightning war*. Of the 350,000 trucks used by the motorized German Army as of 1942, roughly one-third were Ford-made... Indeed, the Cologne plant proved to be so important to the Reich's war effort that the Allies bombed it on several occasions.

"In 1942, Ford Werke/Works was duly officially incorporated into the German armaments industry.

"When Hitler declared war on the U.S. on December 11, 1941, the company later announced that, 'Ford has become a purely German company.'...However, the Nazis never nationalized Ford's German property...Dearborn maintained its 52% share through the duration of the war. Ford Werke even set aside dividend payments due to Dearborn, which were paid after the war....

"By 1943, half of Ford Werke's work force comprised foreign captives, including French, Russians, Ukrainians, and Belgians. In August 1944, a squad of SS men brought 15 prisoners from the Buchenwald concentration camp to Ford Werke...Ford's worker-inmates toiled for 12 hours daily with a 15-minute break. They were given 200 grams of bread and coffee for breakfast, no lunch, and a dinner of spinach and three potatoes, or soup made of turnip leaves.

"Robert Schmidt was appointed in 1939 to run Ford Werke...The fraternal ties between Ford and the Nazis is perhaps best symbolized by the company's birthday gift to the Führer of 35,000 Reichsmarks on April 20, 1939."

For Hitler's 51st birthday on April 20, 1940, the company magazine ran the Führer's picture on the cover. The April 1941 issue wrote, "The management of the Ford Werke salutes our Führer with grateful heart." Schmidt was appointed a Military Economic Leader by the Nazis:

"The Nazis also put Schmidt in charge of overseeing Ford plants in occupied Belgium, Holland, and Vichy France. At one point, he and another Cologne executive bitterly argued over who would run Ford of England when Hitler's troops conquered Britain....

"Ford was quite prepared to do business with the Nazis if Hitler won the war...Six key executives from the Nazi era moved back into important positions in the company after 1945...In 1948, Henry Ford visited Cologne to celebrate the 10,000th truck to roll off the postwar assembly line there. Two years later, Ford rehired Schmidt, [who] remained with Ford until his death in 1962....

"Before its fall, the Nazi regime had given Ford Werke about $104,000 in compensation for damages caused by Allied bombings."

TABLE 2.2. *Motor-vehicle production in selected countries, 1933–1938* ('000)

Country	1933	1934	1935	1936	1937	1938
Canada	65	117	173	162	207	166
France	189	181	165	204	201	227
Germany	118	186	248	303	331	340
Italy	40	45	48	45	71	67
UK	286	342	404	461	507	447
USA	1,920	2,753	3,946	4,454	4,808	2,489

Source: Society of Motor Manufacturers and Traders, *The Motor Industry of Great Britain: 1938* (London, 1939).

TABLE 2.3. *Vehicle ownership in Europe and USA, 1935* (per 1,000 pop.)

Country	Vehicles[a]	Country	Vehicles[a]
USA	204.5	Switzerland	21.7
France	49.0	Irish Free State	17.8
UK	45.2	Netherlands	17.6
Denmark	41.6	Germany	16.1
Sweden	24.4	Italy	9.5
Norway	22.3	USSR	1.5

[a] Excluding motor cycles.

Source: League of Nations, *World Production and Prices, 1925–35* (Geneva, 1936), 90.

TABLE 2.8. *Estimated employment created by roads and cars, 1938*[a]

Reichsautobahnen	120,000
Ordinary roads (1936)	40,000
Motor industry (excluding parts)	170,000
Components and parts	150,000
Garages (1935)	100,000
Supply industry, roads	250,000
Motor trade	60,000
Chauffeurs, drivers, etc. (1934)	260,000
TOTAL	1,150,000

[a] Estimated jobs, including figures for earlier years where 1938 figure not known.

Sources: *WS* 18 (1938), 569, and 19: 3 suppl. (1939); *Wochenbericht*, 9 (1936), 553, and 6 (1933), 4–5; *Das Archiv* (1934), 713–14; *DDV*, Special Issue 5 (1934/5), 19–20; *Der Vierjahrsplan*, 5 (1941), 316.

Cars, roads, and economic recovery in Nazi Germany, 1933-39, from *War and Economy in the Third Reich* by R.J. Overy. (LC)

Henry Ford (third from right at center) poses with both the first (left) and last—the latter the 15 millionth Model T Ford, with his quadri-cycle in between. The first Model T rolled off the production line in 1913, and revolutionized the auto industry worldwide virtually overnight. The genius of his assembly line was that it "Took the work to the man, not the man to the work" for the new concept of mass production, assumed in Germany only with resistance as being incompatible with quality production. Both Hitler and the Porsches recognized the wisdom of Ford's mass production techniques of cars, as opposed to the hand assembly of individual components then favored in the specialized German automotive industry that custom built such expensive cars as Mercedes-Benz. VW was designed to be the antithesis of Mercedes and Daimler-Benz in virtually every way. (LC)

A small fleet of Porsche-built VW W30 car models. (PM)

Road signs of the Third Reich and the early Volkswagen such as these now cover Europe, and there are many in the U.S. as well, (From *Flags of the German Reich* by John D. Griffin, 1968.)

VW logo and those of its competitors during the Nazi German epoch. Noted Rex Curry in 2005, "Volkswagen's iconic buttressing of V and W is attributed mainly to the engineer Franz Reimspiess, the same man who perfected the engine for the Beetle in the 1930s....Before World War II, when the car was still National Socialism's 'Strength Through Joy' car, the logo was surrounded by the gear-shaped emblem of the German Labor Front (DAF)." On July 17, 2005, a graphic designer named Nikolia Borg in a story bylined by Bojan Pancevski in *The Telegraph* from Vienna claimed "That he was commissioned by the Nazis to design the VW logo for Volkswagen, and is suing the company for allegedly failing to recognize his work." (LC)

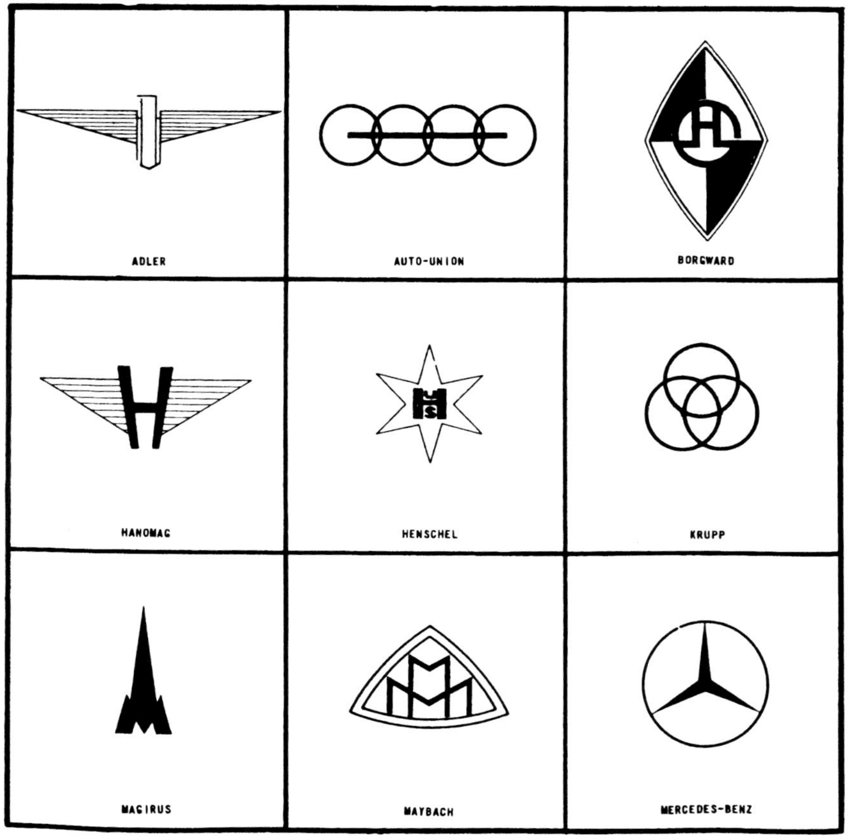

Logos of the German rivals of the Volkswagen, 1930-45, from *Wheeled Vehicles of the Wehrmacht* by Chris Ellis. (LC)

Interior view. (VWM)

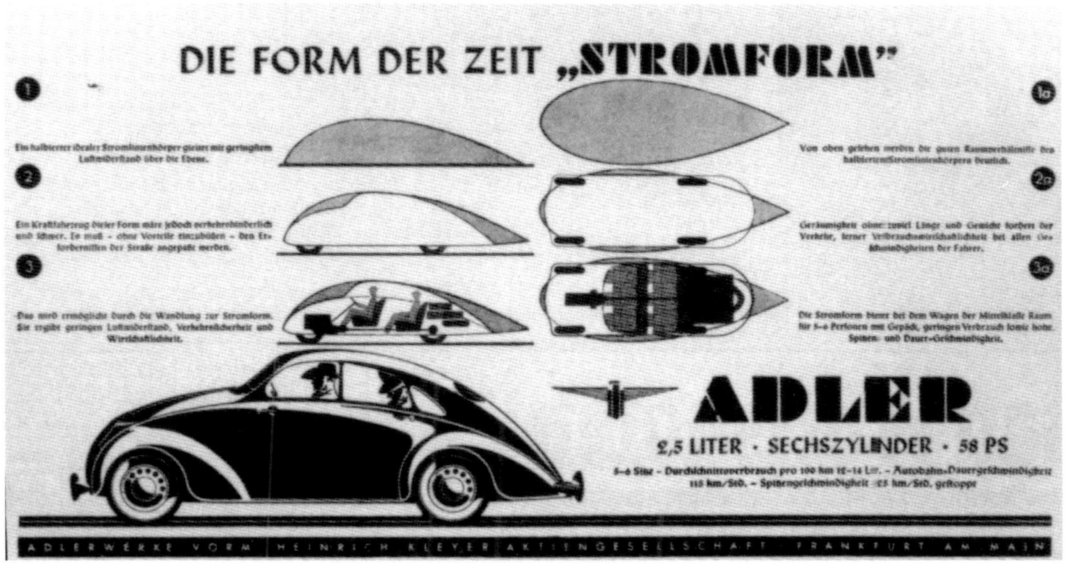

When Hitler proclaimed that, "There can only be *one* Volkswagen, not 10!" this is but one of the many imitators he had in mind, in this case built by the Adler Company, as seen in the Berlin *Illustrated News*. (LC)

Another Adler Company small car model in hype intended to impress the German car-buying public, as seen in this trio of photos by Berthold Fischer in the Berlin *Illustrated News*. (LC)

The Mercedes-Benz Type M 230 Kleinwagen/Small Car: another threat to Hitler's cherished small car dream was his "own" company of Daimler-Benz attempting to muscle into that new market with this 1933-34 entry, even as he was then planning the birth of VW with the two Drs. Porsche. Added Beverly Rae Kimes in *The Star and the Laurel*, "The Type M 23D of 1933 used a rear-mounted, three-cylinder 30hp diesel engine. Severe vibration problems resulted with the diesel, and twice as many cylinders were tried next. Though the trial runs were many, news of these cars never leaked out." (Daimler-Benz Museum, Stüttgart.)

The 1934 Mercedes-Benz Type 150 rear-mounted engine sports sedan racer. Stated Beverly Rae Kimes in *The Star and the Laurel*, it "was built to ride in Germany's 2,000-mile reliability trial. Seven of these Mercedes finished in good order, but the German public remained skeptical about rear-engine cars," and thus here, too, Hitler had his work cut out for him to change the public's perception, and buy the VW. He succeeded. (DPM.)

Twin views of another VW Beetle imitator—or did the Bug copy *it*? Dr. Ferdinand Porsche had worked at Daimler-Benz before founding his own Porsche Design Bureau. (DBM)

The Mercedes-Benz Type M17 Kleinwagen/Small Car: According to German author Werner Oswald in *Mercedes-Benz Personal Cars, 1886-1984*, this is the 1931-32 prototype, proving that the Drs. Porsche weren't the "only game in town" in pre-Hitlerite Germany so far as a Volksauto was concerned. Added Kimes, "The Type M17 of 1931 carried an air-cooled, 1.2-liter, 25 hp, four-cylinder boxer engine in the rear of a 100" wheelbase chassis." (DBM)

The Mercedes-Benz Type 130 of 1934, a VW competitor, with advertising copy. (DBM)

Mercedes-Benz VW imitator. In the center of the hood is the famed tri-pointed star logo emblem. (DBM)

The 1935-36 Mercedes-Benz Type 130 convertible model. (DBM)

Other views of the Type 130. Noted Kimes in her authoritative work *The Star and the Laurel: The Centennial History of Daimler, Mercedes, and Benz, 1886-1986*, "The Type 130—introduced at the Berlin Automobile Show in February 1934—was a complete surprise. Not only was it the smallest Mercedes ever (00" wheelbase, 50" track), but its 1.3-liter (not quite 80-cubi-inch) rear-mounted engine and advanced chassis design were hailed as revolutionary on both sides of the Atlantic. The 1935-36 cabriolet limousine is seen here." (DBM)

The Daimler-Benz 130H car was built during 1933-36, and has a more than accidental similarity between it and the Porsche VW30 design. (DBM)

Mercedes-Benz Type 130 convertible limousine small car model, 1935-36. Hitler wanted none of these to go into mass production, so they didn't. (DBM)

Mercedes-Benz Type 130 cabrio-limousine convertible model. (DBM)

Above Left: The Mercedes-Benz W133 Type 160 Model, 1935-36: Starting to look dangerously close to the real thing! Moreover, according to *Mercedes-Benz, 1886-1986, Volume 2*, "The rear-engine cars were also given more power: the Type 160 W133, of which 992 were built, developed 38 hp. Since the engineers working on the chassis had given a great deal of attention to the problem of all the weight at the back, the handling of this more powerful car was reckoned to be a great improvement." By launching VW Werks at Wolfsburg under the DAF, Hitler closed the door for good on mass production. (DBM) Above Right: The Mercedes-Benz Type 130 saloon car model. (DBM)

Mercedes-Benz Type 130 chart graphic. (DBM)

Mercedes-Benz Type 170H:. The VW imitator that hit close to home: the 1936-39 Limousine model—a fight-to-the-finish with the Porsche-built Volkswagen! (DBM)

Note the center-mounted headlamp on the front hood of this Type 170H at the Mercedes-Benz plant at Üntertürkheim, Germany. According to *Beetlemania*, "In 1962, the Beetle truly proved its remarkable strength and reliability. It became the first officially registered car on the sixth continent—registration number *Antarctica 1*." (Previously unpublished photo, Mercedes-Benz Albums, Library of Congress, Washington, DC)

A copy as close to the real thing as you're likely to get: the 1936-39 Mercedes-Benz Cabrio-Limousine. (DBM)

Where no man (or woman) has gone before…into a galaxy far, far away: the streamlined experimental car of the aerodynamic experimental city of Göttingen, 1938. This Mercedes-Benz design by engineer Karl Schlor was really a leap into the automotive future when it was introduced the year before the start of the Second World War, or perhaps merely just a reflection of the popular movie serial *Flash Gordon* epics of the day starring Buster Crabbe. The VW killed this design as well, but, who knows, we may yet see something similar on the roads, or levitating in the next decade or so. (DBM)

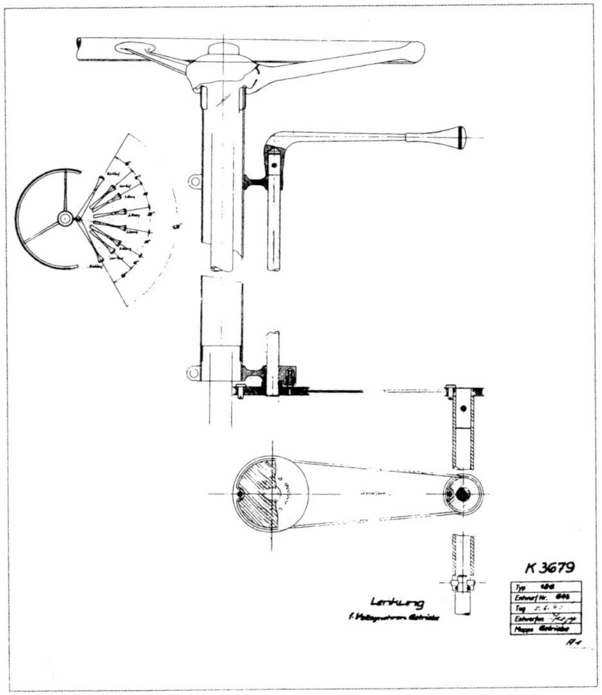

Type 126 fully synchronized transmission K 3679 design. (VWM)

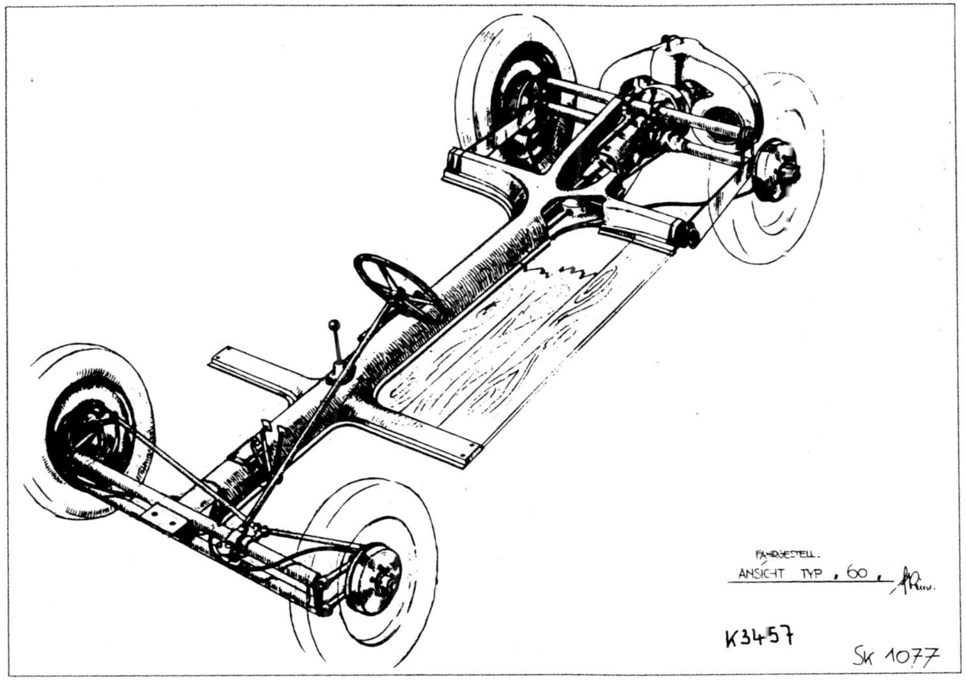

The 1077 chassis drawing of March 1935 by Franz Reimspiess. (VWM)

The Porsche-designed Zundapp Project 32 chassis. A forerunner of the eventual VW Beetle, Zundapp cancelled its productions when motorcycle sales took a sudden upswing in the Depression. This only prototype was destroyed during an Allied air raid in World War II. (PM)

The origin of the Beetle shape, the 1932 project 12 Volksauto Wanderers. Asserted *Great Marques of Germany*, "The origin of the Beetle's shape (was the) 1932 3.5-liter Type 8 Wanderer prototype, designed by the Porsche Bureau; used daily by Porsche. [This is] Komenda's Wanderer bodywork...scaled down for the 1932 Type 12 Zundapp with rear-mounted, 1.2-liter five-cylinder engine." Noted Dr. Ferry Porsche, "We proceeded to build a special Wanderer chassis (later known as the Type 8) for our own use. This enabled us to incorporate all our best ideas for a nice, modern line that would suit a convertible. We liked the car so much that for the next year it was constantly in use by us. At about the same time, we completed the second prototype of the Type 8 Wanderer. Both bodies were made in Stüttgart at the Reutter coachwork shop. They were of course the result of our own styling...They became known as #8 and #9, and had identical engines. This, however, was not our original plan. Number 9 was intended to feature a Rootes-type supercharger that never materialized, but the car had what might be called the first truly streamlined body. My father liked it so well that he used it almost exclusively for the next four or five years!" Of this same picture, author Clive Prew stated in *VW Beetle*, "One of the three Type 12s parked outside Porsche's house. This is one of the two sedans designed by Erwin Komenda and built by Reutter in 1932." (LC)

The Porsche Type 32 with rear-mounted, four-cylinder, air-cooled engine; forerunner of the later Volkswagen. Stated *Great Marques of Germany* of this photo, "The 1933 Type 32 for NSU outside Porsche's offices at 24 Kronenstrasse/Crown Street, Stüttgart. This is one of two fabric-bodied examples." (PM)

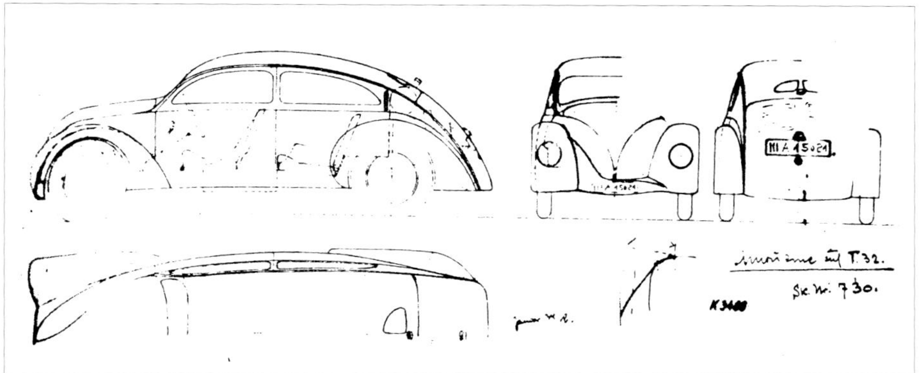

Dr. Ferdinand Porsche's own drawings for the Type 32 small car, one of two he designed for the NSU motorcycle firm of NSU at Neckarsulm near Nürnberg in 1934, the site of the annual Nazi Party Congresses. Dr. Ferry Porsche, in *We at Porsche*, asserted that there was a trio of prototypes completed, adding, "The combination of a rear-mounted, air-cooled engine, torsion-bar suspension, a central backbone 'chassis,' and a unitized flat floor and body were to lay the groundwork for the as-yet-unborn Volkswagen." (PM)

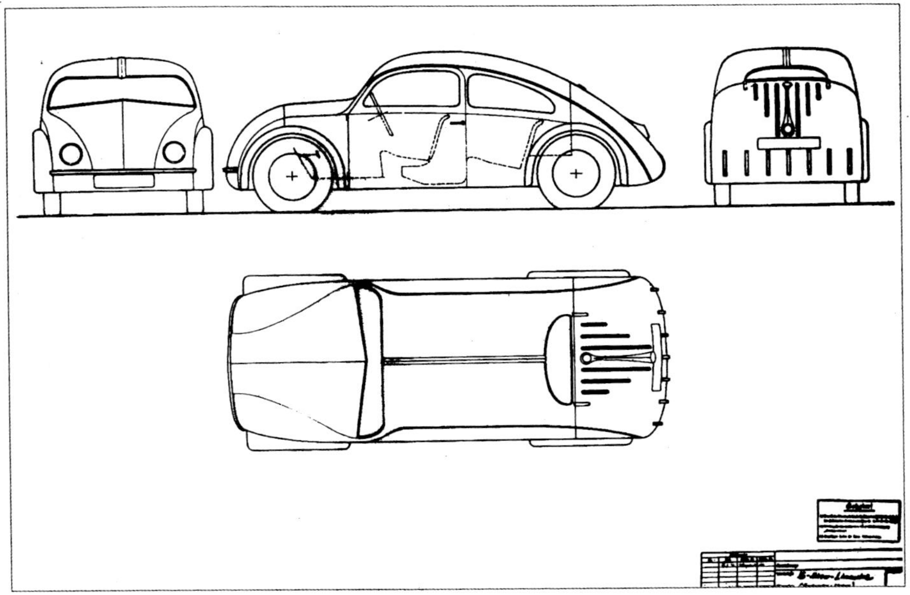

Design Sk 803 of April 28, 1934, entitled "5-seater limousine." (VWM)

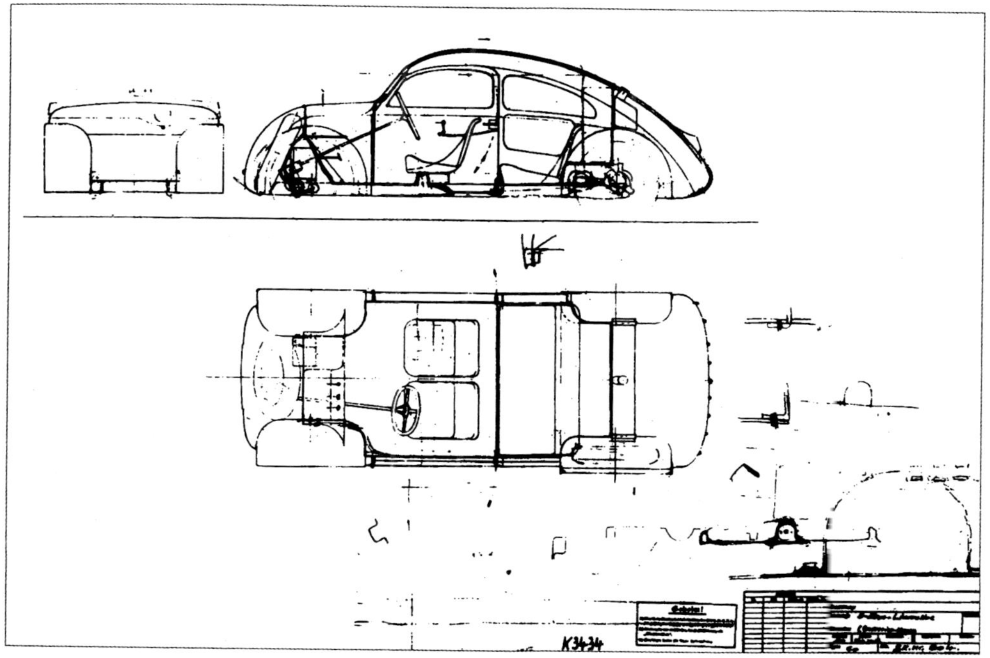

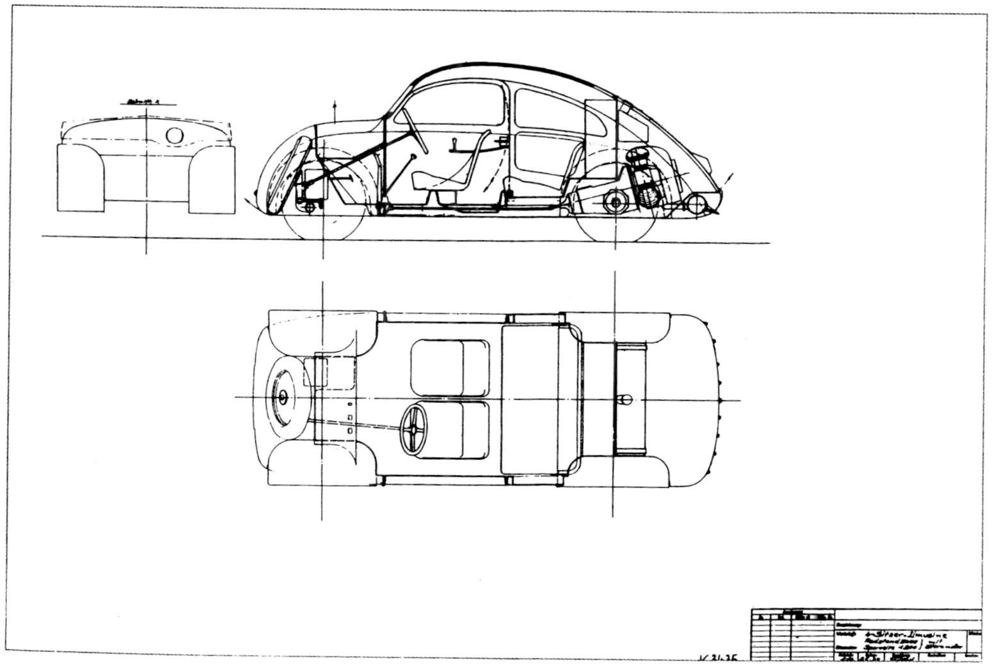

(Top) Design Sk 804. "Sk" stood for *Skizze/Sketch*. (bottom) Design Sk 838 of June 2, 1934. (VWM)

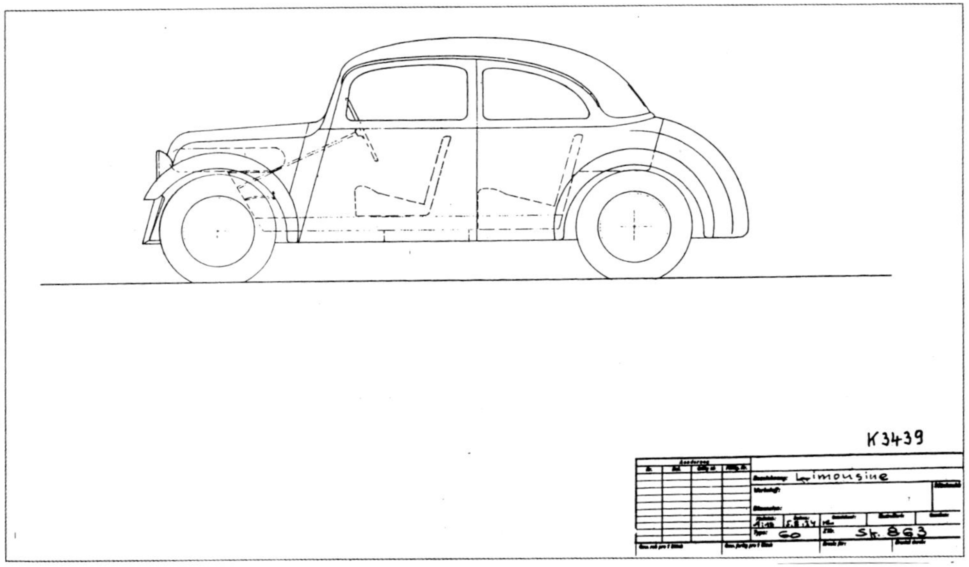

Design K 3439 of August 5, 1934. (VWM)

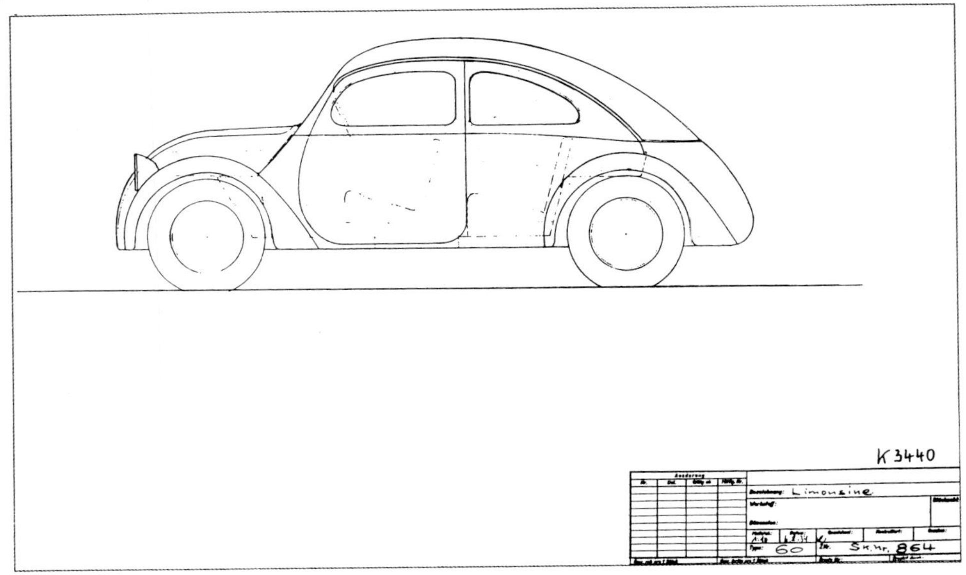

Second Body Design K 3440 of August 6, 1934. (VWM)

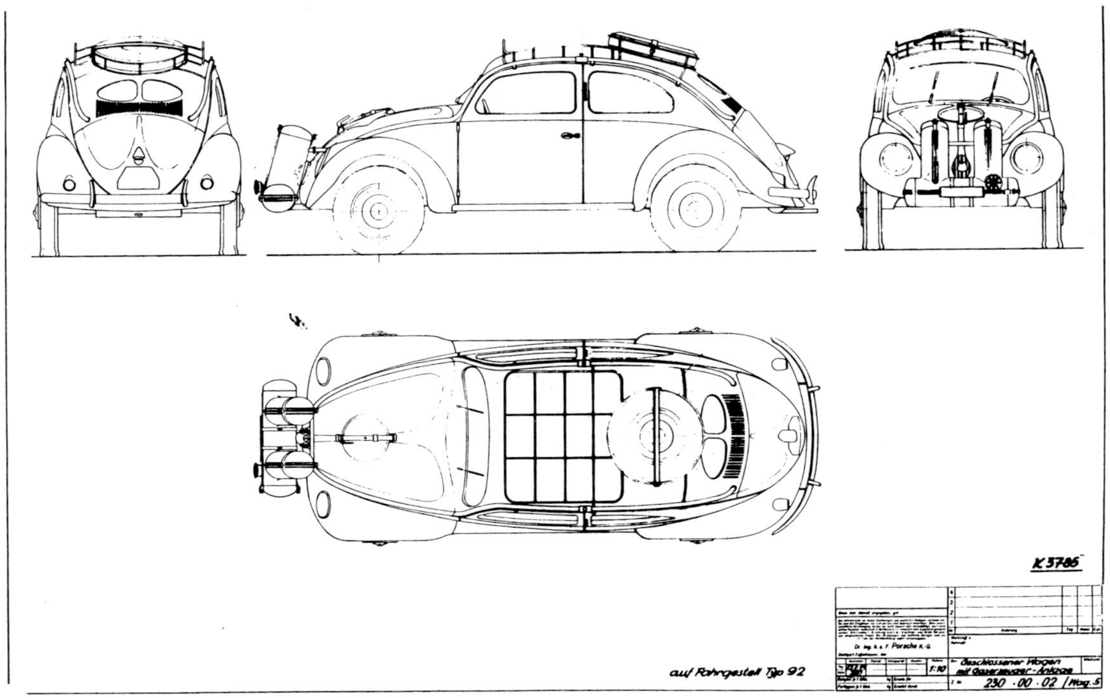

Design K 3785 of March 27, 1944, for the rebuilding of an off-road Type 92 sedan with gas generator from wood gas drive Type 230. Noted one source, "On the front end of the car is the generator. The spare tire is attached to the roof. All generator-powered vehicles had a roof rack on which the fuel was carried." (VWM)

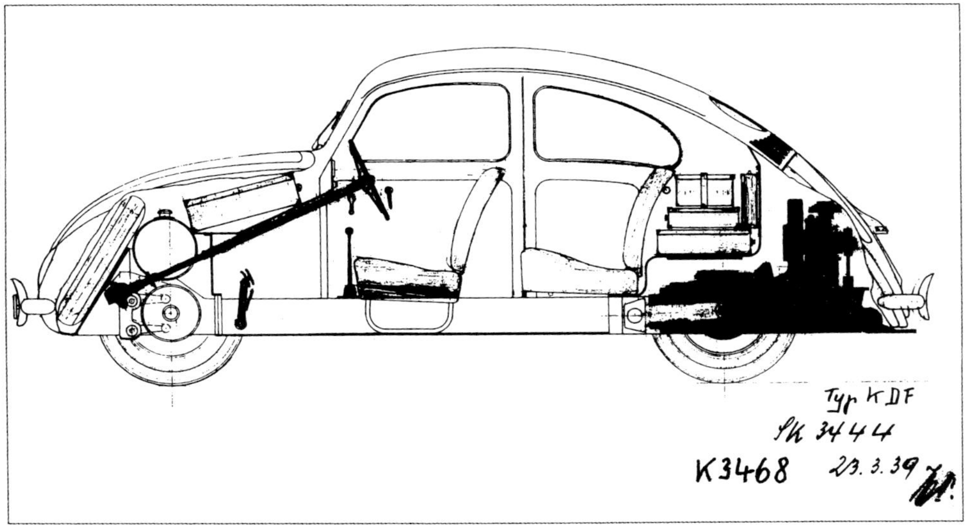

March 1939 Design Sk 3444 VW38 series model. (VWM)

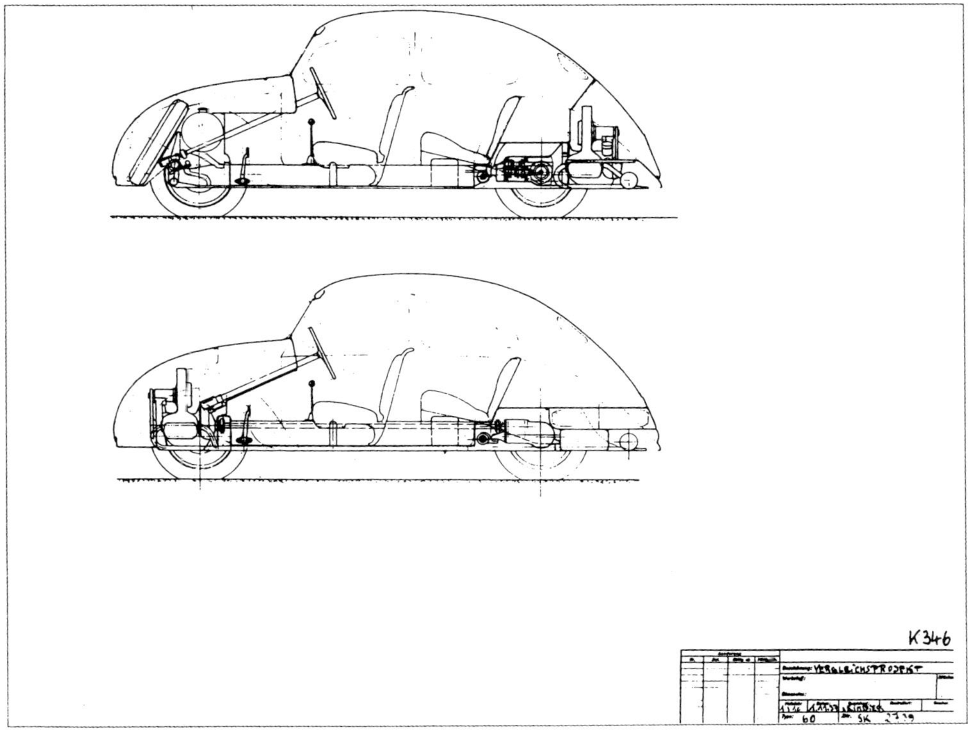

Design K 346. (VWM)

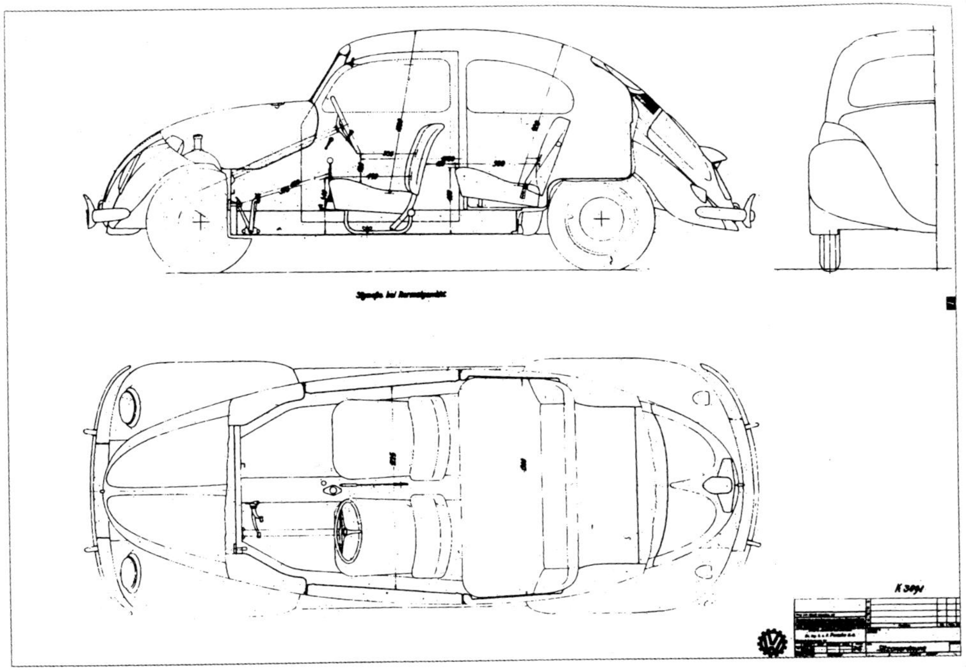

Design K 3091. (VWM)

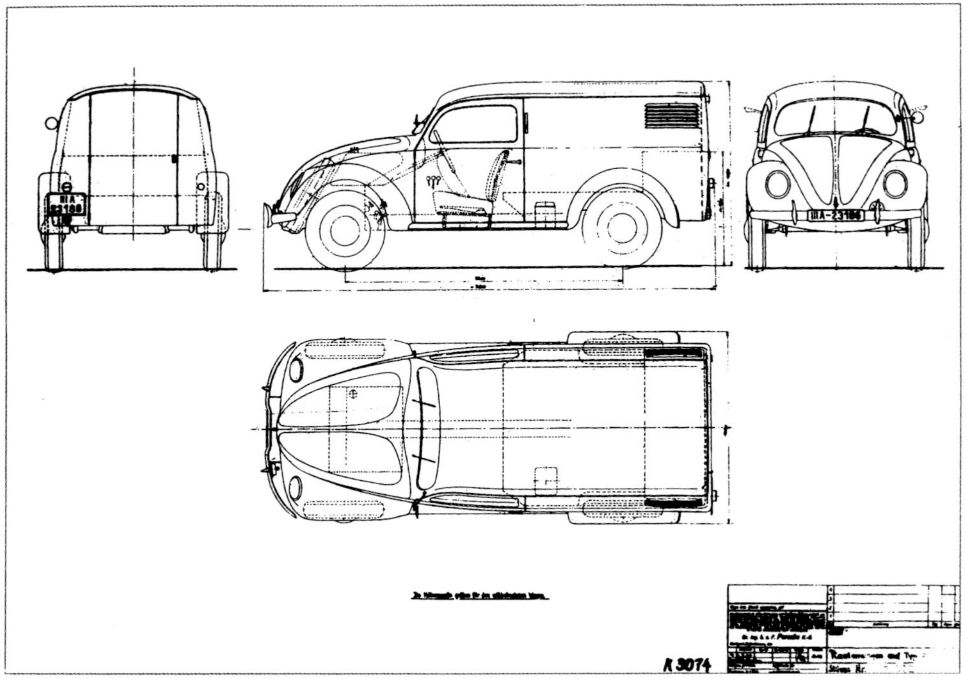

Design K 3074. (VWM)

Design K 3659 of Type 61, 1936 (VWM)

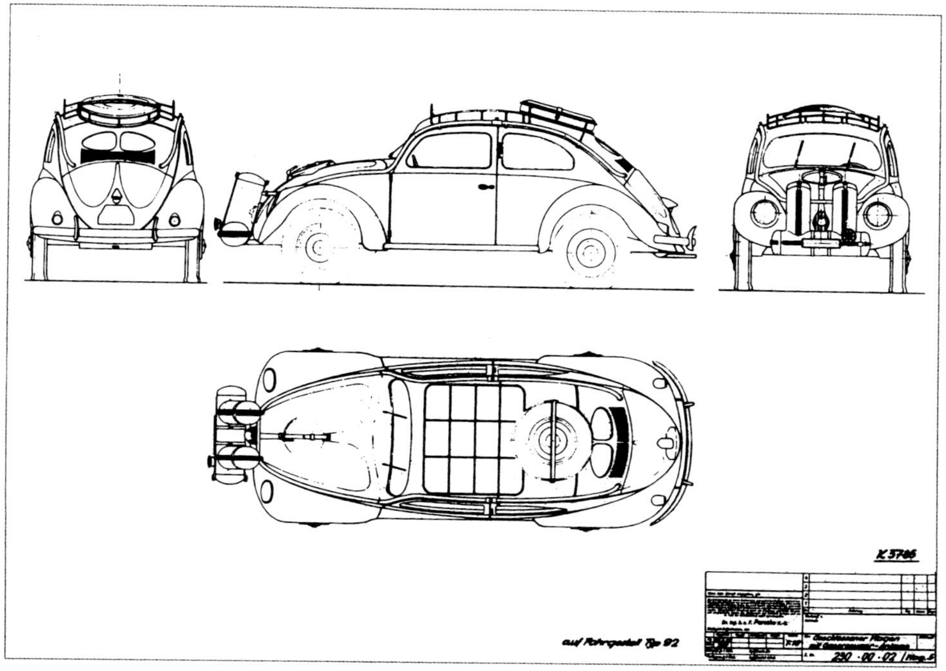

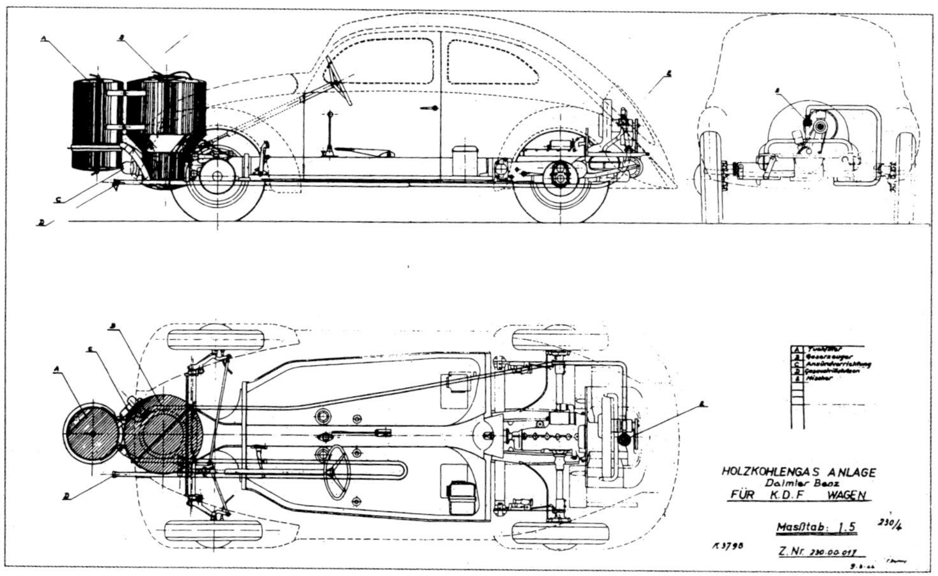

Daimler-Benz Type 230 gas-generator car. (VWM)

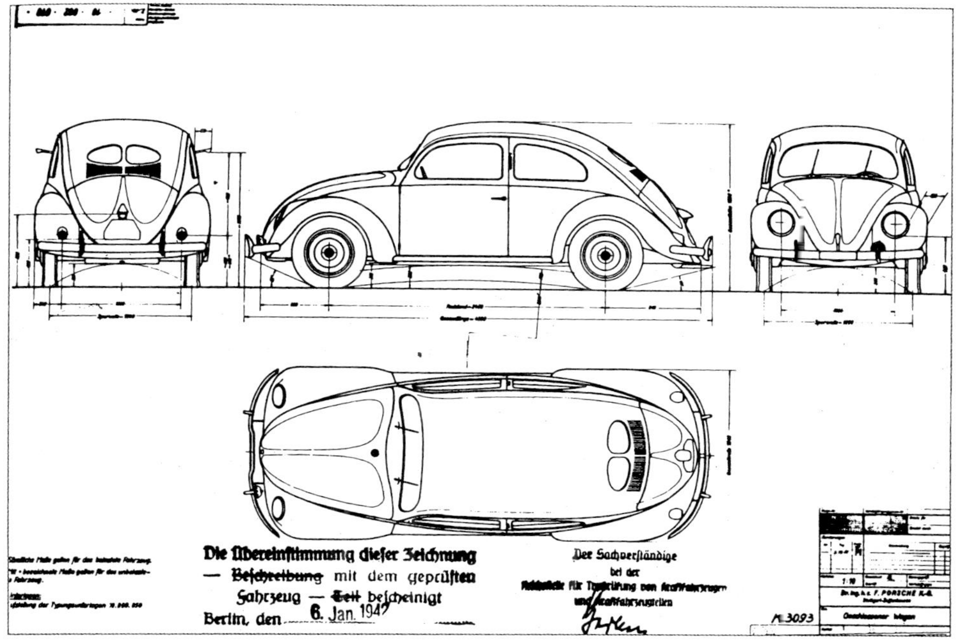

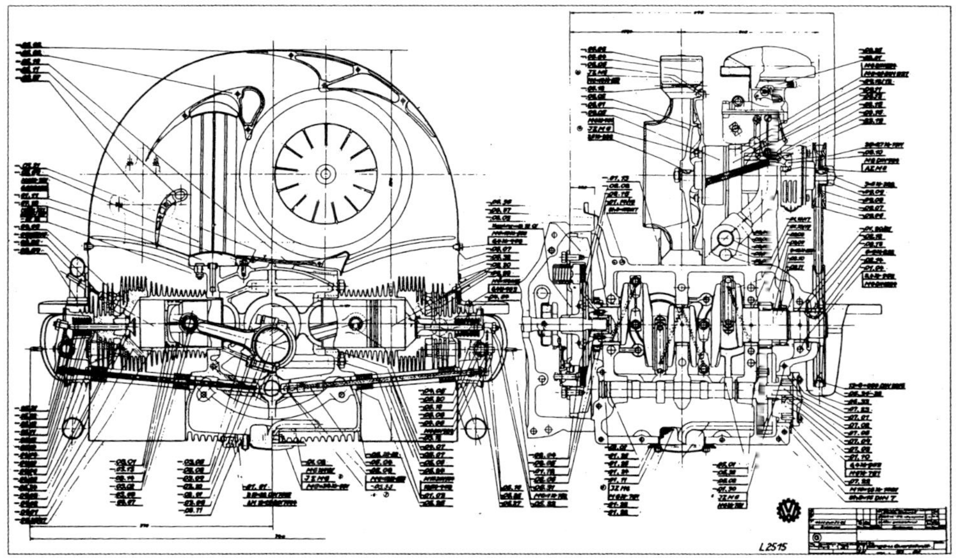

(top) Body design and (bottom) engine schematic. (VWM)

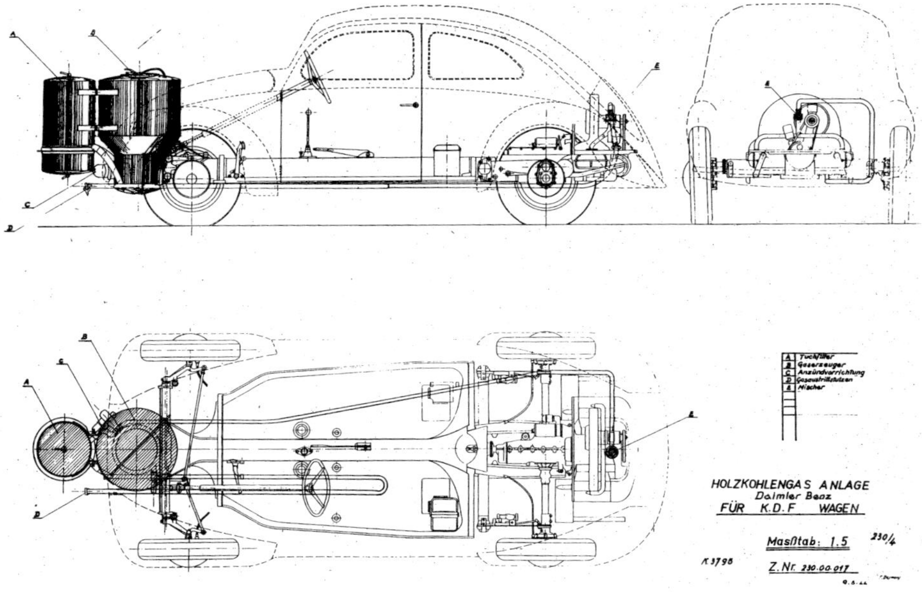

May 5, 1944, design K 3795 for the VW/Porsche Type 230/4 with Daimler-Benz wood-gas system. (VWM)

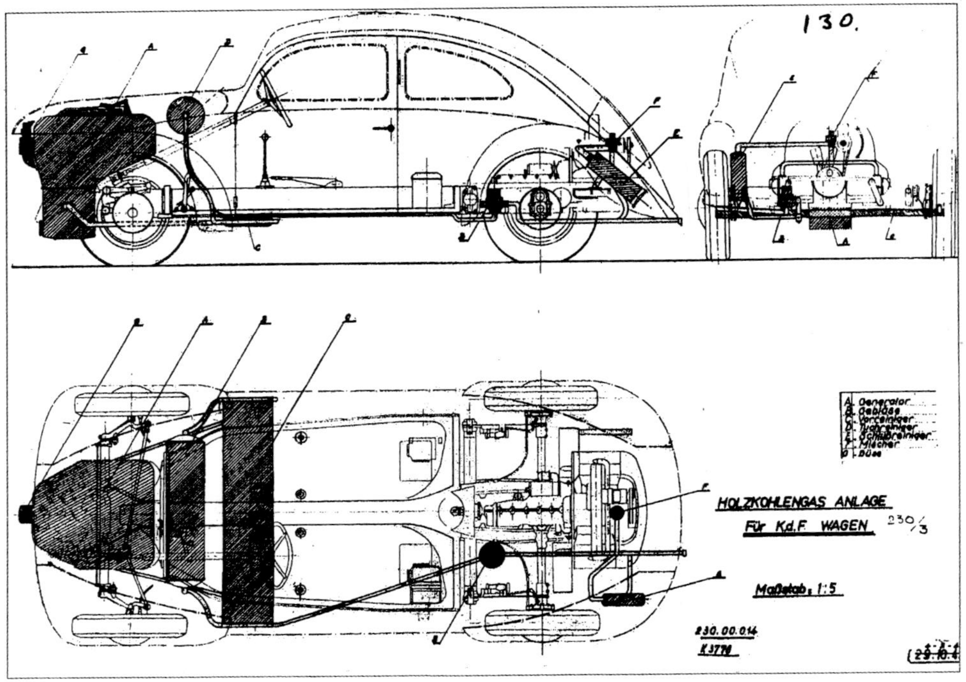

Design K 3778 of 1944 showing technology for a combustible gas production powered car. (VWM)

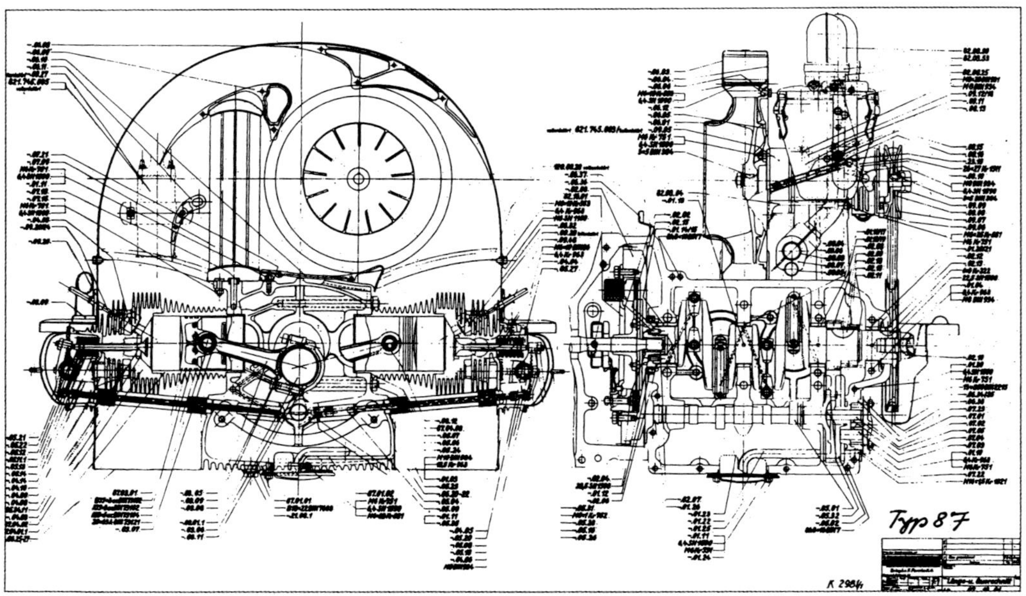

Design 2981/1 for a type 87 engine with large bore cylinders. (VWM)

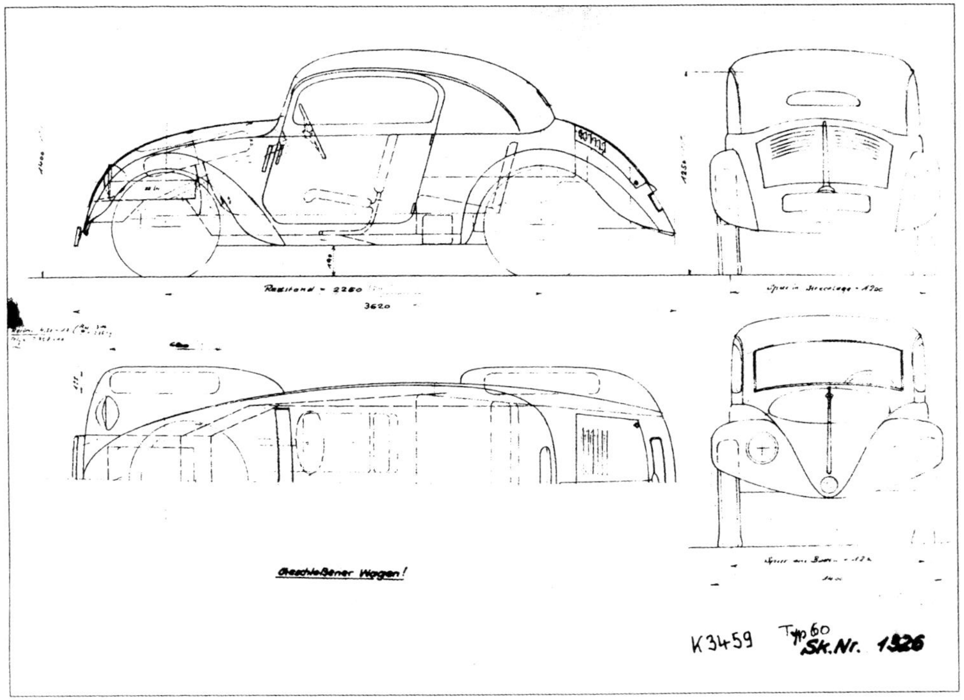

Design Sk 1326 for a closed Type 60 car. (VWM)

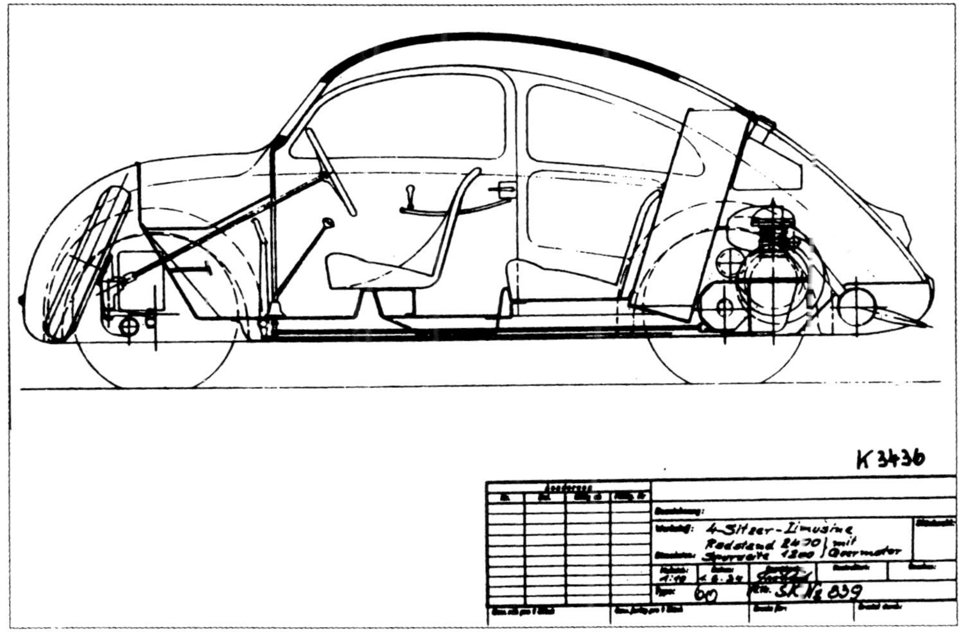

Design K 3436 or Sk 839 with a twin-cylinder engine. (VWM)

1935 Third Body Design K 3449. (VWM)

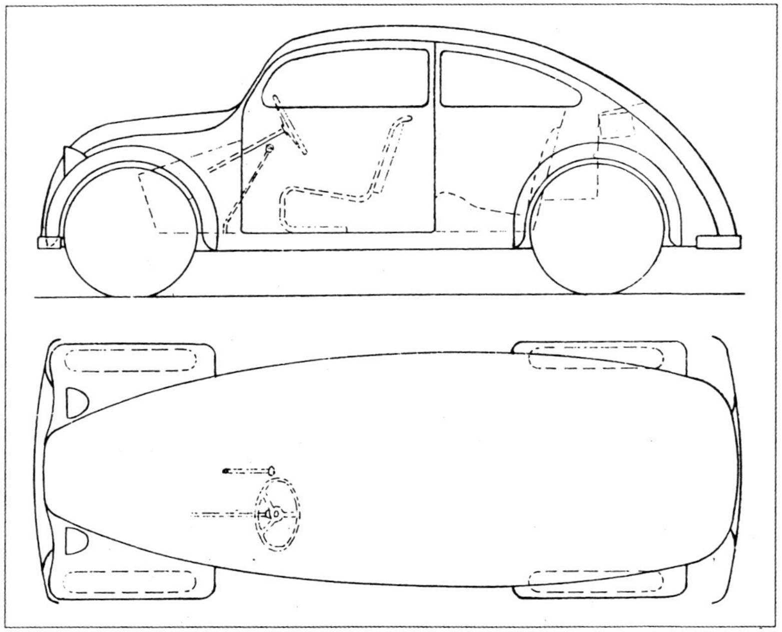

How the VW appeared in Porsche's famed *Exposé* of 1934. (VWM)

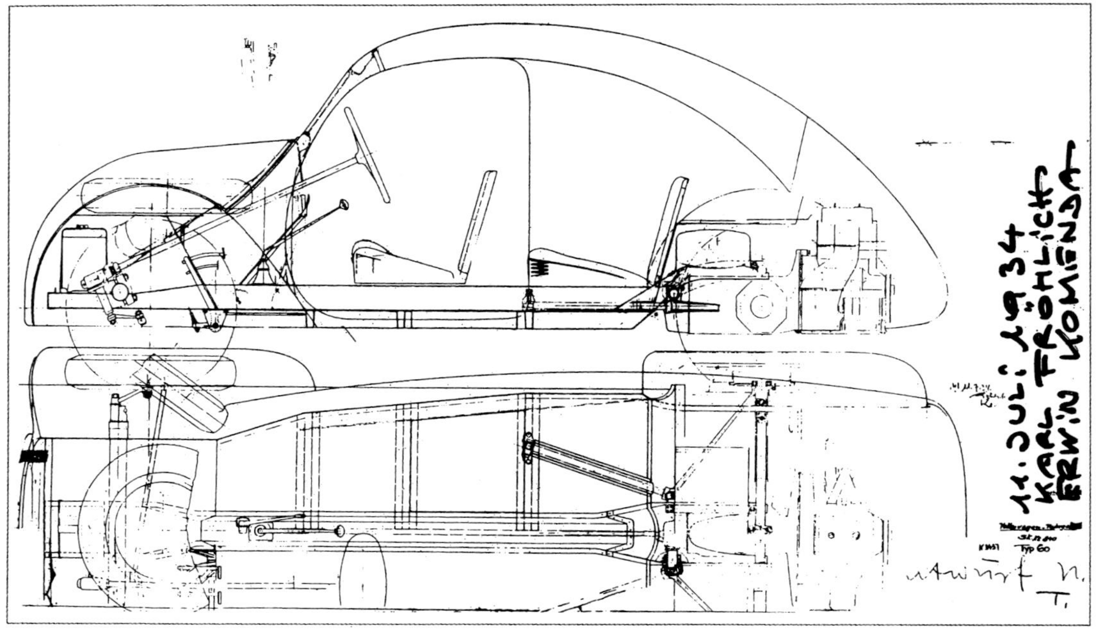

July 11, 1934, design by Karl Frölich and Erwin Komenda of Type 60. (VWM)

Fourth Body Design of February 18, 1935. (VWM)

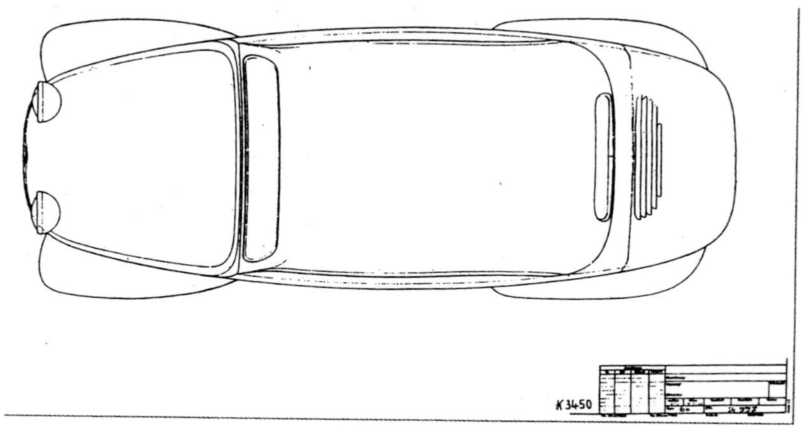

Design K 3450. (VWM)

Fifth Body Design of 1935 for the initial VW convertible, Sk 998. (VWM)

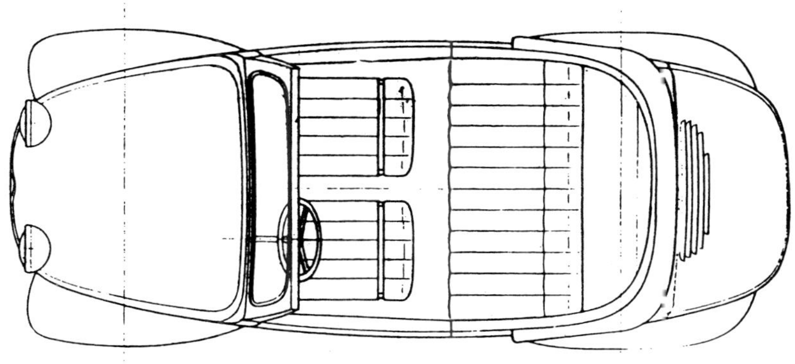

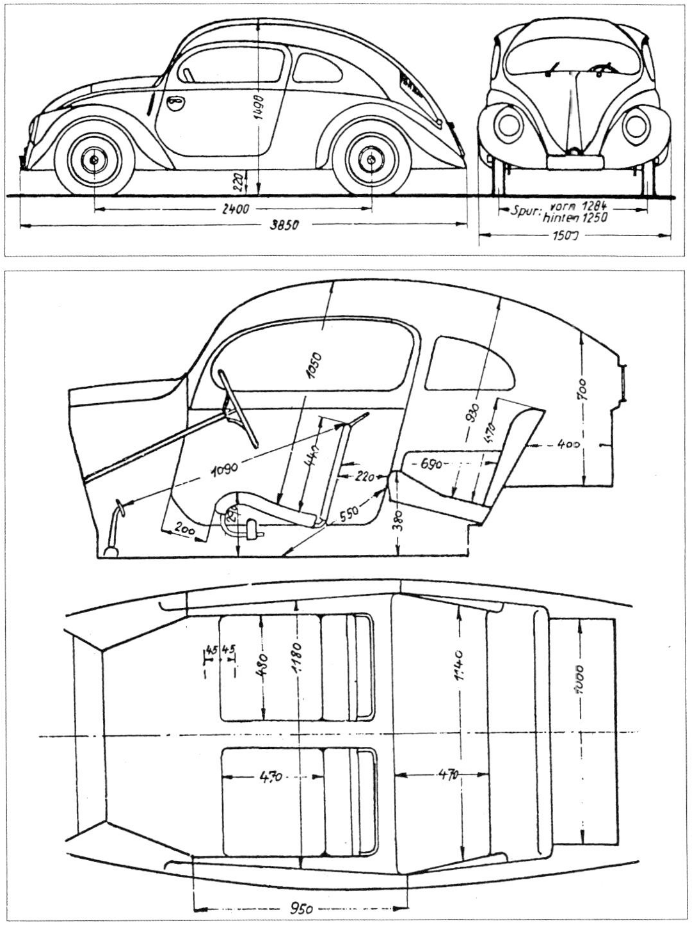

VW W30 body designs from V3 report. (VWM)

According to German author Werner Oswald in *German Autos, 1920-45*, this is another view of the Porsche Type 32 NSU Experimental Car of 1933-34. (VWM)

A V3/2 car parked near the Porsche office in downtown Stüttgart at Kronenstrasse/Crown St. 24, license plate IIIA 0428. (VWM)

The 1934 VW Series 30 Prototypes. Built without rear windows in 1937, 30 of these were put through arduous road tests for thousands of kilometers, according to Robert Gilmore in *VW Trends Magazine*. He added, correctly, "There was a definite need for rear windows, that were incorporated in the next series release." Note, also, the "Venetian blind" louver air vents. (VWM)

Far Left: Car 19 with reflector on the left rear fender. (VWM)

Left: Half body. (VWM)

Wrote Gilmore, "Dr. Ferdinand Porsche developed the VW Series 30 in October 1936, and this represented the birth of the Volkswagen. Also called the Type 60 W 30; 30 were built, and driven over 30,000 miles in tests, and was the concluding prototype." (VWM)

The 1934 VW Type 30 prototype was one of 30 hand built in 1936, and had a 985cc engine. With no rear window, there were large louvers on the engine hood and a central pillar for the door hinges. According to Gilmore, "Dr. Porsche built three prototypes of the VW Series in October 1936…that represented the birth of the Volkswagen." (VWM)

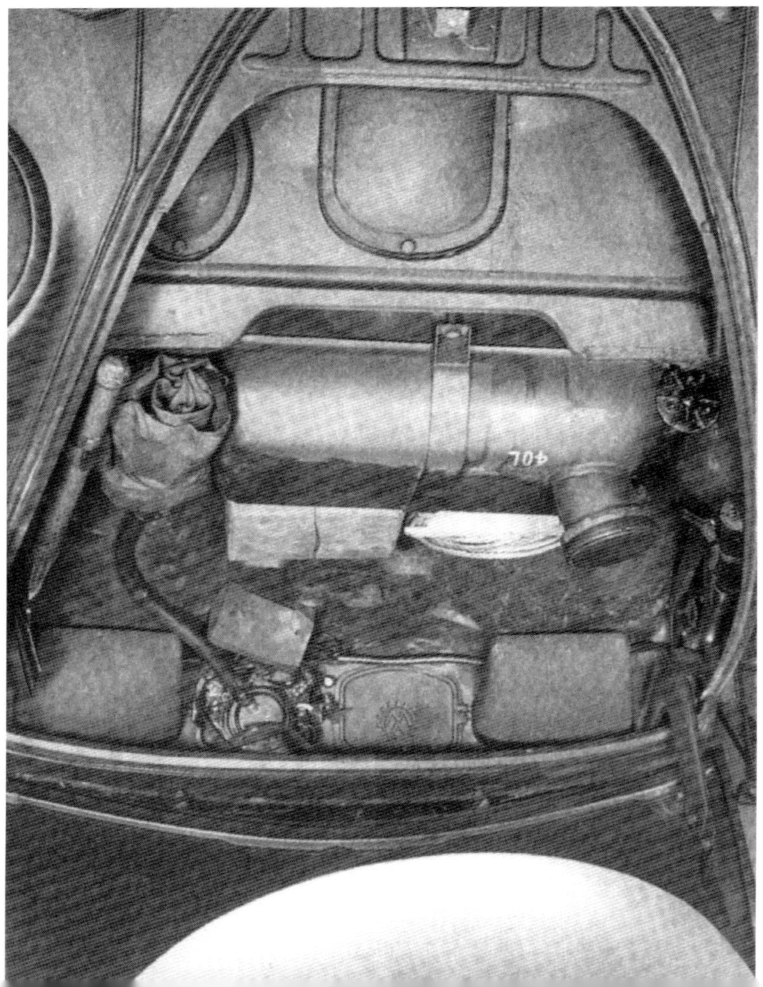

Interior storage area. (VWM)

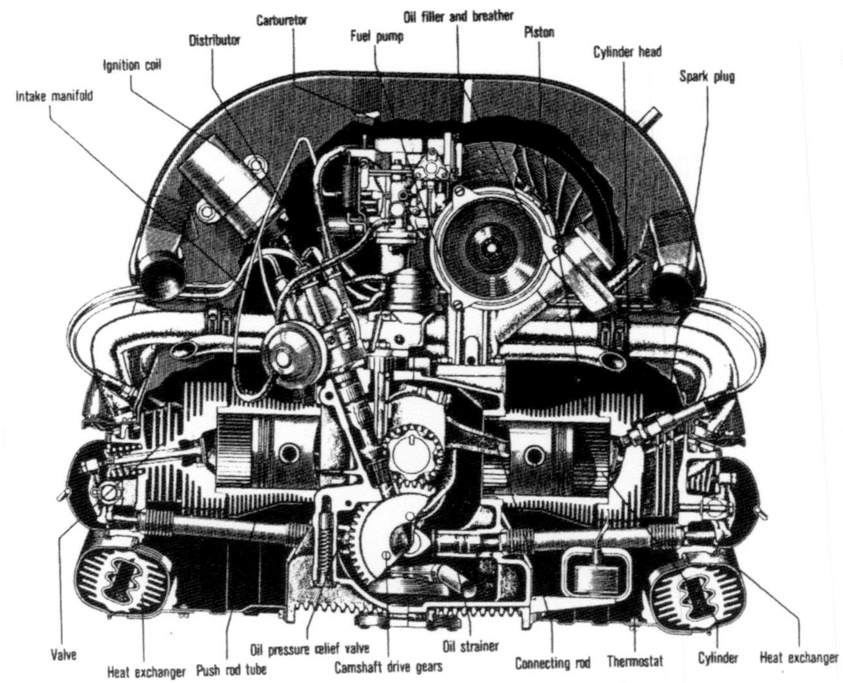

"Cutaway end view of late model Beetle engine showing typical arrangement of air-cooling components," as seen in *Fix Your Volkswagen* by Larry Johnson, 1974. Stated Hitler on April 9, 1942, "The ideal standard engine which I envisage must possess two characteristics: a) It must be air-cooled; b) It must be easy and swift to dismantle and change. This latter characteristic is particularly important, because, as this war has shown, it is more difficult to get spare parts than to get a complete engine unit. Obviously, too, there must be a great measure of standardization and simplification in the manufacture of the engine envisaged." (LC)

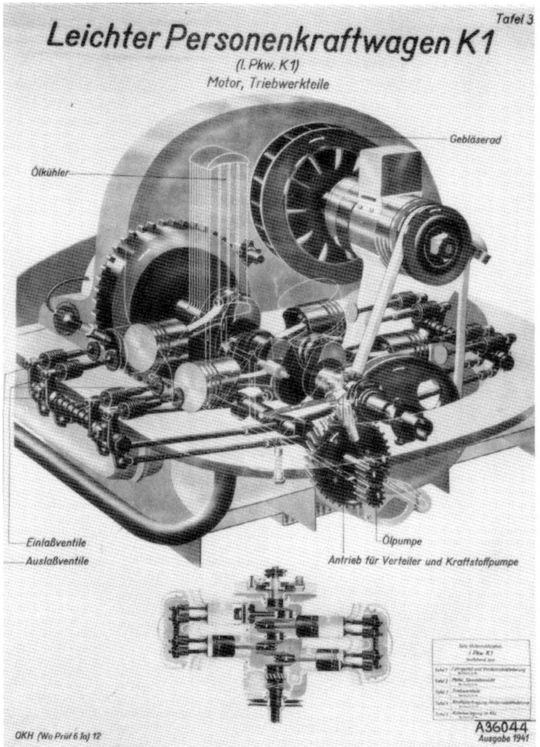

A trio of VW rear-mounted V38 engine views. Attested Hitler on April 9, 1942, "After the war, we must—for military reasons—limit the German motor industry to the production of a dozen models, and the primary objective of the industry should be the simplification of the engine. Higher power must be achieved by increasing the number of standard cylinders, rather than by the introduction of a variety of new cylinders. The dashboard, too, must be simplified, but the most important task will be the design of one single engine that can be used just as well for a field kitchen as for an ambulance, a reconnaissance car, road haulage, or a heavy artillery tractor. The 28 horsepower engine of the Volkswagen should be able to meet all these military requirements. This war has proved that great speeds are of no particular military use, and we must get away from this craze for 'performance!' Provided that the military vehicles mentioned above can attain a speed of between 10-20 kilometers an hour, they will be perfectly adequate." (VWM)

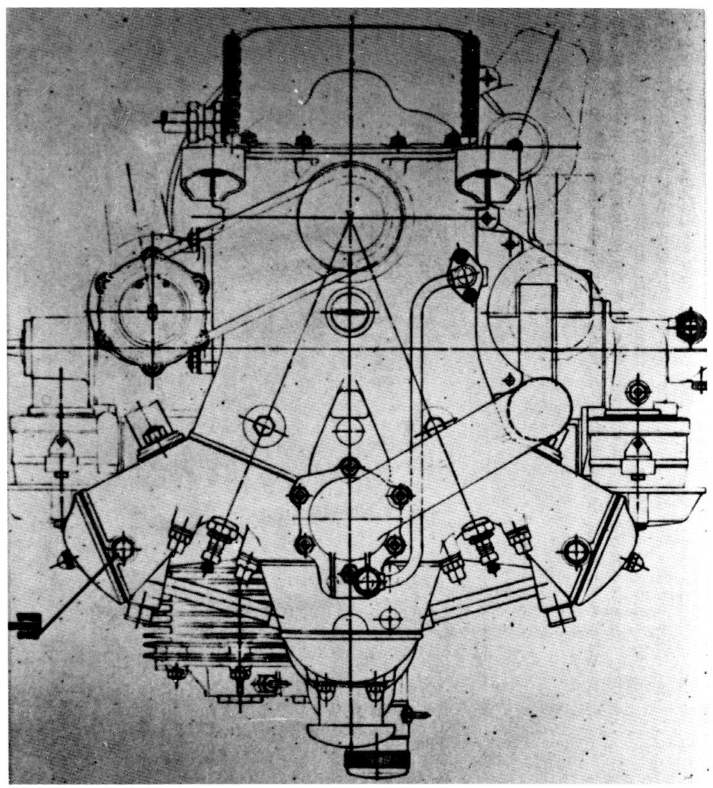

"A 1932 technical drawing by Ferry Porsche showing front view of the proposed 16-cylinder Auto Union engine At top is the casing for the centrally-located overhead camshaft, operating the exhaust valves via transverse pushrods. Two sparkplugs per cylinder were provided," according to *We at Porsche*. (LC)

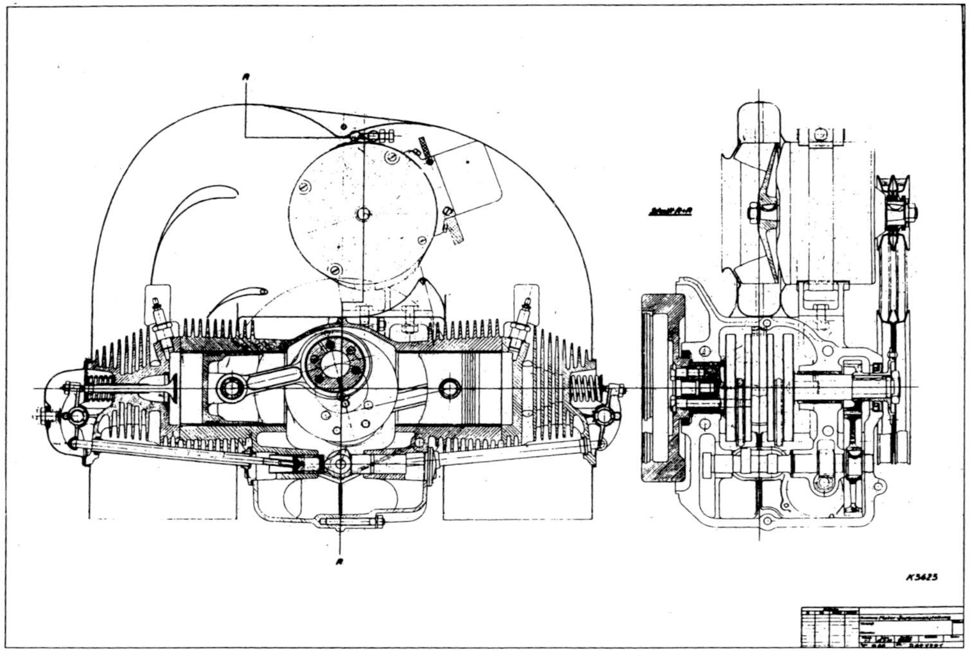

1935 VW motor Design K 3625. (VWM)

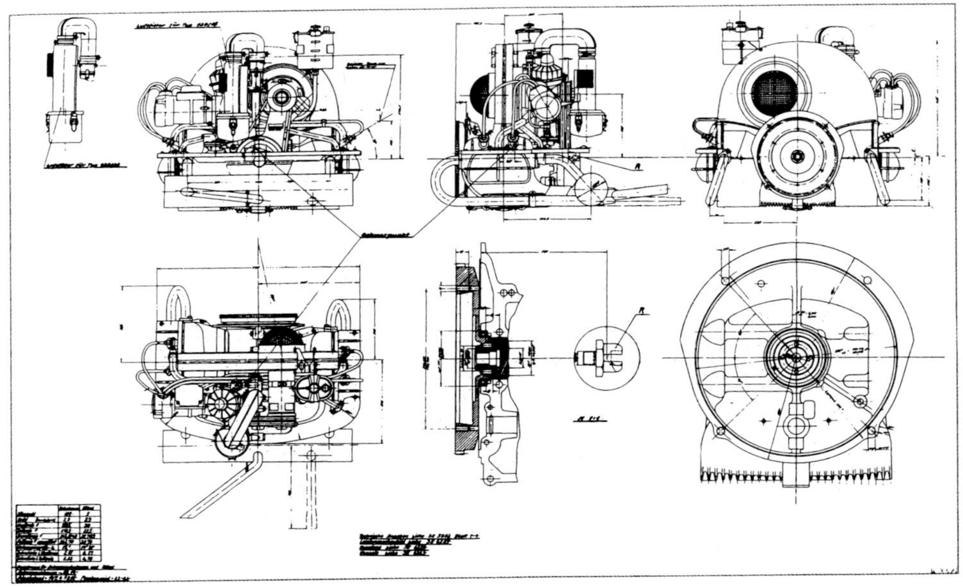

VW engine design schematic. (VWM)

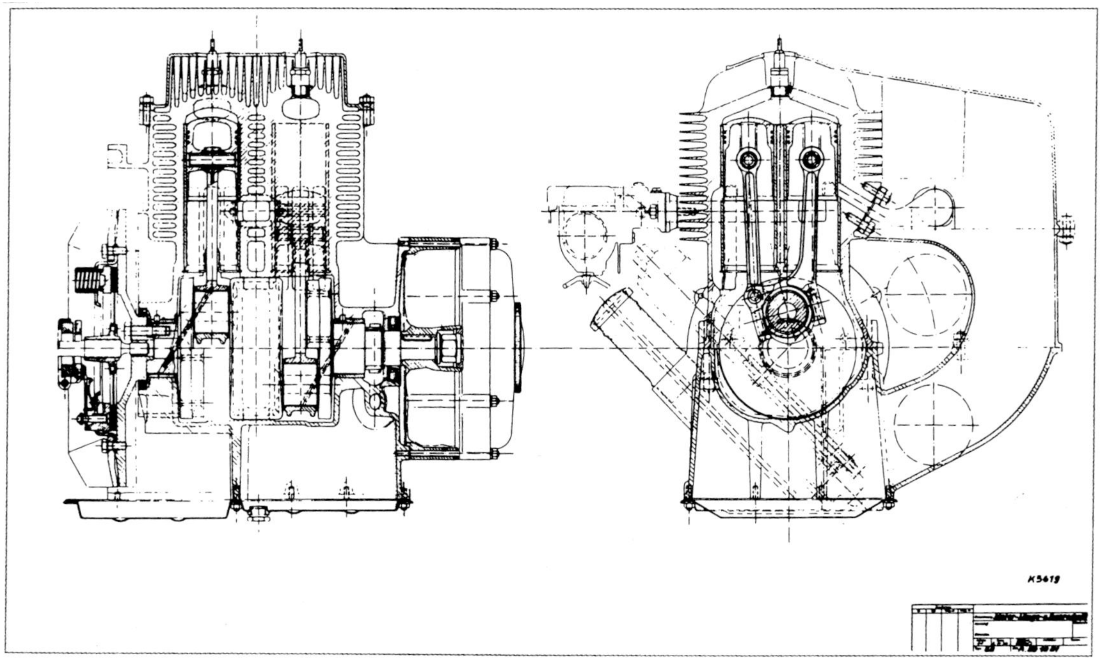

Engine Design K 3619. (VWM)

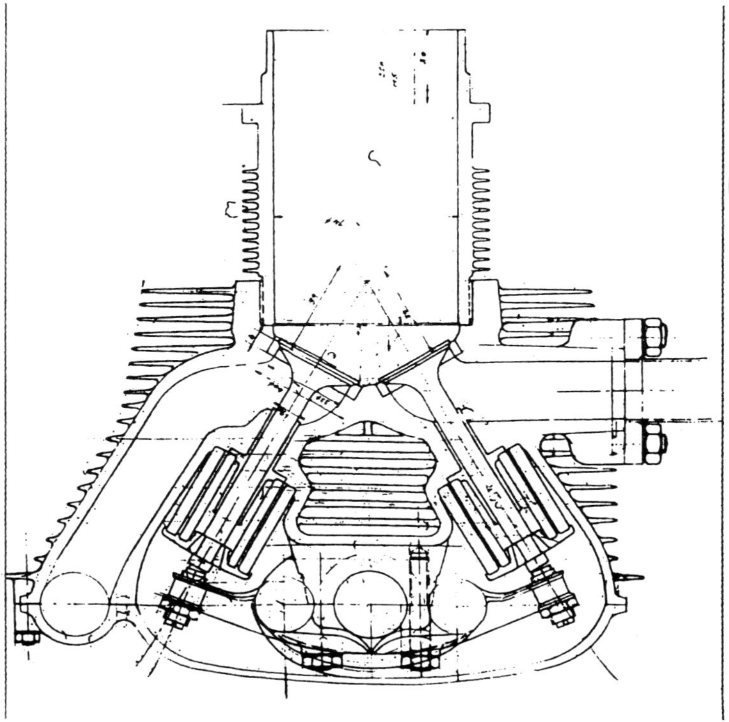

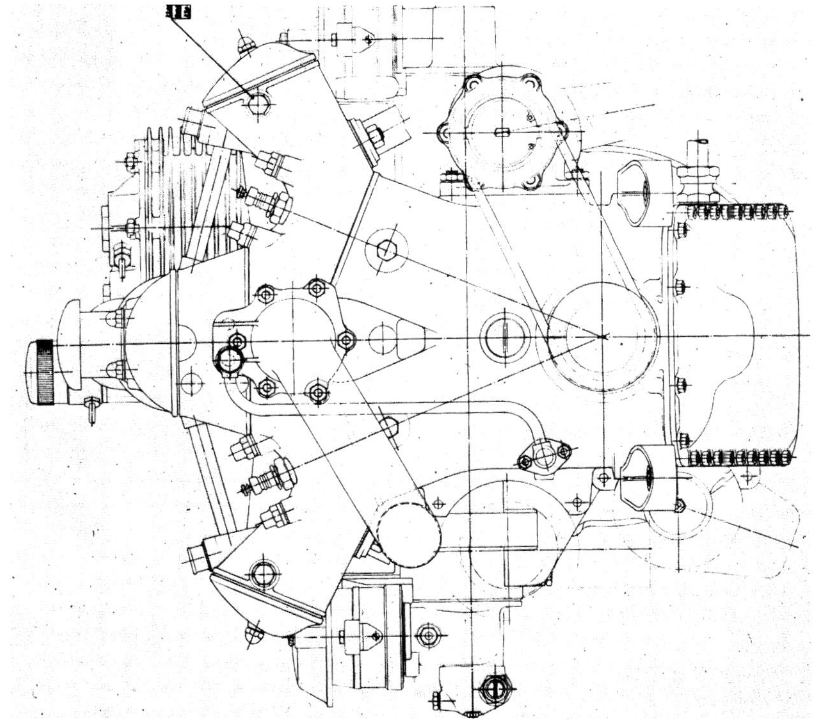

VW engine schematics. (VWM)

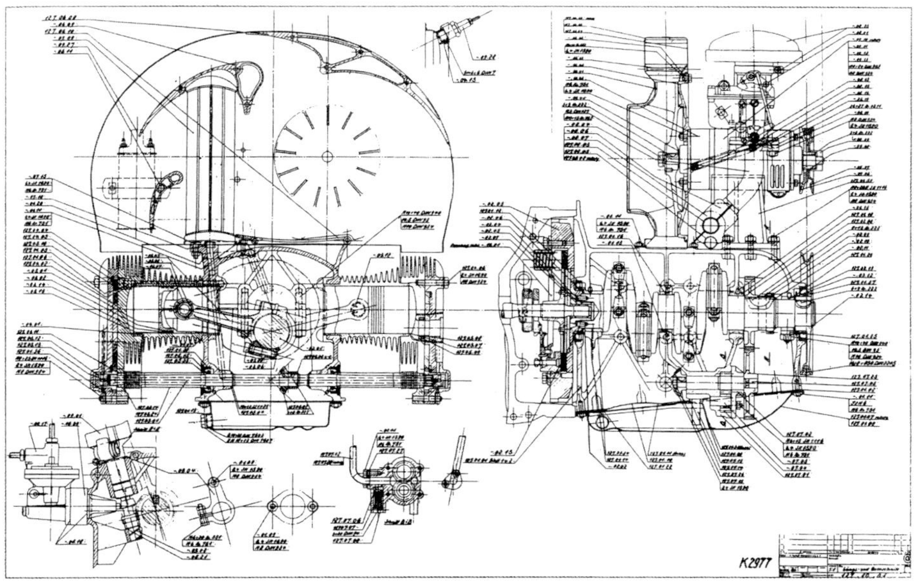

The VW Logo

Nazis stole my idea for VW logo, claims designer **by Bojan Pancevski, *The Telegraph*, Vienna, July 17, 2005, excerpts:**

"A graphic designer who claims that he was commissioned by the Nazis to design the VW logo for Volkswagen, the German car giant, is suing the company for allegedly failing to recognize his work.

"Nikolai Borg, 86—who has a heart condition—has been fighting VW since the 1950s without success. He accuses it of being too embarrassed by its Nazi past to acknowledge its debt to him, a charge the company denies. Mr. Borg has now resorted to legal action in a last attempt to bring VW to account before he dies.

"Mr. Borg claims that his involvement with VW began in June 1939…According to Mr. Borg—who was born in Germany to Swedish and Russian parents—he was asked on the eve of the Second World War to design the VW logo by Dr. Fritz Todt, the Nazi transport minister (sic) in charge of building motorways [the Autobahn].

"'I was a 20-year-old student, and had just won a top award for a logo for the Reich's youth hostel association,' Mr. Borg said… 'That brought me to the attention of Dr. Todt, who a year later became Minister for Weapons, Munitions, and Armament. He read about me in the papers, and was very impressed by the work I had done, and the fact that I was so young.

"'He called me to his office at the Ministry, and gave me three assignments: to design a logo for the company building the motorways (Autobahn), a lakeside resort, and Volkswagen. He said that the car logo was a new project, and wanted me to get working on it straightaway.'

"Mr. Borg said he created three logos for the different names he was given for the new car company: VW, KdF or *Kraft Durch Freude/Strength Through Joy*—which was what Hitler called the project—and VWW, or Volkswagen Werk/Factory.

"Almost 60 years after he first started hounding VW, Mr. Borg will get his day in court…after a pre-trial hearing failed to resolve the dispute. Lawyers for VW were prepared to accept unofficially that Mr. Borg was involved. An official creator of the VW logo has never been registered. Public acknowledgment of Mr. Borg's work could mean that he is entitled to compensation.

"Yet from his home in the Austrian Tyrol, Mr. Borg—still frail after returning from his latest hospital visit—said, 'I am not after money. I just want to live to see my work acknowledged. I will not settle for anything less than historical acceptance. I feel that VW not only fears financial retribution, but is also wary of confrontation with the Nazi past.

"'The company used prisoners-of-war and concentration camp inmates as slave labor, and produced Nazi weapons and military machinery. Its policy has always been to avoid that kind of publicity as much as possible.'

"Michael Walter—a lawyer for VW—said that Mr. Borg could not prove that his designs were sent to VW. The company had no record of receiving them, he said, and similar designs had been patented a year before Mr. Borg claimed to have sent in his work. Mr. Walter said the dark chapter in VW's past was common knowledge. 'It is a fact that it was founded by the Nazis, and relied on slave labor. I do not believe that issue is related to this particular case. It is all about copyright.'

"These have been troubled times for VW. Profits tumbled last year, and plans announced…to cut costs were overshadowed by claims that management had used slush funds to pay for perks, including prostitutes, for trade union officials on the works council, the body that gives German unions a joint say in management decisions. The scandal has resulted in the resignation of Peter Hartz, VW's personnel chief and a close ally of Chancellor Gerhard Schröder. He denied any involvement in a series of alleged abuses, but stepped down, 'for the good of the company.'

"Meanwhile, Mr. Borg's claims—that will be heard by a court in Vienna—are supported by a witness who remembers Dr. Todt summoning him to a second meeting after he was recruited into the *Wehrmacht/Armed Forces*. Mr. Borg, who was given permission to attend by his company commander, told his comrades about the meeting when he returned to barracks.

"Mr. Borg claims that VW acknowledged his work in letters that were lost in the war. He has witnesses, however, who remember their contents. Adolf Schmoll—a professor of art history from Münich who served in the Army with Mr. Borg—said, 'I remember a courier bringing him a letter from Todt. It was a big deal, as we were down in the ranks, and Todt was a senior Nazi.'

"In a court statement, Prof. Schmoll describes seeing drawings that made the original images Mr. Borg has provided as evidence for the trial. Mr. Borg made copies of the drawings that he sent to the VW factory, and claims to have received a reply, thanking him, but confirming that the project was on hold. He was surprised, therefore, to spot his logo on a military vehicle during the war.

"After the war, Mr. Borg contacted VW. He said correspondence from the time shows that they rejected his claim without making any close study of the evidence. Mr. Borg, who has since built up a successful advertising agency, never gave up his quest. His legal costs are being met by an Austrian trade association and legal aid."

Added Rex Curry in 2005:

"In a bizarre way, some Nazism may still exist at Volkswagen within Germany. In 1949 Hirst left the company, now reformed as a trust controlled by the German government. VW is said to still be owned by the government of Lower Saxony, though it is not 'run' by the state.

"Ferdinand Porsche's grandson, Ferdinand Piech, was chairman and CEO of the Volkswagen Group from 1993-2002. With half of all voting shares, he also remains the largest individual shareholder of Porsche AG. Stock can be purchased in Volkswagen companies.

"Founded in 1955, Volkswagen of America, Inc. is headquartered in Auburn Hills, MI, and is a wholly owned subsidiary of Volkswagen AG, one of the world's largest automakers. VW AG (the VW Group) consists of the VW plants in Wolfsburg, Brunswick, Hanover, Kassel, Emden, and Salzgitter. It is the parent company of all other companies in the VW Group, that are either wholly owned subsidiaries or companies in which VW AG has majority ownership.

"The company operates 44 production plants in 11 European countries, as well as seven countries in the Americas, Asia, and Africa.

"Volkswagen's iconic buttressing of V and W was the creation of an engineer named Franz Reimspiess. He was also the same man who perfected the engine for the Beetle in the 1930s…

"The original design featured the letter V above a W, and surrounded by a cog. After the war Britain had the cog changed to a circle, and that design was filed for copyright in 1948…The logo of the DAF was a swastika surrounded by a cog, from which the VW logo was derived."

German engineer Dr. Fritz Todt (1891-1942) (HHA)

Noted Rex Curry, "The People's Car was actually based on the Czech *Tatra*," seen here. "The company's legal case was rudely interrupted by the invasion of Czechoslovakia [in 1939], and was remounted successfully in 1961. Unfortunately, *Tatra*—by then in a Communist country—did not do enough with the damages to survive." (LC)

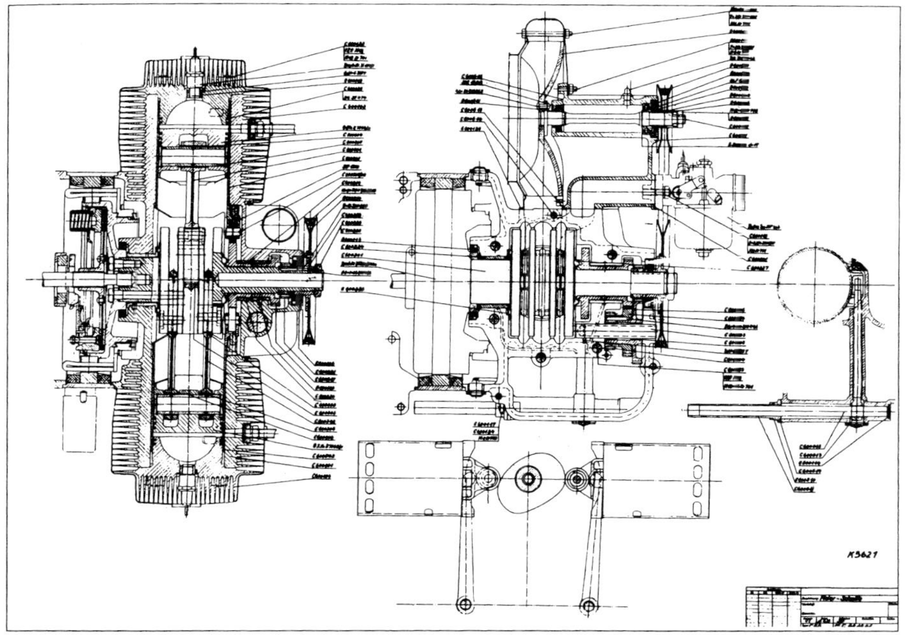

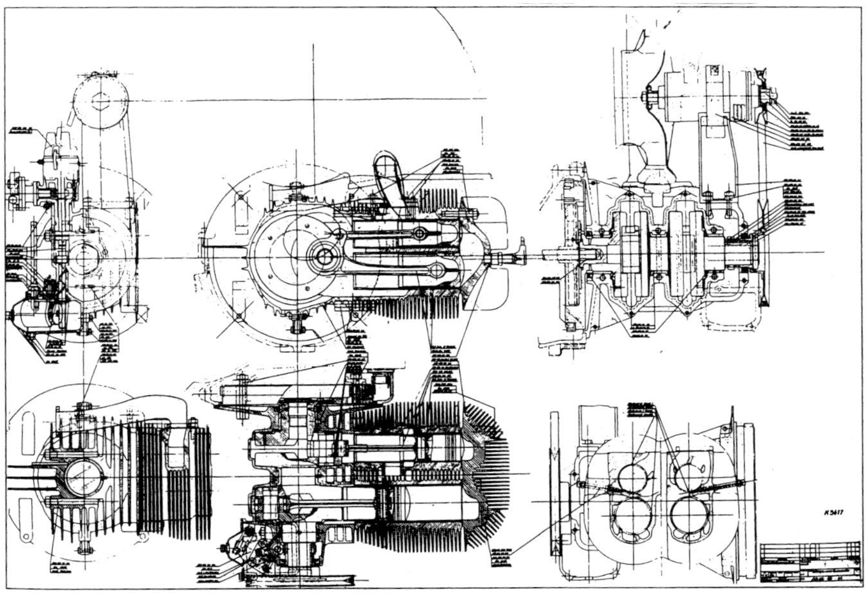

VW engine designs K 5621 (right) and K 5617 (left) schematics. Noted Heinz Nordhoff, "The only decision I am really proud of is that I have refused to change Porsche's design. It's hard to remain the same. You can always sell cars by being new, but we chose a different course. I brushed away all temptations to change model and design. In any sound design, there are almost unlimited possibilities—and this certainly was a sound one. I see no sense in starting anew every few years with the same teething problems, making obsolete all the past. Offering people an honest value, a product of the highest quality, with low original cost and incomparable resale value appealed more to me than being driven around by a bunch of hysterical stylists trying to sell people something they really do not want to have." This was exactly the position that Hitler, Speer, Gen. von Schell, and also the Porsches themselves took during 1938-45, namely, that the German military's mania for creating ever and more unique prototypes would—and indeed, did—help the Third Reich lose the war, with too many models, and not enough spare parts, especially on the battlefield. The Soviets took the "one model only concept" to its ultimate expression by producing the T-34 medium tank, and then simply overwhelming the Nazis and their allies with them. (VWM)

VW W30 Beetle bodies everlasting, awaiting their chassis. As most automobile authorities today concur, Dr. Ferdinand Porsche cannot be said to have actually "invented" the VW as much as he in reality meshed together existent ideas and concepts with readily available component parts—and therein lay his true genius, as well as his persistence in seeing his dream through to accomplishment. (VWM)

Period Beetle with Stüttgart license plate IIIA-42801. Note the front hood handle at bottom. The tubular frame came from the Czech-made Tatra designed by Hans Ledwinka, who, like Dr. Porsche, also came from the former Austro-Hungarian land of Bohemia, which Hitler occupied on March 15, 1939, when he took Prague. (VWM)

German family with Beetle. The now mythic Beetle streamlined shape had its origins in the Twenties, with Dr. Porsche's contemporary designer of Vienna, Paul Jaray (1889-1974), when the Golf model replaced the Beetle in overall sales volume. (VWM)

Small car with rear windows (left) fording Russian road, Fall 1941. At the very beginning Dr. Porsche chose a modern, all-steel body frame with spot-welded body parts attached to it, and this was incorporated into the three prototype models he unveiled on May 26, 1938, at Wolfsburg: limousine, cabrio-limousine, and cabriolet. (CER)

According to author Frederic Spotts in his 2003 work, *Hitler and the Power of Aesthetics*, "Of the various purported drawings by Hitler of what eventually became the Volkswagen, this is an authentic—though undated—one." (VWM)

1935: the VW adventure begins with the design and hand tooling of prototypes. "Look to nature for the shape of the Beetle," Hitler said, and this is the Porsche Design Bureau's drawing for the 1935 VW prototype series, with hood-mounted headlamps and cut-off trunk, an instantly recognizable Beetle still around the world today. Conversely, the V-1 rocket was *produced* by Dr. Porsche, but not *designed* by him. (PM)

Dr. Ferry Porsche (right, center) talking with SS driver chief Albert Liese at the Porsche Shell refueling pump at the family villa with a pair of prewar Beetles. (PM)

The initial two VW prototypes were built by Dr. Ferdinand Porsche and his son Ferry via hand-tooling in their home double door garage at left in the right wing of #48-50 Feuerbacherweg at Stüttgart, Germany, as seen here in 1935. (PM)

Dr. Ferdinand Porsche (center) and son Ferry (kneeling at right) hand-tooling the very first VW in their backyard at home. After having tried two-cylinder, two-stroke engines first, Dr. Ferdinand Porsche finally settled on a four-cylinder opposed engine, and it was this basic construction overall that stayed with the Beetle until the mid-1970s for its high-grade stability and rapid body-change capability. (PM)

VW Beetle chassis undercarriage view. In 1935, according to author John Bentley, "The first convertible VW Porsche was actually the second Volkswagen ever built. Known as Model V2, it was assembled in Prof. Porsche's extended garage at his Stüttgart home, license plate # IIIA-37013." (VWM)

"Dr. Ferry Porsche at the wheel with his new bride Dorothea Reitz Porsche sitting next to him. At right rear sits friend Hellmuth Zarges (right) and Herbert Kaes (left), one of Ferry's cousins (not visible). Note the outstandingly good finish of this prototype," stated Bentley. (VWM)

A Beetle full of VW executives. By 1974, it was simply too "cost-intensive" to manufacture, and thus became a victim of its former success. (VWM)

Two-toned Beetle. Dr. Ferdinand Porsche had first used an air-cooled, boxer motor during 1912-13 while he was with Austro-Daimler at Wiener Neustadt, which was a superb fit for a rear-mounting in a streamlined vehicle like the future Beetle, still a quarter century away! (PM) (VWM)

Dr. Ferdinand Porsche (left) and his own car, with sliding sunroof. These phased out the initial convertibles because the latter were more expensive to build. They made their reappearance in 1943, however—in the very midst of the war! Not a very prudent choice, one would say. Initially, all VWs were available in only one color, according to Robert Gilmore: dark blue-gray. (PM)

Mercedes-Benz workers crowd around an Experimental VW model car in 1940, this one with hubcaps, even though it is wartime! (Previously unpublished photograph from the Mercedes-Benz Albums, Library of Congress, Wash., DC)

Prewar Beetle. Noted Gilmore, upon acceptance of the program by prospective buyers, "The DAF then issued a KdF savers card or booklet that was to be filled out with the weekly purchased 5 RM stamps until 990 RM was accumulated. Actually, more stamps could be purchased, but one stamp per week was the minimum. Several cards had to be filled out, since one card held only 50 stamps. These 5 RM stamps looked similar to small postage stamps, and had a small, embossed white KdF Wagen, and had either red or green background color design. An additional two-years' auto insurance plan was also provided, costing 200 RM. The sunroof model was an additional 60 RM. Upon completion of the 990 RM and the 200 RM requirements (took about 4 ½ years), the worker would be required to travel to the KdF factory and pick up his new KdF Wagen." (VWM)

According to Gilmore, "The KdF Wagen was available in a sunroof model...." The split rear window design remained until 1952, when it was replaced with an oval window style that persisted right up until the 1970 convertible that the current author purchased while a college student. As for the savings program, he added, "There were even special coin banks made (with lithographed KdF Wagen on the sides) that would keep track of daily coin deposits (100 Reich Pfennig = 1 RM) until 5 RM was accumulated. Then the bank was opened and a savers board was introduced in which players rolled the dice and advanced their game pieces." (VWM)

The 1938 VW 38 "pretzel" rear window, as seen here. Stated *Great Marques of Germany* by Jonathan Wood, "The VW's shape resolved on this 1938 VW 38 with split rear window and running boards [far left and second from left]. This is during a presentation of the vehicles outside the Wolfsburg plant in the distance." As I noted in a talk to students at then-Towson State College in 1971 entitled *Adolf Hitler, Human Being*, "On August 2, 1938, the *New York Times* stated that the Nazis planned the VW as an inexpensive car for every German citizen to be able to own: the cost would be 574.20 marks, or about $ 230. Due to the foot-dragging of the German automobile industry, which saw the VW as a potential threat to it (as, indeed, it later developed)—and the onslaught of the war, the VW did not reach mass production in Germany until the end of the war." With the model seen here, the final VW shape had been established at last. Its interior dashboard had a place for the gearshift diagram that could be removed if desired for a radio; it remained basically unchanged until 1953, the year of Dwight D. Eisenhower's Inauguration as U.S. President, as well as the death of Soviet dictator Josef Stalin. (VWM)

Small car with split rear window with hanging dead in the USSR. (CER)

Right: Workers about to install in place the roof of a VW38 model at the Reutter Coachworks, where they were built until the completion of the VW factory at Wolfsburg. The famous "pretzel" window design can be clearly seen in the rear. A total of 44 VW38 series cars were built in all, with the final Beetle shape thus achieved. (VWM)

VW with louvers at left rear, but no pretzel split window yet. (VWM)

According to Barber, "At Reutter (Coachworks), there was a lot of activity in the tiny production hall, where two—even three (!)—bodies were being made, by hand, at the same time. Two complete bodies were finished during summer 1938." (VWM)

VW bodies in production mode. (VWM)

Far Left: Continued Barber, "Throughout the war years, the Porsche workshops were full of interesting vehicles...In autumn 1941, this picture shows a VW38 or VW39 in the center, surrounded by various Schwimmers. The Stuka was still there, and several chassis were lying around." (PM)

Stated Barber, "The air-cooling slots were newly painted on, and a new number plate—IIIA-62148—was given to the car, this time black-on-white." (VWM)

"The KdF Wagen between Italian workers in Factory Fallersleben," from a German publication. Asserted Nelson, "By the mid-1950s, there were over a million Beetles on the roads of more than a hundred countries. The factory at Wolfsburg employed 28,000 people, and turned out 1,230 cars a day." (VWM)

Postwar abandoned VW body shells without chassis—and everything else, too! Continued Nelson, "The basic working week was 42.5 hours, and the workers were paid 2.53 DM per hour [in the 1950s]. They also had three weeks' paid holiday each year." (VWM)

The 1938-39 VW chassis: a good frontal view of the cylindrical gas tank that held 40 liters of fuel showing its placement at the center of the front axle between the wheels, and the location of the steering wheel at right. The battery can be seen at left rear, and the rear-mounted engine at center back. Note, too, the pattern of the tread on the tires. In 1984, as sales of the postwar built VW Beetles were winding down at last, still 14,000 were sold in Europe alone, but U.S. imports had been halted altogether in 1981, according to an August 28, 1985, Reuters dispatch in the Baltimore *Sun*, "'On economic grounds, it's not viable to import them anymore,' says VW spokesman Peter Schelin. 'It's just too expensive.'...For people desperate to buy a new Beetle, all is not lost. They can still import one privately at great expense—from Mexico, Brazil, or Nigeria, where a total of 120,000 Beetles are made every year, and continue to sell well locally." (VWM)

Far Right: Noted Barber, "Although—reportedly—all previous prototypes were destroyed during 1942-43, this picture shows the Porsche factory at Züffenhausen after the American bombing raids during 1944, and there—in the foreground—Car V3/2!" (VWM)

The end in 1945 for this VW 82E "pretzel" rear window model VW on Hitler's very own doorstep in the *Ehrenhof/ Honor Courtyard* of the New German Reich Chancellery in Berlin, built by architect Dr. Albert Speer in 1939, to be replaced 11 years later in 1950 when Nazi Germany had won World War II with the new Führer's Palace. It was never built, however. Red Army officers (left) stand about the bullet-riddled hulk, and a dead body appears to be hanging out of the driver's side door. (Sovfoto, LC.)

The reverse view of a VW Beetle chassis. According to the Baltimore *Sun* of December 20, 1999, "Model T tops Mini, Beetle, in 'Car of the Century' vote…by an international jury of 133 automotive journalists…beating the Mini and the Beetle among others…The Model T beat the other finalists with a tally of 742 points, compared with 617 for the British Mini, 567 for the Citroen DS 19, 521 for the VW Beetle, and 303 for the Porsche 911." (VWM)

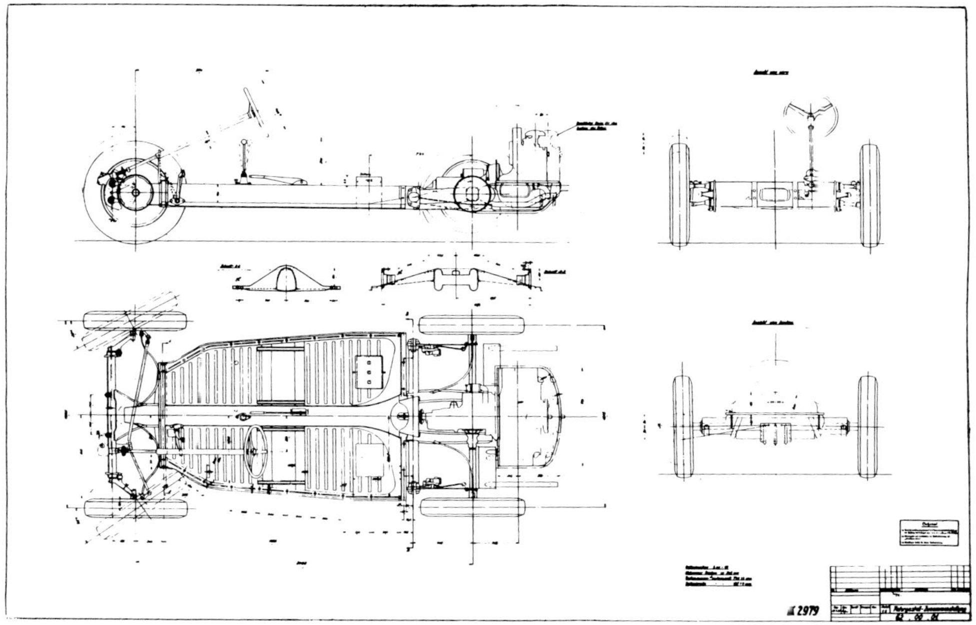

Chassis Design K 2979 of Type 62, January 21, 1939. Noted the Baltimore *Sun* on March 29, 2007, "Porsche boosts Volkswagen stake. Porsche AG completed its acquisition of more shares in VW for a total stake of 30.94%, triggering a formal takeover offer to VW's shareholders, the German carmaker said yesterday. Porsche had said over the weekend that it would acquire another 3.6% stake in VW in a move aimed at shielding Europe's biggest automaker from hostile takeovers. Though Porsche recognized that the additional shares would trigger a mandatory takeover under German law by bringing its total stake to greater than 30%, it said such a takeover was not its intent at this time." (VWM)

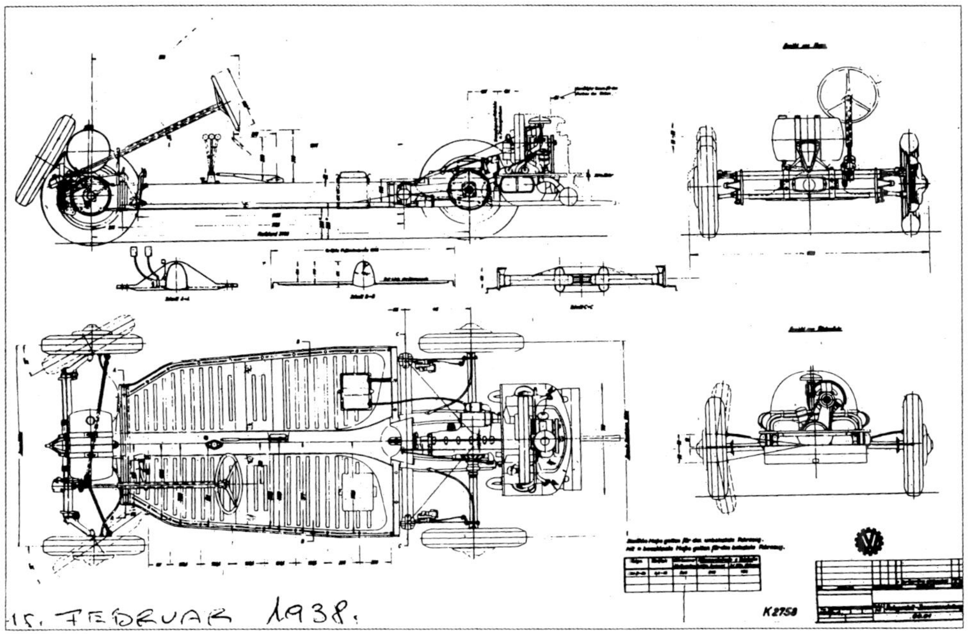

Chassis Design K 2758 of the VW38 series, finished on February 15, 1938. Asked in 1973, "Did you ever see Hitler?" a German civil servant born in 1912 answered, "In 1938, at the inauguration of the VW Works. I was deputy commander of a regiment of the Hitler Youth. What do you think? He impressed me because his appeal was to our pocketbooks. 'This car costs 900 marks, and everyone will be able to drive it.'…I figured it out myself as a young teacher—our village had three cars at the time!—It will take you so and so long to buy one. The appeal to the pocketbook! There were the first cars, right there, and Hitler drove [sic] the first round in the stadium. The Head-of-State helps the simple people to acquire a car, and at the same time builds the highways, eliminates unemployment. Proof, exposition, and demonstration were so compelling that it all seemed so inescapably right." (VWM)

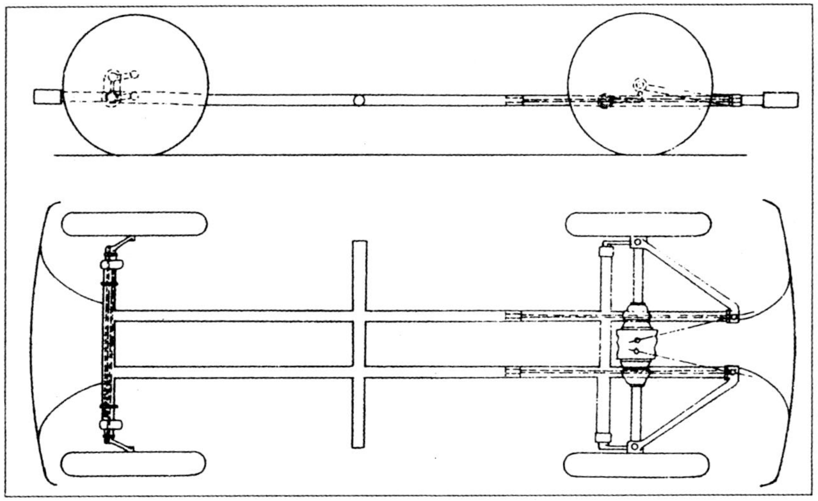

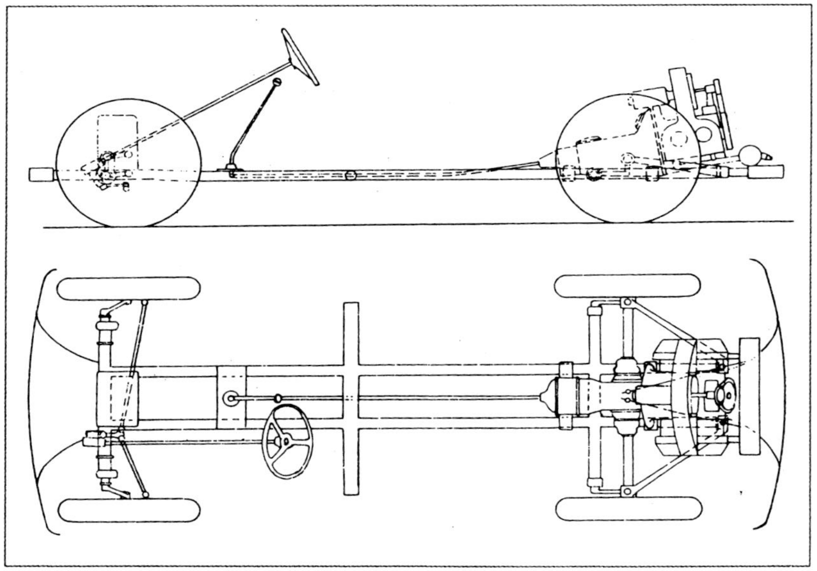

The bare "ladder frame" chassis designs (X 35 and X 36) from the files of Karl Rabe. Noted author Richard Grunberger in his work, *The 12-Year Reich: A Social History of Nazi Germany, 1933-45*, "The total weekly expenditure on a car would've accounted for between a third and a quarter of the take home pay of most wage earners. The likelihood of the People's Car becoming most peoples' car was therefore highly conjectural, even before the war intervened to kill the project at birth." (VWM)

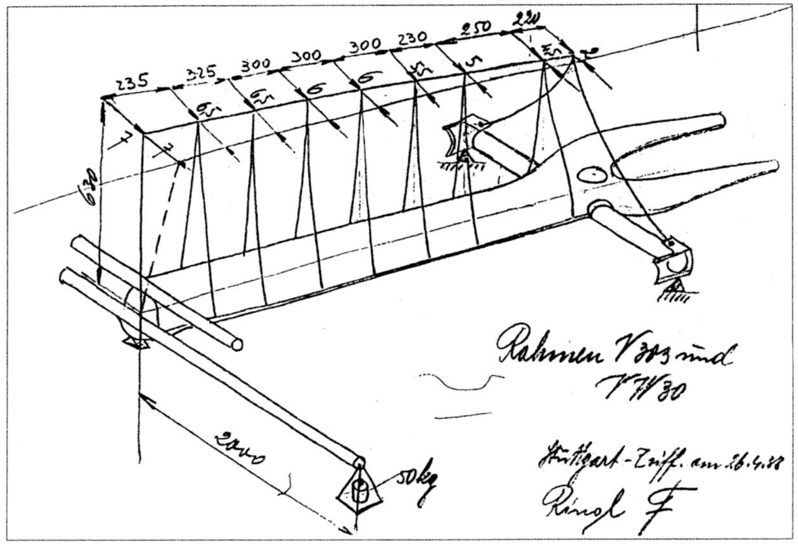

According to Barber, "On April 26, 1938, technician Ringel and designer Fröhlich produced this drawing of how the rigidity of the chassis was tested, which showed the frame of both V303 cars and VW30... This proved that the first three cars with the split rear windows were based on the older VW30 chassis design, not the VW38 chassis." (VWM)

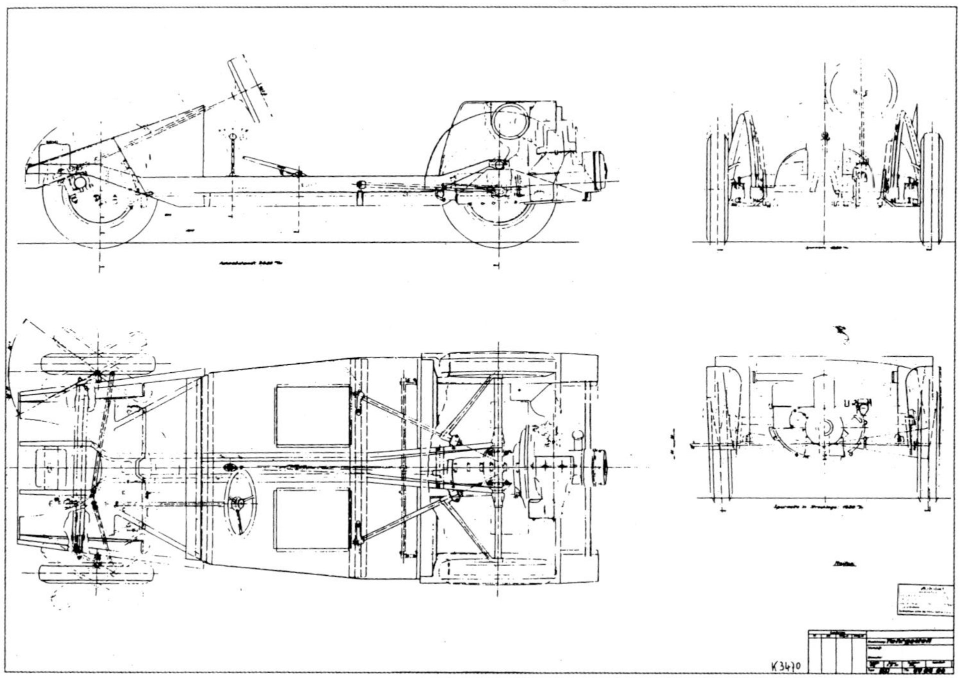

VW chassis Design K 3470. (VWM)

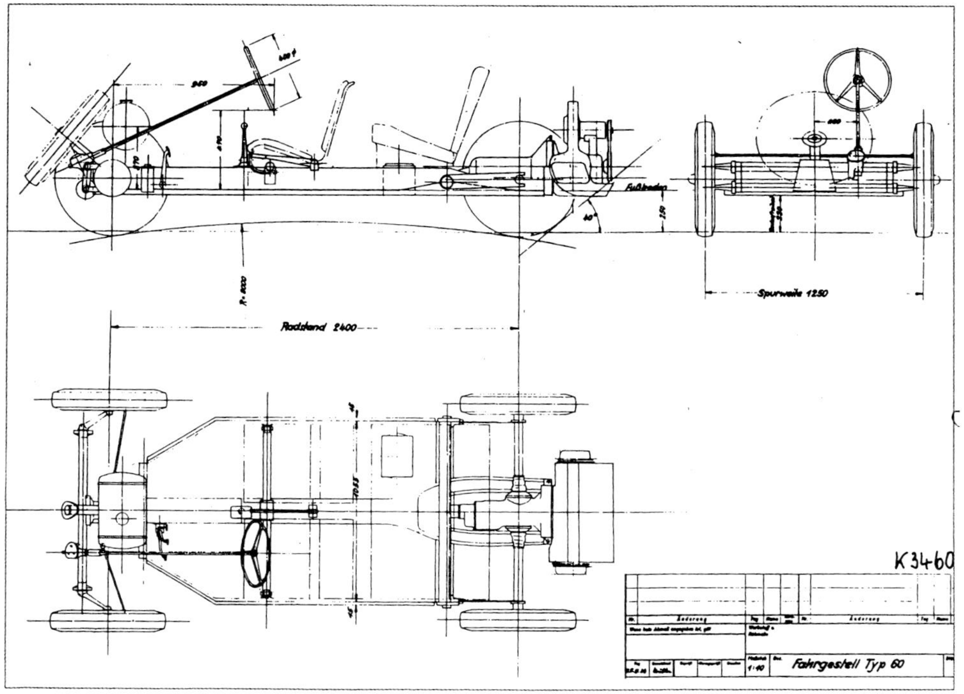

VW seventh chassis Design K 3460. (VWM)

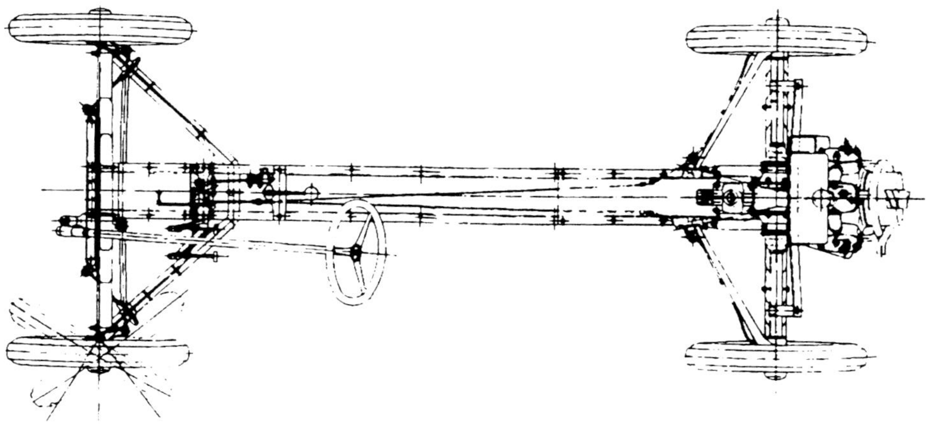

Noted Barber, "Adolf Hitler became obsessed with the idea of a world beating German racing team. His obsession led Porsche to design the superb mid-engine Auto-Union, that had a top speed close to 320km/h (200 mph.)" (PM)

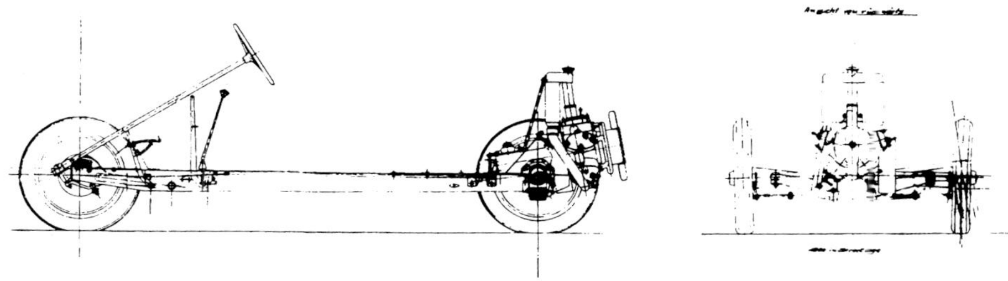

A forerunner of the *kafer/Beetle* was this Project #32 drawing by Dr. Ferdinand Porsche for a Zundapp water-cooled, five-cylinder radial, rear-mounted engine that he wasn't really pleased with. It was, however, an early step on the path to the eventual VW. (PM)

The 1939 Beetle. Asserted Robert Gilmore, "There is no doubt about it, that's a VW at the Berlin Auto Show in 1939! Thousands of refinements would be made over the years, but the basic silhouette remained the same... The funds raised by the savers program were put in a special account of the DAF treasury. During the program, more than 700,000 workers of which 336,000 workers had completed their KdF savers program. However, not a single worker received a KdF Wagen!" As VWs, however, the savers' stamps *were* honored by VW after the war. (VWM)

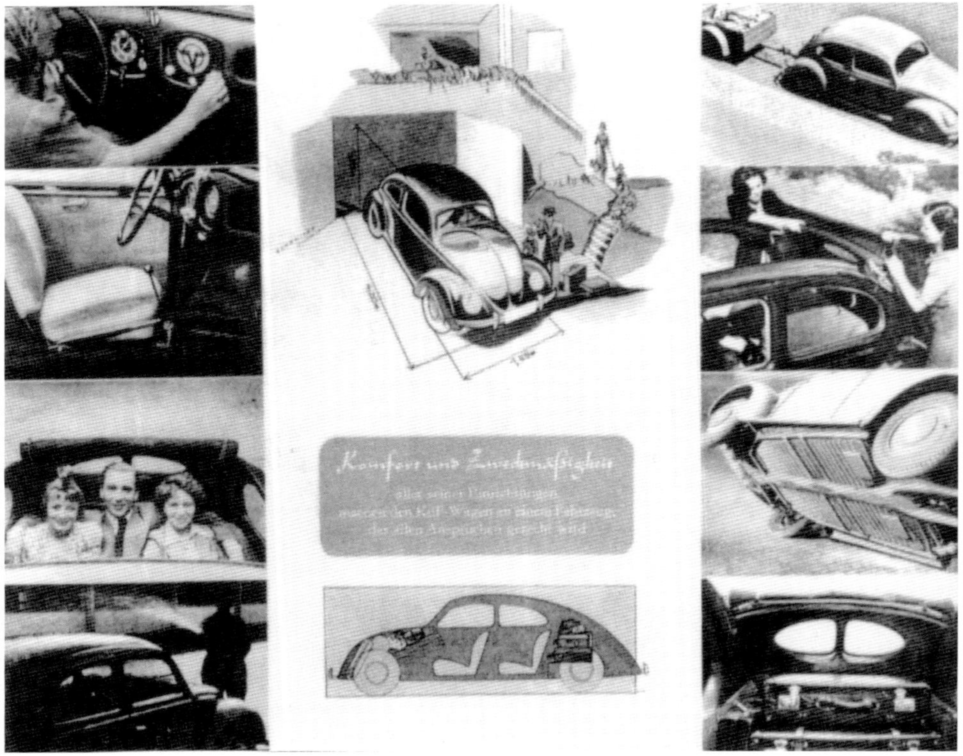

Far Left: The 1939 Beetle. An American-style car sales brochure—but for the VW in 1939 under the Third Reich's DAF Organization. Clockwise: the radio with logo in the center, driver's seat with stick shift, sunroof rolled back to reveal a trio of grinning passengers, cleaning the car, side-diagram revealing what went where, luggage in the rear, the undercarriage, rolling back the fabric sunroof, and towing a load. In the center, ironically, is depicted what most Germans then did not have: a personal garage, much less a 1960s-style home! Had Hitler won World War II, no doubt they would've gotten them, from the Atlantic to the Urals, in his projected new Nazi European Empire. (VWM)

Left: VW interior dashboard with writing desk and wooden grids on the floorboards, seats attached with visible wing nuts at lower left. (VWM)

Right: VW30 dashboard and interior. (VWM)

Far Right: W30 dashboard close-up view, complete with key in the ignition at center right. (VWM)

The outer shell of the VW Beetle hardtop model has been removed on April 20, 1938, at the ORC in Berlin, and the bare chassis is being examined by, from left to right, Dr. Bodo Lafferentz, Dr. Ferdinand Porsche, unknown Nazi aide, Hitler, three unidentified men behind the Führer, and Jakob Werlin. (HHA)

VW38 scale model and shipping box sent to DAF chief Dr. Robert Ley in Berlin, February 1938, that was produced by the Porsche Design Firm on a scale of 1 to 15, given as his birthday present. (VWM)

In April 1938, there was produced by the PDB a series of five models scaled about 1 to 12. According to Barber, "The first was presented to Hitler on his 49th birthday, April 20, 1938. One of the models is today in the German Museum in Münich, built by architect Dr. Ludwig Troost, and that still stands.(Herbert Kaes, LC.)

Enter Hitler and Speer

Stated Dr. Speer in his 1976 work, *Spandau: The Secret Diaries*, during the war "Himmler was on the watch everywhere, seeking any possibility of becoming active in industry. Himmler had been working toward this goal for more than two years. Thus, on January 11, 1942—four days before Werlin's appointment as automotive tsar—"by means of an order of Hitler's, he took over the 'manufacture, expansion, and management…of the foundries in the Volkswagen Works, especially in the light metal foundries.' With Hitler's promise that it would also be responsible for the factory, the SS could feel that it was in charge of production. The Führer's order said: 'The SS *Reichsführer/National Administrator* will employ the necessary manpower from concentration camps. He will assume responsibility for the implementation of this assignment within the shortest possible time. The factory must be in operation by 1942 at the latest.' This edict had been submitted to Hitler by Porsche and Werlin, the Führer's Deputy for Motor Vehicles. Porsche had resolved to forge ahead with the project of the Volkswagen Works even in wartime conditions; and he thus managed to realize a major portion of his plans. It was only four weeks later that I became responsible for all these matters upon being appointed Minister of Armaments. Six weeks later, I gave Hitler reports by the appropriate group leaders of my newly created self-responsibility of industry; these reports explained that the additional capacity of the light metal foundry of the VW Works would be necessary only if all Volkswagens were equipped with light metal cast parts. However, Hitler had already decided that only the vehicles and amphibious trucks meant for Africa should be fitted with such light metal components. Thus, Himmler's order had been nullified by the events." This example also shows to what degree technician Hitler was prepared to intervene in a specific automotive decision!

Top Nazis at a prewar Berlin Automobile Show, held each year in February, from left to right: Göring, Hühnlein (leaning over, facing camera), two unknown men, Werlin (civilian coat), and Hitler. (HHA)

DAF plaque: DAF Training School. (Mercedes-Benz Archives, LC.)

A 1937 bout of drunkenness caused an international incident during the visit of the British Duke of Windsor (left) to Germany, seen here being lectured by Dr. Ley, who wears his Nazi Party Golden Membership Badge (with swastika) above the two First World War decorations. (HHA)

Dr. Robert Ley

Like Joachim von Ribbentrop and Julius Striecher, few in the Nazi Old Guard had anything good to say about the Third Reich's drunken German Labor Front Leader Dr. Robert Ley, but what cemented his longevity in Nazi Germany was a crucial meeting on September 30, 1925. Ley—whom Dr. Josef Göbbels called "a fool"—was the sole member of 25 top Party leaders to vote for Hitler's position in declaring that the Bavarian branch of the Party, that led by Hitler, was superior to the northern Strasser brothers, Gregor and Otto.

Gregor would be murdered in 1934, and Otto forced to flee for his life in exile in Canada, but Robert Ley would go from being virtually penniless to great wealth, having four lavish homes, a special train, and a fleet of shiny black Mercedes-Benz limousines. He had backed the right horse early on—and won.

His self-created German Labor Front (DAF) tackled one of the thorniest problems facing the new Nazi regime in the spring of 1933—what to do about the massive German labor movement of the Weimar Republic? The simple solution adopted by Hitler and Ley on 1 May was to outlaw them, then seize all their offices and assets. Overnight, the portly Rhineland *Gauleiter/Regional Leader* became one of the most powerful men in Germany, as the head of the new Nazi DAF.

Although not as well known as the other Nazi factotums—such as Göring or Hess, perhaps—Ley's primary place in the Third Reich's pantheon of leaders has come down in history as the head of the Strength Through Joy movement that provided German workers with vacations on luxury cruise ships in the Baltic and elsewhere, but he was much more than that. He was classified by at least one biographer as a rabble-rouser from the beginning to the end of his career (death by suicide in a jail cell awaiting trial as a war criminal). It was to Ley that Hitler assigned the task of escorting the Duke and Duchess of Windsor when they came calling in 1937. It was also to the drunken, womanizing Dr. Ley that the following year Hitler gave the ambitious task of building what became after the war the best-selling car of all time: the Volkswagen.

Had the Third Reich won World War II, Dr. Robert Ley's name would've figured prominently among the century's other great automakers: Ford, Kaiser, and Studebaker, to name but a few. But Germany *didn't* win the war, and so the man Hitler called "my greatest idealist" died ignominiously, strangled by a towel tied around a toilet pipe, alone and dejected in his cell. It was a sad end for a man with a doctorate in chemistry who truly believed that cradle-to-grave, Communistic-style Nazism would take care of all Germans throughout their lives.

The shameful death had been preceded by defeat at the hands of his more ruthless Nazi Party rivals: Rudolf Hess (whom he vainly tried to succeed as Deputy Führer in 1941 when Hess flew to Scotland), Martin Bormann, and Fritz Sauckel among them.

Intimidation was part of his complicated character. Recalled Kurt Ludecke of one Propaganda Ministry reception, "After the speeches, Dr. Ley and I strolled out to help ourselves to drinks. Göring, as we passed him, beckoned to Ley as one would signal a waiter, and Ley—subaltern that he was—trotted meekly over and listened, as though Göring were the Almighty himself."

Hitler he saw as a father figure akin to God, and he never got over his self-view as a humble peasant, once unable to believe that he was actually speaking from the same platform as one of the six sons of the former German Kaiser, Prince August Wilhelm (nicknamed "Auwi").

Born in the Rhineland in 1890 as the seventh of 11 children, Ley suffered from the poverty induced when he was six when his father torched the family farm in an insurance scam that netted him a four-year prison term. Plunged into shame and gloom, young Robert was determined to succeed through education, and in 1910 at age 20 entered the German university system.

With the onset of the First World War four years later, Ley in 1915 joined an artillery regiment fighting French mountain troops in the Vosges range, but in 1916 transferred to the German Flying Corps, where he was trained as an artillery observer. His machine gun jammed on a mission, and he was wounded in the thigh when shot down by a British fighter plane behind French lines.

Dr. Robert Ley (right, 1890-1945), head of the German Labor Front (DAF) and also VW. The Führer (left) greets Dr. Ley as a white-belted member of the Adolf Hitler SS Bodyguard Regiment (far left) salutes with port arms at the NRC in Berlin. (HHA)

Stated biographer Robert Smelser, "The thigh wound almost cost him his leg—to keep it he had to endure six operations while in captivity. In the course of one of them, Ley had cardiac arrest and came close enough to death to have had an out-of-body experience." Moreover, upon impact, Ley suffered frontal lobe damage that would become chronically worse over the years, leaving him with a stammer and an alcohol problem. He would remain a POW, however, until 14 months after the war ended, being released only in January 1920.

Ley finished his doctoral dissertation barely six months later, "On the theme of mixed glycerides in butter fat, that qualified him as an expert in the field of food chemistry," asserted Smelser. Soon afterwards both married and a father, Dr. Ley went to work for the famed I.G. Farben chemical firm, where he believed his colleagues laughed at him. He became a Nazi at age 33, and the man later called the "Reich lush" firmly hitched his wagon to Hitler's star when it was still unpopular to do so.

In 1924, Ley began organizing for the Party in Cologne, delighting in his new found reputation as a "brawler" in Communist sections of the city, where he deliberately founded Party cells. Despite his stammer, Dr. Ley became an orator sought after almost as much as Hitler and Göbbels, and founded a Nazi newspaper that would be published throughout the later war with the Führer's personal backing.

Notorious for his rowdy meetings and shady financial dealings that led him to a brush with the law and investigation by the Party's Münich headquarters, Ley nevertheless took the plunge, and devoted full time to Party affairs when he gave up his job at Farben at the worst moment of the Party's fortunes, and Hitler never forgot this.

Attacked within the Party for alleged Jewish parentage, Ley endured a Communist assertion that he'd left his swastika armband at a local whorehouse, and was even horsewhipped by an irate former SS leader. Still Hitler kept him on, and in 1928 he was elected to the German Landtag as a deputy. One Prince who heard him speak—impressed by his evident conviction—asserted, "No *wonder* Hitler keeps this man on!"

Despite a failed media business venture using the Prince's funding, Ley was confirmed by Hitler as both a Reich Speaker and Rhineland *Gauleiter,* although even the Führer admitted that, "Ley is a much better evangelist than a bookkeeper!" After a political setback in which his *Gaue* was split in two, Ley was nonetheless appointed Inspector of the Party on October 21, 1931, in effect becoming Hitler's hand-picked spy within the Strasser branch. In 1933 Hitler rewarded him once more, this time with the post of Reich Organizational Director in charge of the Party's growing political leadership cadres that would become all-important as the Third Reich was established in earnest.

The second leg of Ley's emerging empire within the Nazi bureaucratic morass was the creation of the German Labor Front, and here Ley's almost unrivalled personal greed after the years of struggle led him to be investigated for corruption and swindling by the Nazi Party Court in 1938, but Hitler had the probe quashed instead out of loyalty to his man.

That same year, Dr. Ley divorced his first wife (divorce was rare among Nazi leaders, as Hitler virtually forbade it) to marry beautiful blonde soprano singer Inge Spilker, by whom he had three children. By all accounts, the second Frau Ley was the love of his life, but he could be insensitive and cruel to her as well, once displaying a topless portrait of her to his dinner guests that left them in shock.

On another occasion, he actually tore her clothes off so his guests could admire her body. She once commented, "He treats me outrageously. He'll end up killing me someday." Rumored to be addicted to alcohol and drugs, Inge Ley shot herself on December 29, 1942. Attested Smelser, "More likely, she was the victim of her husband's alcohol problem, that was getting worse along with his brain disease." By this time, Ley himself was almost perpetually drunk.

Ley's drunkenness became such a well-known scandal that Heinrich Himmler's doctor refused to treat him because he could never find him sober during repeated house calls. Recalled Smelser:

"Perhaps the most embarrassing incident resulting from Ley's penchant for alcohol came in 1937. The Duke and Duchess of Windsor were visiting Germany, officially as guest of the DAF, and Dr. Ley thus hosted them.

"…An inebriated Ley insisted on chauffeuring the couple in his big Mercedes around workers' barracks at a factory on the outskirts of Münich. 'He drove the car through the locked gates, and then raced up and down at full speed between the barracks, scaring hell out of the workers, and nearly running over several. The next day Hitler told Göring to take over the Duke's visit before Ley killed him.'"

And yet, Ley wasn't without a social consciousness, coming out in favor of a minimum wage and better worker housing, and two luxury cruise ships were launched under his regime—one named the *Wilhelm Gustloff* (after a murdered Swiss Nazi), and the other for himself! Violently anti-aristocrat by the end of the war, Ley's anti-German Army writings after the July 20, 1944, officers' plot to kill Hitler had to be suppressed.

Along with von Ribbentrop, Ley was one of the few top Nazis to welcome the start of the Second World War in 1939, since it gave him renewed opportunity to attack his favorite targets, the Communists and the Jews, but like the former, he desired a classless society in the Reich as the ultimate political form.

The war ended his ambitious plans to build "Six million Volkswagens in 10 years"—or by 1948, but at least the plant site was launched at the current headquarters of Wolfsburg, and prototype production was started as well. It can be truthfully said that both Hitler and Ley fully intended to build the cars, and not defraud the German people. They paid for the cars in advance, the opposite of how Americans buy cars on payment plans *after* delivery. The money was still in the vaults of the Reichsbank at the end of the war in 1945, untouched; the Red Army seized it, however.

The coming of the war, though, brought Ley into conflict with two new opponents, Hitler's two successive Ministers of Armaments and War Production, Drs. Fritz Todt and Albert Speer. Prior to Todt's death in an airplane crash early in 1942, he vigorously opposed the further growth of the DAF, while Ley dreamed instead of greatly expanding his empire in the conquered Eastern territories, that brought him yet another foe in the Nazi hierarchy: Alfred Rosenberg, whom Hitler had earmarked to administer the USSR when and if it was ever fully beaten.

History ruled otherwise, however, making at least this particular internecine Nazi struggle a moot point for good. Thwarted in the east, Ley nevertheless won an important—if phantom—victory in that other area dear to his heart, namely future housing for the nation's workers. Thus, on October 23, 1942, Hitler appointed Dr. Ley Reich Housing Commissar—just as the Battle of Stalingrad was heating up. Ironically, Ley had inherited the social mantle of his old nemesis, Gregor Strasser, who—along with Dr. Göbbels—represented the "socialistic" side of National Socialism.

After the flight of Rudolf Hess to Scotland in May 1941, the former Deputy Führer's own number two man—Martin Bormann—became Dr. Ley's greatest enemy, as he also did for many other leading figures of the Third Reich. Thus—in the shifting sands of Nazi political alliances—Ley would find himself one day fighting with Göbbels over turf (such as his inopportune speeches being censored), and the next allied *with* him against Bormann. It was all very confusing.

As 1945 opened, however, Ley found himself at one with both of them in urging Hitler to use poison gas against the Allies, that the Führer—who'd been gassed himself in World War I—rejected. He did, though, accept Ley's idea of creating post-Third Reich guerillas to harass the victorious Allies; the vaunted but paper tiger *Werewolf* organization.

He saw Hitler for the last time on the Führer's final birthday on April 20, 1945, then hurried south to organize resistance. Nor did the Leader forget his faithful paladin, naming him Minister Without Portfolio in the new shadow government he bequeathed to his successor, Navy Grand Adm. Karl Dönitz. Ley never took office, but was captured instead by troops of the American Army 101st Airborne Division.

How low had he fallen? Shorn at last of the brown Party uniform, "He was a wretched figure, dressed in blue pajamas, a green hat, and sporting a four-day growth of beard. From his once portly 200 pounds, he had shrunk to 135 pounds." To add insult to injury, his disguise was given away when he was positively identified by another old Party enemy, treasurer Franz Xaver Schwartz, who'd audited Ley's books many times in dismay over the years of Nazi power, and even before.

Ley's indictment as a war criminal by the International Military Tribunal at Nürnberg cracked his fighting spirit at last, and led directly to his suicide on the night of October 25, 1945, as described by Smelser:

"Ley fashioned a noose from the torn hem of a bath towel, and tied it to the stand pipe of his corner toilet, the only place where he could not be directly observed.

"He then stuffed his mouth with rags to stifle any sounds, sat on the toilet with the noose around his neck, and leaned forward until he had strangled himself. It was not a pleasant way to die, and demonstrated Ley's determination to depart this world at any cost."

His suicide note read, in part, "Farewell. I cannot stand this shame any longer…Everything is in order, but the fact that I should be a criminal…This is what I cannot stand."

In a cruel twist of fate, Dr. Ley ended his life as had his father—in prison. Autopsied, Ley's brain was flown to the United States for further examination. His old boss at the Nazi Four Year Plan—Göring—stated, in a sort of requiem: "It's just as well that he's dead, because I had my doubts about how he would behave at his trial." Less than a year later Göring, too, would die a suicide. The wheel had turned full circle for both men.

Relations of Hitler and Dr. Ley with the Drs. Porsche

"I must say, the impression one got of Adolf Hitler in person was a very different one from what appeared, say, in pictures. I think he was more simpatico/sympathetic if you knew him personally, and in my father's case, the situation was rather a special one. At most, a half-dozen men in all of Germany dared to speak their minds openly before Hitler, and my father was one of them," recalled Dr. Ferry Porsche.

"What was more, he could do so without fear of being criticized or 'put in his place' by the Reich Chancellor. The situation, in fact, was in some respects as though my father were also Hitler's father. In all fairness, I must say that, whenever I met Hitler, he was courteous and correct with me as well.

"From the time he came to power, and during the first 10 years of his era, I had the impression that he was well informed about most things that were going on all over Germany. It was only later that this impression changed.

"In any case, the fact that my father did have direct access to the Führer, and could always freely speak his mind on technical matters, did not please the coterie of Hitler's hangers-on who took increasing pains to hide the truth from him. With one exception they resented my father's privilege, but the exception was an important person—none other than Dr. Ley. The man behind the Volkswagen enterprise was Ley, who...was also the founder of the KdF movement and chief of the German Labor Front.

"Of course, there were efforts made to discredit my father with Dr. Ley, but they failed completely. Accusations that he was costing the government too much money with all our experiments, and that Germany could not afford him had no effect on the leader of the German Labor Front, and Ley made quite sure that everyone knew it. 'If Prof. Porsche would like a golden equipage,' he once told a complainer, 'I would give it to him, and do you know why? Because he is an extraordinary man!'...

"As the war progressed and Germany was faced with one problem piled on top of another, I had fewer and fewer occasions to meet Adolf Hitler in person: but at the time of the Type 166 amphibian (Kübelwagen) demonstration, despite outward appearances, I sensed a distinct change in the man.

"While World War II ground deep into its fourth year, Hitler still *appeared* to be the dominant figure of the Third Reich, and the sole arbiter of everything and everyone, but as he fell under the influence of those closest to him, his attitude of dictatorial power became more and more of a façade.

"It was by now fairly obvious that if his clique made a sort of god out of the man, it was only so as to elevate themselves to the status of demigods. It had the feeling of an atmosphere where an insidious technique prevailed. No one contradicted Hitler anymore. They took great pains, in fact, to pretend to agree with him so that the picture he got of what was going on around him no longer related to reality.

"He therefore reacted to a set of imaginary facts and cleverly contrived distortions and half-truths in a manner which he might not have done had he known what was really happening. Of course, this is just one man's opinion, based only on personal experience when seeing the Chancellor.

"The general belief prevailed that once Hitler had set his mind on something, there was no way to make him change it. My father, however, saw another side of the German leader. He found that he *was* able to influence Hitler's opinion, though of course only in technical matters, since we at Porsche remained steadfastly nonpolitical at all times.

"We simply had no interest in political matters. Our territory was designing and building machines of one kind or another and overcoming the numerous problems associated with this work."

Thus, it was this kind of "non-political attitude" that would have permitted Dr. Ferdinand Porsche in 1932 to have gone to work just as easily for Soviet dictator Josef Stalin as he did for Hitler the very next year, with the supreme irony that the Porsche-Volkswagenwerk used Russian Red Army POWs in the thousands to build VW Beetles, Kübelwagens, and Schwimmwagens to help the Nazis conquer their native land, Mother Russia.

It is my opinion that these types of "political technicians" are present in all "civilized" societies, even now—*especially now*—in pursuit, really, of but one goal: the financial profit of successful business ventures. They are a dangerous breed, for that very reason!

Ironically, Dr. Ferry Porsche was not alone in his observations on Hitler and that inner circle of ambitious men around their Führer. Stated controversial English revisionist historian David Irving in his 1977 work *Hitler's War*, "When his closest crony of all those years, SS Gen. Josef 'Sepp'/Joe Dietrich, was asked by the American 7th Army for an opinion of Hitler on June 1, 1945, he replied, 'He knew even less than the rest. He allowed himself to be taken for a sucker by everyone.'"

Or *did* he?

Recalled Dr. Speer in his 1970 work, *Memoirs: Inside the Third Reich*:

"Hitler must already have realized the immense drama that his life was, the high stakes he was playing for, by the time he had a long conversation with Cardinal Faulhaber at Obersalzberg in November 1936.

"Afterward, Hitler sat alone with me in the bay window of the dining room, while the twilight fell. For a long time he looked out of the window in silence. Then he said pensively: 'There are two possibilities for me: to win through with all my plans, or to fail. If I win, I shall be one of the greatest men in history. If I fail, I shall be condemned, despised, and damned.'"

Dr. Ley (right, smiling) gives a ride in his VW convertible to Italian Fascist leader Tullio Cianetti, for whom a hall was named at the Wolfsburg VW plant. Cianetti was an industrialist, Italian Minister of Propaganda, a member of the Fascist Grand Council, and Undersecretary for Popular Culture to the Duce. On July 25, 1943, he voted to oust Mussolini from power in the wake of the lost war at Germany's side in a majority motion of the Council. After the Duce was restored to office by Hitler that September, Cianetti was tried and convicted of treason in January 1944, but his was the sole pardon issued by the court. The rest of those captured were shot in the back by a Fascist Republican firing squad. (HHA)

DAF chief Dr. Robert Ley (center) stands between two of his longtime rivals within the Nazi Party: Deputy Führer Rudolf Hess (right) and *Reichsleiter/National Leader* Martin Bormann (left) at a Nürnberg Congress in this previously unpublished photo. (HHA)

Dr. Ley's Nazi boss within the economic Four Year Plan of 1936-40 was Hermann Göring. In this previously unpublished photo from the Hermann Göring Albums are seen Luftwaffe Field Marshal Göring holding baton and cap (third from left) and Dr. Ley also holding cap (seventh from left) on May 31, 1939, at Hamburg, where they are welcoming home the German Kondor Legion, back from the just concluded Spanish Civil War, where its members flew on behalf of Franco's Nationalist Air Force. Stated author Charles Hamilton in his 1984 anthology, *Leaders and Personalities of the Third Reich: Their Biographies, Portraits, and Autographs*, "A chemist by profession, Dr. Ley was an aviator in World War I, and spent nearly four years as a French prisoner. In 1925, he joined the Nazi Party...In 1933, Dr. Ley founded the DAF, or German Labor Front... Slated for prosecution at Nürnberg, the imprisoned Dr. Ley rigged a noose from towel rags, hitched it to a toilet pipe, and hanged himself on October 25, 1945." Göring believed it was probably best that he didn't live to stand trial, feeling he would've been an embarrassment to the rest of the defendants, as were Streicher, Hess and von Ribbentrop. (LC)

Dr. Ley (center) visiting the Reich Textiles trade show before the war. (HHA)

Dr. Ley (left) with Dutch Fascist Labor Movement leader Noudenberg (right) in Berlin. Dr. Ley is wearing "walking out dress that featured the double-breasted jacket and dark blue trousers, white shirt and brown tie," according to noted authority Roger James Bender. (Bender)

At the famed Berlin Sports Palace indoor arena for Dr. Josef Göbbels' epochal "Total War" speech of February 18, 1943, following the great German defeat of the war at the Battle of Stalingrad. From left to right, Drs. Speer, Ley, and Göbbels clap. All three men were associated with the VW in the end: Speer being responsible for the wartime production of Kubels and Schwimmwagens after February 8, 1942; Ley via his KcF Organization; and Göbbels to promote the Beetle ownership program for "after the war" as a further inducement toward victory on the Home Front. (HHA)

Hitler (center) and Dr. Ley (center, right) review the DAF leader's own private army of DAF men before the war, one of several within the overall Third Reich. (HHA)

A bearded, disheveled looking Dr. Ley at his capture by U.S. Army troops of the elite 101st Airborne Division in 1945. (U.S. Army Signal Corps, USNA, College Park, MD)

PRISON OFFICE

SUBJECT: Statement concerning Suicide of Dr. Ley.

TO : Major Teich

At 2010 25 October 1945 the Corporal of the Guard, Cpl Glaskell, came into the prison office and asked me to come to cell # 9, Dr. Ley's cell immediately. I rushed to cell #9/in the latrine recess with a rag stuffed into his mouth and an improvised noose around his neck fastened to the latrine flushpipe. I tried to lift him in order release the noose from the flushpipe but he was to heavy. The corporal of the guard cut the material and Dr. Ley fell forward. I caught him and we laid him on the floor. I told the corporal of the guard to get our German interned doctor, Dr. Pfluecker, tell him the situation AND TO COME IMMEDIATELY

The Sergeant of the Guard, S/Sgt John J. Daley, was told to remain in the cell. I returned to the prison office and called Dr. Juchli, informing him of the situation. I told Dr. Juchli to inform the colonel. He said he would and he was coming right down.

I returned to cell # 9 and found Dr. Pfluegker and our German interned dentist, Dr. Hoch, giving Ley one cc of cardiazol and one cc of lobulin. The German doctor then ordered Ley to be placed on the bed, which the sgt and corporal did. I told the Sgt of the Guard to go out and check the posts on the first floor. The German doctor began artificial respiration at approximately 2020. I told the corporal of the guard to assist Dr Pfluecker.

I checked the guard on post # 8. Questions asked at this time were later covered in detail by Major Teich in his talk with the guard. I then checked the remainder of the guard on the first floor and returned to cell # 9. Dr. Pfluecker then told me that Ley was dead and to the best of his knowledge had been dead about fifteen minutes. He continued artificial respiration. Col Juchli, Maj Teich and Lt Durkee arrived at 2028. Col Juchli examined the body and pronounced him dead at approximately 2032.

The door to Dr Ley's cell was kept closed. There was little confusion or noise. I returned to my normal duties.

PAUL H. GRAVEN
2nd Lt Infantry
Ass't prison Officer on Duty

U.S. Army *Statement concerning Suicide of Dr. Ley.* (USNA)

Level of unemployment at the end of every month in the years 1933–39

	1933	*1934*	*1935*	*1936*	*1937*	*1938*	*1939*
January	6,013,612	3,772,792	2,973,544	2,520,499	1,853,460	1,051,700	301,900
February	6,000,958	3,372,611	2,764,152	2,514,894	1,610,947	946,300	196,800
March	5,598,855	2,798,324	2,401,889	1,937,120	1,245,338	507,600	134,000
April	5,331,252	2,608,621	2,233,255	1,762,774	960,764	422,500	93,900*
May	5,038,640	2,528,960	2,019,293	1,491,235	776,321	338,400	69,600
June	4,856,942	2,480,826	1,876,579	1,314,731	648,421	292,200	48,800
July	4,463,841	2,426,014	1,754,117	1,169,860	562,892	218,300	38,400
August	4,124,288	2,397,562	*1,706,230*†	1,098,498	509,257	178,800	34,000†
September	3,849,222	2,281,800	1,713,912	*1,035,237*†	*469,053*†	156,000	77,500
October	3,744,860	2,267,657	1,828,721	1,076,469	501,847	163,900	79,400
November	*3,714,646*†	2,352,662	1,984,452	1,197,140	572,557	*152,400*†	72,600
December	4,059,055	2,604,700	2,507,955	1,478,862	994,590	455,700	104,400

*216,000, including Austria and the Sudetenland.
†The italicized figures are the lowest level in each year.

The Development of Wages 1929–1939:

	1929	1932	1933	1934	1935	1936	1937	1938	1939
Nominal hourly wages (official)	122	100	97	97	97	97	97	97	98
Nominal hourly wages (actual)	133	100	97	99	101	102	105	108	111
Actual hourly wages (real)		100	99	99	99	100	101	104	107
Actual weekly wages (nominal)	149	100	102	110	112	117	121	126	131
Actual weekly wages (real)	118	100	104	109	110	112	115	119	123
Wages as a % of National income	56.6	57.0	56.0	55.5	54.6	53.5	52.7	52.4	51.8
Official cost of living index	128	100	98	100	102	103	104	104	105
Undistributed profits of private business as a % of national income			0.5	1.4	2.6	3.6	3.9	4.9	
Gross wages in the machine building industry			100	113	118	120	122		
Gross wages in the food processing industry			100	101	101	101	102		
Gross wages in the clothing industry			100	96	91	96	95		
Average hours of work per week for each worker in the processing industries	46	41.5	42.9	44.6	44.4	45.6	46.1	46.5	47.0[1]

[1]First six months.

Leisure-time activities organized by 'Strength through Joy' in 1934 and 1938

	1934		*1938*	
	number	*participants*	*number*	*participants*
Concerts	1,020	576,594	5,291	2,515,598
Popular entertainments	725	285,037	54,813	13,666,015
Operas, operettas	959	540,841	12,407	6,639,067
Theatre	2,839	1,581,573	19,523	7,478,633
Variety, cabaret	1,315	481,855	7,921	3,518,833
Evening variety shows	3,189	1,228,457	10,989	4,462,140
Films	3,372	316,968	3,586	857,402
Exhibitions	72	237,632	555	1,595,516
Guided tours	1,528	90,242	676	58,472
Others	9,653	3,772,464	15,084	11,118,636
Events for the Autobahn workers	—	—	13,589	2,658,155
Total	24,672	9,111,663	144,434	54,568,467

Dr. Ley's German Labor Front (DAF) and unemployment, wages, and leisure time activities of the KdF Organization, 1933-39. (From *Nazism: A History in Documents and Eyewitness Accounts, 1919-45*, edited by J. Noakes and G. Pridham.)

Glory days, from left to right: three unknown Nazis, Dr. Ferdinand Porsche, unidentified man, Hitler, Dr. Bodo Lafferentz behind him, and DAF leader Dr. Robert Ley examine VW Beetle convertible license plate IA-148564 in 1939. (HHA)

Dr. Ferdinand Porsche (center, in light civilian overcoat and hat) is welcomed by German DAF leader Dr. Robert Ley (fifth from left) in brown Party uniform at the 1939 Berlin Auto Show with VW Beetles at left. Visible behind Dr. Ley is the taller Dr. Bodo Lafferertz, his deputy in building the VW. (HHA)

RAD: Reich Labor Service

The Reich Labor Service (RAD), "The Soldiers of the Spade," who helped clear the way for both *Autobahnen/Highways* and Volkswagen, 1933-42. In his 1941 book *Berlin Diary*, the late CBS radio broadcaster and celebrated author William L. Shirer noted on September 6, 1934, at the Nürnberg Party Rally:

"Hitler sprang his *Arbeitsdienst/Labor Service Corps* on the public for the first time today, and it turned out to be a highly trained, semi-military group of fanatical Nazi youths. Standing there in the early morning sunlight that sparkled on their shiny spades, 50,000 of them—with the first thousand bared above the waist—suddenly made the spectators go mad with joy when, without warning, they broke into a perfect goosestep...I felt for the first time this morning what an inner chord it strikes in the strange soul of the German people.

"Spontaneously, they jumped up and shouted their applause. There was a ritual even for the Labor Service boys. They formed an immense Spechor—a chanting chorus—and with one voice intoned such words as these: 'We want one Leader! Nothing for us! Everything for Germany! Heil Hitler!'"

Part of this chanting is captured forever in Leni Riefenstahl's epic 1935 film "Triumph of the Will" of the 1934 rally of which Shirer here writes.

Here is a rear view of the assembled RAD men facing the Zeppelinfield. (Previously unpublished photograph from the Heinrich Hoffmann Albums.)

Hitler reviewing the RAD from the tribune of the Zeppelinfield, from left to right: Göring, Hitler, Hess, RAD Leader Konstantin Hierl, two RAD leaders, Interior Minister Dr. Wilhelm Frick, and another RAD leader watch a similar event in another year at the same location and event. The creation of the RAD and the expansion of the Wehrmacht were part of the overall solution to German unemployment launched by the Nazis, as well as the growth of industry and the building of the Autobahn superhighways. The law making such RAD service compulsory for all German males was signed June 26, 1935, affecting those born before 1925. Many went to work on farms and road and irrigation projects, with no distinction made for class background or previous occupation: workers, artisans, peasants, and intellectuals were all melted into the same pot, to help mold the German people behind the Führer. At Nürnberg in 1936, he claimed he'd reduced unemployment by five million down to one million. (Previously unpublished photo from the Hermann Göring Albums, Library of Congress, Washington, DC)

Hühnlein's Motor Corps

Korpsführer/ Corps Leader Adolf Hühnlein (1881-1942), the Nazi Motor Corps, and VW.

As noted by Lt. Col John R. Angolia and David Littlejohn in their excellent 1994 work, *NSKK/NSFK: Uniforms, Organization, and History*:

"'Without the car, the plane, and the loudspeaker, we could never have conquered Germany,' Hitler declared in 1935. There is little doubt that paramount among the reasons for the success of the Nazi movement was its grasp of the importance of mobility and propaganda. Hitler was master of mass psychology, using convoys of trucks, cars, and even small squads of motorcyclists to traverse the cities, towns, and countryside with swastika banners and slogans to create an impression of the omnipresence and authority of the NSDAP/Nazi Party…The NSKK, as much as the SA/Storm Troopers, played an essential role in the battle for the hearts, minds, and attention of the German people."

As we shall see, the motorized formations of the NSKK were an important feature of the overall motorization of the German people and, thereby, their preparation of the new lifestyle that Hitler was preparing for them with his vast, expansive, and growing Autobahnen and Volkswagen programs. To have these things, however, Nazi Germany needed a motor-conscious people and—above all—drivers, and these he lacked when he took office as Chancellor in 1933.

In Vienna, March 1938, from left to right: Hitler, Dr. Göbbels (four steps up from bottom) and, on step below Hitler at far right, NSKK Korpsführer Adolf Hühnlein. Two men up from him on the far right is the head of the German Regular (Order) Police, Gen. Kurt Daluege, and, next to him at left (wearing coffee can-style kepi cap) Hühnlein's liaison officer with Hitler, Albert Bormann. Just under his outstretched arm in Nazi salute (in SS black peaked cap) is Hitler's longtime personal aide, SS Gen. Julius Schaub. Rudolf Hess is seen to the left of Dr. Göbbels and one step above him. (HHA)

"Once Hitler took national office, he used the NSKK and the DDAC/German Automobile Club, an organization comparable with the Automobile Association of America, to make German youth 'motor-minded'....Through defeat, Germany had learned the lessons of the World War; these were largely ignored by the victors. The NSKK became the training formation for future armored drivers..." The NSKK Motor Sports School at Bayer (seen here) in the Ostmark/Eastern March, the Nazified name for the former Austria after the Anschluss/Union with Germany of March 1938, pose for a group photo in 1939. State Angolia and Littlejohn, "Although post-World War I Germany lagged behind the Western world in vehicle ownership, by the end of 1938, they were able to boast over 3.2 million trucks of various sorts on the road. Hitler used this interest in things mechanical to further his own ends. Motorized units of the Party were vital to the dissemination of propaganda, and the transport of Party members to the many rallies." (CER)

A popular picture postcard of Korpsführer Hühnlein sold by Heinrich Hoffmann's photo shop in Münich throughout the Third Reich. On Hühnlein, Angolia and Littlejohn attested, he "Had been a regular soldier, but with the end of World War I, his career was ended. At an early date, he decided to join Hitler. He possessed no specialist or technical skills of any sort. Celebrated car designer Ferdinand Porsche—who knew Hühnlein well—described him as 'A humorless man who seemed to have absolutely no qualification for his job, as he had no mechanical knowledge at all,' and 'appeared always to be in an ill temper.' His advancement seemed to stem from his association with Hitler from the early days, and his blind devotion to the Führer. With the rank of SA Grüppenführer/Major General Hühnlein took command of the new NSKK, and subjected it to military-style discipline." (HHA)

A trio of top Nazi automotive chieftains takes a wartime stroll along a pathway at Ft. Wolf, Rastenburg, East Prussia; from left to right are Hitler, Korpsführer Hühnlein, and Albert Bormann. The painted stripe on the tree at right was to light the way at night during blackouts for the walkers, according to the late Dr. Richard Raiber of Hockessin, DE, whose information came from one of Hitler's wartime SS aides, Richard Schulze-Kossens, and thus was passed along to me kindly by Dr. Raiber in 2001 at my request. Continued Angolia and Littlejohn on Hühnlein, "When SA Capt. Ernst Röhm created a new territorial structure in July 1932, Hühnlein was promoted to the rank of SA *Obergruppenführer/Lt. Gen.*, the second highest rank in the SA. Members of the Motor SA were automatically also members of the NSKK; however, the reverse did not apply." Added author Charles Hamilton, "Hühnlein served as a major in World War I. After the war, he joined the SA...and took part in the Beer Hall Putsch of 1923. He rose gradually in Nazi ranks, becoming, in 1934 chief of the NSKK, an organization devoted to paramilitary transportation that developed many soldiers who subsequently served in *Panzer/Armored* divisions." (Previously unpublished photo, HHA)

Hitler (left) and Hühnlein (right) review an NSKK honor guard outside the NRC in Berlin before the war. (HHA)

On March 8, 1936, NSKK Korpsführer Hühnlein (right) places a wreath for Heroes' Memorial Day (Veterans Day) at the Drivers' Monument near Potsdam outside Berlin as a company guidon bearer (left) stands at attention. Note the bas relief trucks on the concrete side of the monument and the tank atop it. Noted Angolia and Littlejohn, "The NSKK took part in the much publicized 'total mobilization' of the Party's uniformed formations held in the city of Brunswick on October 17-18, 1931, when it was able to muster some 5,000 vehicles. The event received a great deal of attention in the press, and was a considerable propaganda coup for Hitler." (HHA)

Hühnlein (center left) shakes hands with famous German race car driver champion Rudolf "Rudi" Caracciola, seen wearing NSKK uniform and cap. Note, too, the NSKK German Motor Sport Badge enlarged on the curtain at upper right. (HHA)

Before Hitler became Chancellor in 1933, the Federal and State governments of the Reich temporarily banned by law the wearing of the Nazi brown shirt, leading the men of the NSKK to wear instead either white shirts or none at all, as seen here, in protest. Their distinctive metal badge was also removed from the black leather crash helmet, also seen here. Once Hitler became Chancellor, the NSKK expanded to 30,000 members and—after Röhm's murder during the June 30, 1934, Blood Purge—the Motor SA was merged with the NSKK, its former "junior partner," and was made an "Independent formation of the Party," responsible only and directly to the Führer, thus escaping the rule of new SA Staff Chief Viktor Lütze, just as Himmler's SS had done. It also jumped in membership during 1934 to a whopping 350,000. (HHA)

At the 1935 annual Nürnberg Party Congress—held each September from 1927-39—Hitler "consecrated" new Nazi banners with a touch of the "Blood Flag" of the November 8-9, 1923, "Beer Hall Putsch," as seen here. SS Man Jakob Grimminger stands behind his Führer with the Blood Flag, while Hitler solemnly touches the other with his left hand, and shakes with his right the standard bearer. This trio of NSKK men each wear a different style of headwear. Noted Angolia and Littlejohn, "The *Sturmabteilung/SA/Stormtroopers* had possessed a motor section of sorts as far back as 1923, when trucks were employed to transport the elite *Stosstrupp Adolf Hitler/ Hitler's Personal Guard*, but progress in this respect had been rather slow. In 1928, the SA created mobile units, known as *Kraftfahtstaffeln/Motor Squadrons*, but these lacked proper organization. The following year, Martin Bormann suggested to Hitler that the Party would greatly benefit from having a nationwide pool of motorized transport to enable rapid mobilization during a show of strength. Hitler approved the idea, and directed Bormann to create such an organization." Bormann thus had made an important and early step on his rise to power, and also a significant contribution to our own story of the motorization of Germany and, ultimately, the twin births of the Autobahns and Volkswagen. (Previously unpublished photo, HHA.)

NSKK period postcards. (HHA)

NSKK motorcyclists on a field maneuver. (HHA)

Nazi propaganda poster touting the NSKK, with helmet emblem logo seen at upper right, enlarged. The legend below the motorcycle rider reads, "Adolf Hühnlein Motor Sport School of the NSKK Nordmark." (HHA)

Driver's Service Badge

According to *Orders, Decorations, Medals, and Badges of the Third Reich* by Littlejohn and Col. C.M. Dodkins, 1968:

"The Driver's Service Badge was instituted on October 23, 1942, and awarded to all drivers (including civilians) of military transport vehicles who had been engaged in any campaign since Dec. 1, 1940. The badge is in three classes: bronze, silver, and gilt. The Bronze badge was awarded for a) being a dispatch rider for 90 days' service; b) as a frontline supply driver for 120 days' service, and c) as a driver of any other form of military transport for 135 days' service. The Silver and Gilt versions were given for longer periods of service. The Badge could be awarded for shorter periods if the driving had been under particularly arduous conditions of climate or terrain (as in Russia or North Africa), or irrespective of length of service, for a display of merit in transport maintenance, or some special driving achievement. Awards to military personnel were made by the commanding officer of the unit; to civilians by the Ministry of the Interior [headed until October 1943 by Wilhelm Frick, afterward by RFSS Himmler]. The Badge, attached to a round or diamond-shaped piece of cloth of a color corresponding to that of the uniform, was sewn to the left cuff. It could also be worn as a miniature on the left lapel of civilian clothes. It could be forfeited if the holder were convicted of careless driving, etc., or involved in a road accident due to his own negligence, or if he maltreated his vehicle in such a way as to lower its efficiency. Awards could also be made to non-German auxiliaries serving in the Wehrmacht, but not to members of Germany's allies."

Since Korpsführer Hühnlein died on June 18, 1942, he did not live to see the institution of this badge, but he did witness in 1935 the first annual "national contest" of the NSKK in which its members competed against DDAC and Hitler Youth (HJ) teams from all over Germany. Added Littlejohn and Angolia, "It proved to be so popular that it became an annual event." (CER)

The German Motor Sport Badge, according to Littlejohn and Col. Dodson, was:

"A Badge to be conferred annually for outstanding achievement in the field of motor sport, and was instituted on Feb. 18, 1938. The first awards were made on Jan. 30, 1939 [as part of the Party's celebrations of its six years in office]. The Badge is in three classes: iron (black), silver, and gilt. It was awarded on a point basis; 50 points were required for an award of the Badge in Iron, 100 for the Silver badge, and 150 for the Gilt version. For winning first place in an international car race, 12 points were given; for second place, eight points. The winner of a long distance rally received nine points. The Badge—which is sometimes called the NSKK Sports Badge—could be worn on the left breast pocket of any uniform." Added Littlejohn and Angolia, "In March 1938, Austria was incorporated into the Greater German Reich. This same year marked the growth of the NSKK to over 500,000 members [making it a major factor in Allied prewar numbers' estimates of German paramilitary forces available on time of war]. In September, Hühnlein was rewarded by being made a 'Reichsleiter/National Leader' of the Nazi Party, the highest Party rank." (CER)

Period postcard of a popular NSKK driver. (CER)

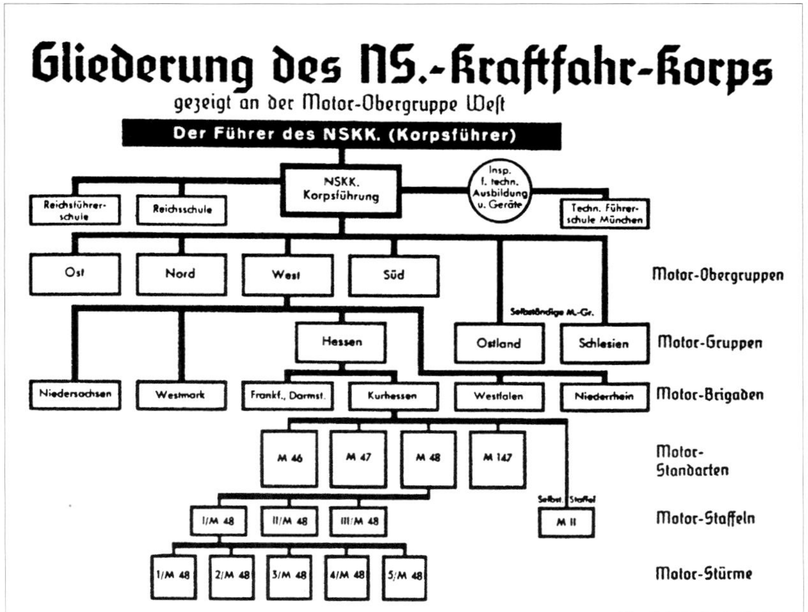

The organizational breakdown of the NSKK under Hühnlein, as shown in the 1936 *Organization Book of the Nazi Party*, depicting the various Motor Standartes, schools, districts, and sections. During the Nazi *Gleischaltung/Coordination* of German society in 1933-34, they combined all existing motor clubs into a single national German Automobile Club/Der Deutsche Automobile Club, or DDAC, by the first September of their rule in 1933. Stated Angolia and Littlejohn, "The *Kraftfahrstaffeln/Motorized Section* of the Stahlhelm/Steel Helmet, or VFW of Germany, organization had been incorporated into the NSKK earlier that same year. In December 1934, Hühnlein was promoted from NSKK *Obergruppenführer/Lt. Gen.* to the rank of Korpsführer der NSKK. He was, by this time, also Chief of the ONS/Supreme National Sports Authority for German Motoring, as well as being a member of the Board of Directors of the Reichsautobahn/National Super Highway, and an honorary Army major general." (LC)

One prominent member of the NSKK was former Imperial German Crown Prince Wilhelm of the House of Hohenzollern (hands in pockets at center) at age 50 in 1932, wearing what he would later call the "funny pants." His father—the exiled Kaiser Wilhelm II in Doorn, Holland—was not amused. During the First World War, Wilhelm had been a German Army Group Commander, nominally in command of the 1916 Battle of Verdun that Göring had photographed from the air as an artillery observer. (Previously unpublished photo, HHA.)

Prussian Prime Minister Hermann Göring (center) salutes an honor guard of NSKK men on a visit to Hamburg on December 6, 1935, for a work session at the Blohm and Voss shipyard. Note the leather crash helmets the men are wearing at right, first introduced at the 1935 Nürnberg Party Congress three months earlier. According to Angolia and Littlejohn:
"The crash helmet/sturzhelm of the Motor SA was carried over into the NSKK without design modification, except to the helmet badge [that was an eagle-with-swastika-pattern on the front]. Helmets were made either of black leather or black Vulcan fiber (the leather protective head portion was 2.5-3mm thick, while the Vulcan fiber was only 1.5mm thick, but with greater strength). It took the form of a hard helmet with front visor, and a padded protective roll around the lower edge and across the middle of the head from front to back. There was a leather protective flap with closeable ear covers, and a strap with metal buckle that fastened under the chin. A single 12mm diameter wire mesh air vent was positioned at the right and left of the head portion...The NSKK crash helmet, in addition to being worn during normal driving duties, was worn as part of the full dress uniform when so proscribed, especially at parade formations and special events." (Previously unpublished photograph from the Hermann Göring Albums, LC.)

Göring (left) receives birthday greetings on January 12, 1936, from Korpsführer Hühnlein (right), who wears a 1936 pattern dagger. All Nazi formations wore these—copied from Mussolini's Italian Fascist Blackshirts—but they were purely decorative, not for street battles against the Communists, or other pre-1933 political opponents. State Angolia and Littlejohn, "On Jan. 27, 1939, a 'Führer Decree' created the SA Wehrmannschaften/SA Militia into which all physically fit males on reaching the age of 18 were to be drafted prior to their obligatory military service. The NSKK's part in this undertaking was to be the training of drivers for the Army's motorized units at the various NSKK Motor Sports Schools. With the invasion of Poland by Germany on September 1, 1939, World War II was underway. By this time, the NSKK had built a considerable reserve of motor transport. The NSKK played a major role in the construction of Germany's Western defenses (the 'Siegfried Line'), working in concert with the Organization Todt. A somewhat similar arrangement was entered into by Albert Speer, whose Baustab/Building Staff Speer had been set up to oversee the rebuilding of Berlin to conform to Hitler's grandiose dream" of the replacement capital *Germania*. The NSKK—in the form of NSKK-Baustab Speer—supplied the transport for this project. By the time that the war broke out, transportation facilities outside those of the Armed Forces could be furnished by the NSKK proper, NSKK Transport-Brigade Todt, and NSKK-Baustab Speer. This three-way split in the NSKK weakened Hühnlein's authority, and in 1944 caused his successor to lose control over much of the organization. (Hermann Göring Albums, LC, Washington, DC)

Another high ranking but rather unwilling honorary member of the NSKK was Nazi Germany's first Ambassador to Fascist Italy, Ulrich von Hassell (1881-1944), who did all he could to keep the Nazis and Fascists out of the military alliance that he believed would bring on World War II—a conflict he knew that the Axis Pact powers could not win. Implicated in the July 20, 1944, plot to assassinate Hitler, von Hassell was tried for treason against the State, convicted, sentenced to death, and hanged at Berlin's Plötzensee Prison on September 8, 1944. Here he wears the coffee can-style kepi associated with both the German SA and the French Foreign Legion, which still wears it. The U.S. Army wore it in the Eisenhower Presidential years and into the first years of the New Frontier era of JFK. (CER)

NSKK members with an Army officer (fourth from right) during the war with a portable field kitchen. Noted German author Rudolf Kohl in his work *Uniforms and Badges of the Third Reich*, "During the war, the importance of the NSKK increased so much that—even in the occupied countries—organizations were formed by foreign auxiliaries...The incorporation of the Motor SA and the DDAC into the NSKK showed the new task of the NSKK [after 1934] quite clearly: political indoctrination into the field of motor sport plus training and schooling facilities. In a way, the NSKK also influenced the increasing motor vehicle production and selling, because of its motor-stimulating activities"—exactly what Hitler wanted it to do regarding Volkswagen. (CER)

Dr. Ferry Porsche on Adolf Hühnlein from *We at Porsche*:

"Hitler's prominent Party henchmen brings to mind another individual who certainly deserves mention.... *Obergruppenführer* Konrad [sic] Hühnlein, a man with whom my father came into contact frequently, though without much pleasure...In his position as a sort of overlord of German automotive sports and its related affairs, he wielded considerable power. Besides being the sole authority in issuing competition licenses, Hühnlein had the last word on when and where record attempts could be made, and even in the rules that governed motor racing. Mores the pity, therefore, that he was not a pleasant individual to deal with and—on top of that—was neither an engineer nor held any special qualifications to fit him for such an important job. Still worse, I would go so far as to say he was rather a stupid man whose outstanding feature—to us—was his strong Bavarian accent. Hühnlein looked exactly what he was—a born soldier, robust and aggressive. He had, in fact, served in World War I in a tough Pioneer/Engineer regiment. Later—during the Hitler regime—he had somehow managed to get himself appointed head of the NSKK, though certainly not because of any personal charm. It may have been as a reward for 'loyalty.' The fact remains that he always spoke in a sort of growl and gave the impression of being angry with someone. If he had any sense of humor, he certainly kept it well hidden. I don't think anyone ever saw him laugh, or even smile. The ferocious attitude earned him the nickname of 'Papa Bos.' That can be most closely translated into 'Father Angry.' Naturally, Hühnlein always wore a uniform and high boots, and any form of empathy with this man was quite out of the question. He was too ready to criticize and reject people."

Perhaps that is why Hitler chose to keep him on the top of the NSKK, to rein in on the top magnates of the German automobile industry—including the Porsches and the Volkswagen management team. In any event, here at least is one photo of the stiff Korpsführer (center) breaking into a partial grin with a smiling Führer aboard the German Navy ship *Leipzig* in 1933, surrounded by sailors and a naval officer. (HHA)

Hühnlein at the wheel of a convertible VW Beetle with a pair of victorious German drivers promoting the VW, with a convertible sunroof model following behind. The Korpsführer's car has a Stüttgart license plate. According to Dr. Ferry Porsche in *We at Porsche*, "Returning to the subject of those VW propaganda tours for a moment, all the top Party people were, in one respect, in the same boat. They all felt obliged to praise the People's Car in glowing terms. Even the sour-faced Hühnlein believed that—as a leader of the NSKK, and in his capacity as administrator of all motor sports activities—he should not be left out of any VW tour. However, for his own private use, he swept around in a Mercedes—not a VW!"—as indeed, did not only all the other top Nazi leaders, but even—and especially—Adolf Hitler himself. He never rode a horse or a bicycle so far as anyone knows, and stopped riding the ordinary streetcars of the day when he got his first Mercedes in order to enhance his "image" as the Führer, even in the midst of the Great Depression, that made the socialist-inclined members among what was supposed to be a workers' party grumble. (HHA)

Field Marshal Hermann Göring Meets the Volkswagen Beetle - June 17, 1939

As the current author noted in an article published in *VW Trends Magazine* in July 1992:

"Dr. Ferdinand Porsche's son and successor, Dr. Ferry Porsche, reported that...Göring—who was in charge of the economy—intervened in the project, and almost stopped everything. As Göring growled to Nazi Labor Front leader Dr. Robert Ley and Ferry Porsche, 'I'll be honest with you. As you know, I've always been opposed to nationalizing private industry, and that is what we're doing with the Volkswagen!'

"Ley protested, and stood firm on the position taken by Hitler and the Porsches [i.e., to develop and build the VW]. Dr. Ferry Porsche recalls, 'Göring took his first ride in 1938 [actually, the date was June 17, 1939, as these photos from his personal albums show], when I drove to *Karinhall,* his country estate, to fetch him, but with his very considerable weight, he forced the VW from a straight and level position till it was leaning to his side. There was little I could do about that.'"

Here are the pictures of that historic encounter between Marshal Göring and the Bug, and the truth of Dr. Ferry's recollections can be clearly put to the photographic test. I believe they show he was mistaken. Judge for yourself!

A convertible VW makes its debut at Hermann Göring's country estate *Karinhall.* From left to right: Dr. Bodo Lafferentz, Dr. Ferry Porsche (leaning down to open the hood), Dr. Ferdinand Porsche (dark suit), Göring (behind whom stand three unknown aides), Dr. Robert Ley, and an unidentified SS aide. (HGA)

Drs. Ferry and Ferdinand Porsche, Dr. Lafferentz, Göring, unknown man, and Dr. Ley in a detail of a larger photograph. In the summer of 1936, Hitler and Göring hammered out the final details of the Four Year Plan at the Berghof at Berchtesgaden. (HGA)

The larger photograph, showing Göring (center) making a point to Dr. Ferdinand Porsche. The men to the right of Dr. Ley are unidentified aides. The FYP was announced by Hitler at the Nürnberg Party Congress on September 8, 1936. (Previously unpublished photo from the Hermann Göring Albums, LC.)

As an amused Dr. Ferdinand Porsche looks on, a jovial Göring attempts to push the Beetle down his driveway. The leather jerkin and dagger he wears were designed by and for himself in his role as Reich Chief Master of the Hunt. Note the car's interior and dashboard. (HGA)

A look underneath. How this was accomplished, I do not know! Note the seat coverings. On July 6, 1938, Göring announced that he would discuss the whole raw materials selection with Hitler: oil, gas, synthetic fuels, rubber, iron, and steel, all items that would later vitally affect the production of Volkswagen. (HGA)

Göring in the back seat. If the car is tilting toward his side due to his weight (as Dr. Ferry Porsche alleged), it is *not* evident from these photos. In the open car doorway stand, left to right, Drs. Ley and Porsche. The man in the snappy looking civilian suit and bow tie at left is Göring's aide and Nazi biographer, Dr. Erich Gritzbach, who testified on his behalf at Nürnberg during Göring's trial in 1945-46. (HGA)

Göring (center) surveys the VW Beetle. From left to right are Drs. Porsche and Lafferentz, with Dr. Ley to the right of Göring. The leading conservatives had been invited to attend the Congress, according to British author Richard Overy, but they declined, since they—like their colleague Dr. Hjalmar Schacht—were opposed to the "crazy" and "wild" Nazi notions of pursuing autarky and unrestricted rearmament; the die had been cast, and on 4 September Göring reported to the State Council of Ministers on the scope of his new powers to be delegated from the Führer, rejecting flatly the more cautious economic policies of both Schacht and Dr. Carl Gördeler, Mayor of Leipzig until his ouster that same year. (HGA)

Göring again is seen sitting in the car's rear. Drs. Ferdinand Porsche (dark suit) and Lafferentz (right) look on, while Dr. Ley stands just opposite Göring, his chief. Dr. Gritzbach has his hands ir his suit pockets, third from far left. (Previously unpublished photo from the Hermann Göring Albums, LC.)

An interesting postscript to our story occurred in April 1944 at Salzburg, Austria, a few months before the D-Day invasion of northwestern Europe, as Hitler's own VW Beetle convertible with top up pulls up to the curb. Reich Security Service/RSD watched the happy crowd at left. Note also that the wartime headlamp covers are in place for nighttime driving, as is also the Notek driving lamp at center on the hood. (HHA)

The Reich Youth leader in the front passenger seat of a VW V2 convertible with the top down before the war. Dr. Ferdinand Porsche is in the rear seat, partially obscured by von Schirach's peaked cap. Stated Dr. Ferry Porsche, "With the start of the war, the propaganda sales tour through Germany that Volkswagen had undertaken in 1939 was, of course, cancelled. Hitler received the first convertible model as a gift, but apart from this…it was mainly the Gauleiters/Regional Leaders who got first choice of those 50 initial production cars and were put at the top of the list for 'company' cars. There was, however, another aspect of our involvement with the manufacture of the People's Car that proved very useful to us at Porsche. At about that time, I was given the opportunity to meet practically everyone of importance in the German government, while preserving the first production cars with my engineers. For instance, I went on a propaganda tour for the car with Göring, and another with Göbbels, and on a third tour with Reich Youth Leader Baldur von Schirach." (HHA)

VW Model B delivery van Type 88. (VWM)

Far Left: Hitler's kafer—the Beetle, 1939. A 1939 sedan hardtop model with Stüttgart license plate in front of Berlin's famous Brandenburger Tor/Brandenburg Gate. As he stated in 1943, Hitler planned for production to reach 1 ½ million units after the war, but the Beetle hit 22 million within three decades after 1945. He called it "The car of the future," and he was proven right! (*Berlin Illustrated News*)

Left: Gushed *The Berlin Illustrated News* of the People's Car, "Everybody knows it, and after the war, there will be hundreds of thousands of them on the roads. It was designed on the instructions of the Leader by the German Labor Front for employees and workmen. It costs RM 975—and can be bought on an easy purchase system with weekly payments of RM 5." *(Berlin Illustrated News)*

Automotive artist Hans Lizka's drawing of a Mercedes Beetle as seen through a ladies' millinery shop window. (LC)

Far Left: The Volkswagen Savings Card and other memorabilia. The cover of the 1939 KdF sales brochure entitled *Your KdF-Wagen*, superimposed over the Savings Plan booklet. (CER)

Left: A German Reich postage stamp commemorating the 1939 International Auto Show at Berlin—that Hitler always attended from 1933 on—with the focus on his dream: the "People's Car," or Volkswagen, with an Autobahn overpass seen at rear. (CER)

According to Gilmore's article "The KdF Wagen: Germany's Car for the Masses!" in the February 1992 issue of *VW Trends* magazine, "The 5 RM savers stamps were purchased weekly and pasted on the KdF savers card. The stamps had an embossed KdF Wagen, and the background was either red or green ink." (CER)

Added Gilmore, "The German toy manufacturers sensed the popularity of the KdF Wagen and produced it in miniature form. The two rare die-cast models pictured here were manufactured by Marklin in 1939." (Gilmore Collection, LC)

Far Left: Noted Gilmore, "At the ground breaking cornerstone ceremony for the dedication of the KdF factory in May 1938, these lapel pins were given out to those in attendance." (Gilmore Collection, LC)

Left: Continued Gilmore, "In 1933, Hitler announced the need for a 'People's car,' and six years later the KdF Wagen was on display at the 1939 Berlin Auto Show." (Gilmore Collection, LC)

Asserted Gilmore, "This is the front and back of the KdF savers card [normally it is folded in half]. On the reverse side is room for 50 each of the 5 RM savers stamps. Information on the card shows four booklets have been completed, and this is the fifth booklet. Those are rare 4 RM stamps in the upper left corner for the additional costs of a sunroof model of the KdF Wagen." Note the date on the card, March 11, 1939, and the VW symbol stamped on both front and back—the Nazi spinning swastika-and-gear symbol of the DAF that was then is use for the KdF Wagen as well. The card belongs to Herr Otto Meier. His stamps and records of payments are seen at the left. (Gilmore Collection, LC)

Zur Beachtung!

1. Für verlorengegangene oder sonst abhanden gekommene Sparkarten oder -marken wird Ersatz **nicht** geleistet.
2. Jede voll geklebte Sparkarte ist der zuständigen Gaudienststelle der NSG-KdF, Abteilung Gaukassenwart, **unverzüglich** einzusenden. (Einschreiben.)
3. Sofern innerhalb 3 Wochen Gutschrift nicht eingeht, ist dies der unter 2. genannten Dienststelle **sofort** zu melden.
4. **Wohnungsänderungen müssen der für den alten Wohnsitz zuständigen Gaudienststelle der NSG-KdF, Abt. KdF-Wagen, unverzüglich gemeldet werden.**
5. Im übrigen gelten die Bestimmungen des Merkblatts zum Antrag auf Ausstellung einer KdF-Wagen-Sparkarte.

Nur für den Dienstgebrauch:

Eingangsdatum: ______

Karte Nr.: ______ Wert: RM ______

Die Deutsche Arbeitsfront

KdF-WAGEN-SPARKARTE

(Nicht übertragbar)

Sparer Nr. 11 622

Vor- und Zuname (bei Frauen auch Geburtsname)

Wohnort: ______ Poststation: ______

Straße: ______ Nr. ______

Beruf: ______

Vertragsbeginn: 17.8.1942

Volkswagenwerk

According to *The Volkswagen Story* in *After the Battle* in 1976, "A reproduction of KdF savers card # 11,622. Volkswagen would still honor a card today." This card is dated August 17, 1942, and it is significant to note that the VW has replaced the swastika at last in the final version; soon, the gear wheel would be replaced by a normal circle, and the surrounding broken circles would disappear as well. (ATB)

Stated Gilmore, "An application was required to be filled out to enroll in the KdF savers program. Upon acceptance into the program, a confirmation postcard like this one was sent to the applicant." (Gilmore Collection, LC)

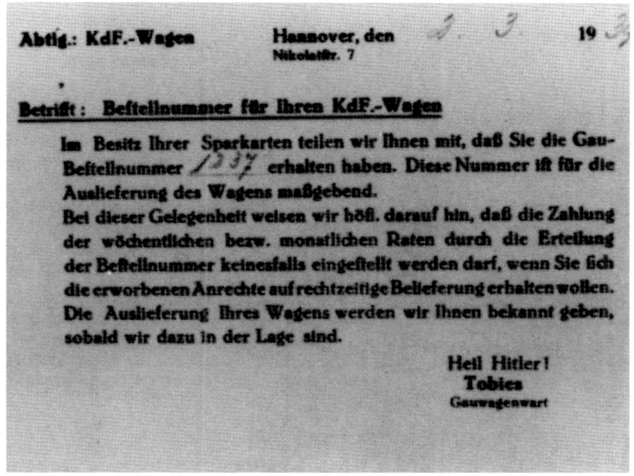

Abtlg.: KdF.-Wagen **Hannover, den** 2. 3. **19** 39
Nikolaistr. 7

Betrifft: Bestellnummer für Ihren KdF.-Wagen

Im Besitz Ihrer Sparkarten teilen wir Ihnen mit, daß Sie die Gau-Bestellnummer 1237 **erhalten haben. Diese Nummer ist für die Auslieferung des Wagens maßgebend.**
Bei dieser Gelegenheit weisen wir höfl. darauf hin, daß die Zahlung der wöchentlichen bezw. monatlichen Raten durch die Erteilung der Bestellnummer keinesfalls eingestellt werden darf, wenn Sie sich die erworbenen Anrechte auf rechtzeitige Belieferung erhalten wollen.
Die Auslieferung Ihres Wagens werden wir Ihnen bekannt geben, sobald wir dazu in der Lage sind.

Heil Hitler!
Tobies
Gauwagenwart

Noted Gilmore, "The reverse of a confirmation post card. The translation, "Department: KdF Wagen Hannover 2 March 1939. Regarding: Reference for your KdF Wagen. In possession of your saver cards, we are informing you that you have received the district reference number 1237. This number is provided for the delivery of the car. At the same time, we politely advise that the weekly installments that were established with the reference number are not to be cancelled if you want to attain the required rights to the timely delivery. We will advise you of the delivery of your car as soon as we are in a position to do so. Heil Hitler! Tobies [name of District Mechanic]." (Gilmore Collection, LC)

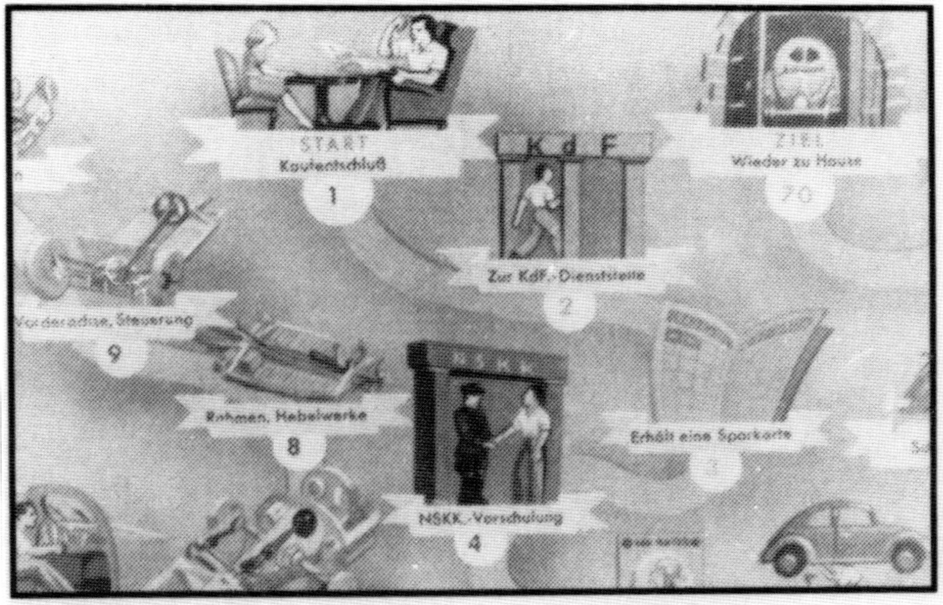

Stated Gilmore, "This close-up view of the KdF game board is the start in which the player decides to purchase a KdF Wagen, takes the application to the DAF, receives a KdF savers card, and then begins the tour of the KdF factory." (Gilmore Collection, LC)

Concluded Gilmore, "There were other board games available. This one shows the little KdF game pieces photographed on top of the game box cover." (Gilmore Collection, LC)

Nazi-era Volkswagen Beetle toys and games. Stated Gilmore, "If you were in the market for a JNF split window tin VW, then this was your day. Here are six to choose from, and that is a CKO flip top VW (one on the right) with the original box." (Gilmore Collection, LC)

"This was a nice display of…a Gamma fire VW, Huki, Tipp and Co., and a CKO flip top VW," stated Gilmore in 1992. (Gilmore Collection, LC)

The popular KdF Gameboard for future owners of the Nazi-produced People's Car. Stated Gilmore, "At the end of the game, the first player to complete the course received the fines accumulated, and this was an incentive to put the winnings towards buying a savers stamp." (Gilmore Collection, LC)

Color Gallery

Hitler dedicates the VW factory at Fallersleben/Wolfsburg on May 26, 1938, with a Beetle hardtop model down in front and an NSKK man standing at right. (Hugo Jaeger Collection)

Dr. Bödo Lafferentz speaks at the lec:ern at left. In front of him are, from left to right, the VW :ollapsible sunroof model, the convertible model with top and all windows rolled down, and the hardtop. The license plates, all from Stüttgart, are, from left to right: IIA-42802, IIIA-42803, and IIIA-42801. (Hugo Jaeger Collec:ion)

At the February 1939 Berlin auto show, the VW Beetle convertible is closely examined. From left to right at center are Dr. Ferdinand Porsche, Dr. Bodo Lafferentz, Hitler, Dr. Robert Ley, Dr. Ferry Porsche, and an unknown SS officer. The display lasted from February 17-March 5, 1939, the last under the Nazis. (Hugh Jaeger Collection)

The scale model belonging to Dr. Ley of the inner workings of the Beetle is examined at the February 1939 Berlin auto show by (from left) Dr. Ley, Hitler, unknown man, and Dr. Ferdinand Porsche, watched by several officers in SS black and officials in Nazi Party brown. Note the spare parts! (Hugo Jaeger Collection)

From left to right: NSKK aide Albert Bormann, Dr. Bodo Lafferentz, Dr. Ferdinand Porsche, unknown official, Hitler, Dr. Robert Ley, six unknown aides, and Dr. Ferry Porsche all looking at the VW Beetle convertible model at the February 1939 Berlin auto show. (Hugo Jaeger Collection)

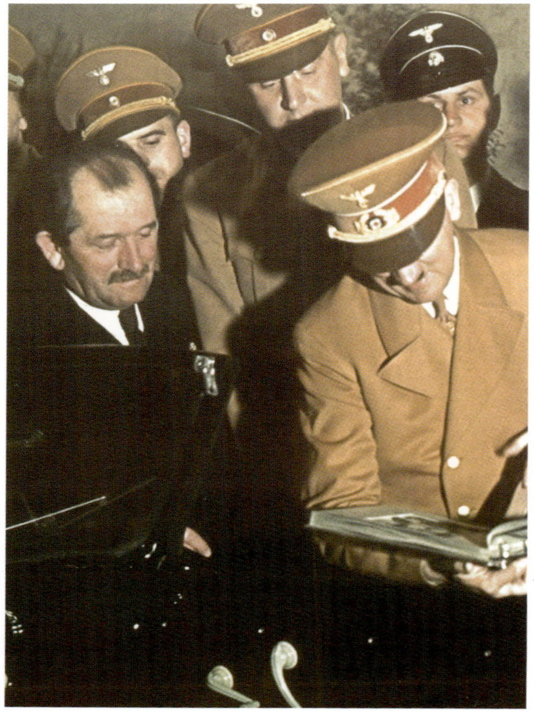

Hitler leafs through a photo album compiled of the first VW's production process, as Drs. Ferdinand Porsche (left) and Bodo Lafferentz (third from left) look on. (Hugo Jaeger Collection)

Volskwagen at the very epicenter of the Nazi empire and madness—literally! The Beetle is backed up by a trio of desert-colored VW Kübelwagens for North African service, surrounded by (clockwise) a Nazi judge in judicial robes; burning, bombed buildings; a Nazi mass rally, the cover of Julius Streicher's *Der Sturmer/The Stormer* with a burning synagogue from Crystal Night in 1938; a guillotine for executions; the railroad tracks to Auschwitz and the yellow Star of David that Jews were forced to wear; the crematoria ovens at a death camp with a striped-uniformed inmate, a black-jacketed SS man and wartime profiteer; the burning of the books and Dr. Ley's ocean liner cruises for DAF employees; the Viking god Wotan with a shield emblazoned with SS runes, the Nazi self-view of their "kultur"/culture, with swastika banner and torch; "back to the soil" with farmers and Göring's Four Year Plan smokestacks, drummers of the Hitler Youth, SA men with banners, a Death's Head, the logo of the film studio Ufa that produced propaganda movies for Dr. Göbbels (seen speaking via radio over top the DAF symbol and German girls of the BDM playing ball atop Panzer tanks); an SA man standing guard in front of one of the joint Hitler-Speer architectural columns, the Führer as prince awakening the sleeping maiden-princess of Germany, the Russian Communist sickle-and-hammer emblem and the triple arrows of the German Red KPD Party; the domed Congress Hall that Hitler meant to build for Berlin after the Third Reich won the war in 1950; Stuka dive bombers dropping bombs, the V-1 and V-2 rockets in which Volkswagen participated, Nazi flags, the "Blood and Soil" eagle with German maidens bringing in the harvest, symbols of the SA and NSFK over top Mercedes-Benz Grosser cars (left) and racers (right); barriers of Dr. Todt's West Wall/Siegfried Line, bombed out Germany in 1945, the Jews and the SS in the 1943 Warsaw Ghetto Uprising, German POWs surrendering to the Allies, the shadow of the Gestapo, the specter of death, Moabit Prison in Berlin, rolling artillery on parade, the crosses of dead buried Germans across Europe with their helmets atop, a U-boat, and the Iron Cross. (Allegorical painting courtesy of John H. Bloecher, Jr., Danzig Study Group, Baltimore.)

"Your KdF Wagen," a poster designed to popularize the new People's Car among young people, much as do current American advertisements in the media. The model is a VW Beetle sunroof car. The term "KdF" stood for Dr. Ley's "Strength Through Joy" organization that was building what everyone popularly called the Volkswagen—the People's Car—but Hitler dubbed it the KdF Wagen during the May 26, 1938, dedication ceremony, and it was thus so advertised during the Third Reich's life. Despite Hitler, however, the simpler VW label stuck fast with the populace, even under the Nazi regime. (Library of Congress, Washington, DC)

The hardtop and convertible model Beetles made the cover of the German magazine *Motor Schau/Show* in July 1938, published in Berlin. Note, too, the Nazi DAF logo displayed prominently at the left above them. (*Military Illustrated*, UK)

The KdF poster headline reads, "You must save five marks a week if you want to drive your own car!" and advertises the unique VW layaway plan. The car is set against a backdrop of a pre-payment plan booklet cover. Unlike the American system of getting the car and paying later, the Germans paid for it in advance by installments, and by the time Nazi Germany fell in May 1945, the fund contained $67 million Reichsmarks left untouched by the Nazis, seized as reparations by the Red Army in fallen Berlin. In this advertisement, note the III on the license plate, indicating the city of Stüttgart; I was for Berlin and II was for Münich. (Blocher/ DSG.)

The Savings Card cover of the KdF Booklet. The headline below reads, "Your KdF Wagen," showing a VW Bug climbing alpine roads. (LC)

A standard wartime VW Beetle with a VW Schwimmer parked in the garage behind it, both painted in desert brown; two Wehrmacht workhorses of World War II. (Captured Enemy records, U.S. National Archives, College Park, MD.)

In 1942 at Führer Headquarters, Hitler predicted during a "table talk" conversation that the VW would become the car of the future, with sales of over a million. Here, he takes a wartime spin in his convertible Bug around his *Wolf's Lair* military headquarters, Rastenburg, East Prussia, driven by an RSD/Reich Security Service man rather than by his usual chauffeur, SS Lt. Col. Erich Kempka, with RFSS Himmler in back, holding his cane Hitler's boast that the VW would one day be the best selling car in the world came true decades after his death in 1945. (Walter Frentz photo.)

The automotive dream of Hitler and Prof. Porsche realized: the hardtop version of the VW as it appeared in a prewar sales brochure, and a cutaway view showing the luggage compartment, passengers, and the rear-mounted engine upon which the Führer insisted. The car was intended to provide affordable popular transportation for the average German to travel on the newly built Autobahn highways of Dr. Fritz Todt. Had the Nazis won World War II, these would've extended deep into the conquered Soviet Union as well. (Roger Wychgram Collection, Aberdeen, MD.)

Two more cutaway views of the VW Beetle during the Third Reich era. Its home plant at Wolfsburg would later rate as one the world's largest factories, to be joined by five more throughout Germany after the war. (Wychgram)

A cutaway view of the VW Beetle. As with the air-cooled engine concept, it was the Führer, too, who insisted that the engine be in the rear of the new car design, and not in front. The New Beetle of the 21st Century reversed his original idea after six decades. (Wychgram)

Bug with U.S. Army star at Omaha Beach Museum, Normandy, France, 2009. (*Volks World*)

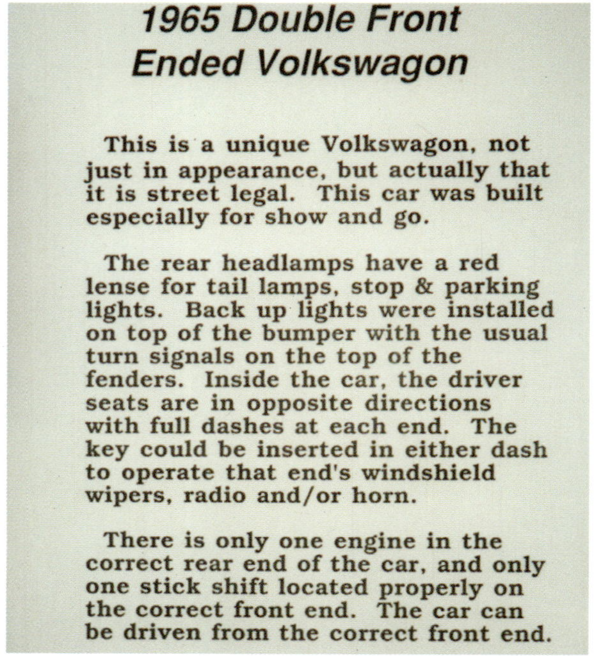

Having it *both* ways: a display during the 1989 Baltimore Convention Center Auto Show. (Previously unpublished photos by Blaine Taylor, Towson, MD.)

It sat two and came in dual colors, with ivory and black being the public's favorites. It was a far cry from 1938, when only dark blue-gray was the sole color available! Today's New Beetle comes in the following shades of choice for prospective buyers: yellow, silver, red, black, white, blue, light blue, and green; and with the following interior shades for seating: gray cloth, black cloth, black leather, gray leather, cream leather, black, gray, and cream leatherette. (VW Museum, Wolfsburg, Germany.)

The rear-mounted engine. (Wychgram)

Hitler (front, right) and RFSS Himmler (rear) in Hitler's Beetle convertible at FHQ, 1942. (Walter Frentz.)

Scale models left to right of the VW Kubel, Schwimmer, and convertible Beetle (bottom), and another, larger Schwimmer (top.) Note the bar mounted machine gun on the latter, the exhaust pipe at rear, and the spare tire on the front. (Previously unpublished photo by Chris Henry, Towson, MD.)

The author in 1971 with his red 1970 Super Beetle convertible. I wanted a convertible, and at that time, VW was the only car manufacturer that made one, but I had to learn driving a stick shift all over again, from my days in the Army! According to authoress Kate McLeod in *Beetlemania*, it was "the most popular convertible ever built…" and cost $2,299, but went out of production in 1975. (Previously unpublished photo by Joyce Lynn Gaston Taylor, BT Archives, Towson, MD.)

Bibliography

Books

General Reference:

Armored Fighting Vehicles by Philip Trewhitt, London, Barnes & Noble Books, 1999

Blood, Tears, and Folly: An Objective Look at World War II by Len Deighton, Edison, NJ, Castle Books, 1993

Langensheidt's German-English Dictionary, New York, Pocket Books, 1960

The Other Nuremberg: The Untold Story of the Tokyo War Crimes Trials by Arnold C. Brackman, New York, William Morrow & Co., Inc., 1987

Strange Victory: Hitler's Conquest of France by Ernest R. May, New York, Hill and Wang, 2000

The Complete Idiot's Guide to 20th Century History by Alan Axelrod, PhD, New York, 1999

The Third Reich Day by Day by Christopher Ailsby, London, Zenith Press, 2001

Collective Biography:

Leaders and Personalities of the Third Reich: Their Biographies, Portraits and Autographs by Charles Hamilton, San Jose, CA, R. James Bender Publishing, 1984

On the Field of Honor: A History of the Knight's Cross Bearers, Vols. I and II by LTC John R. Angolia, San Jose, CA, R. James Bender Publishing, 1979-80

General Nazi/ German Reference Works

Allgemeine SS: The Commands, Units, and Leaders of the General SS by Mark C. Yerger, Atglen, PA, Schiffer Publishing, 1997

Arms and Uniforms/The Second World War, Vol. 1 by Liliane and Fred Funcken, London, Ward Lock, Ltd., 1975

Art as Politics in the Third Reich by Jonathan Petropolous, Chapel Hill, NC, 1996

Battle of the Bulge: Then and Now by Jean Paul Pallud, *After the Battle*, 1984

The Biographical Dictionary of World War II by Mark M. Boatner, III, Novato, CA, Presidio Press, 1996

Combat Medals of the Third Reich by Christopher Ailsby, Wellingborough, Northhamptonshire, United Kingdom, 1987

Deutschland Erwache: The History and Development of the Nazi Party and the "Germany Awake" Standards by Ulric of England, assisted by Otto Spronk, San Jose, CA, R. James Bender Publishing, 1987

Encyclopedia of the Third Reich by Louis L. Snyder, New York, McGraw-Hill, Inc., 1976

The Encyclopedia of the Third Reich edited by Christian Zentner and Friedemann Bedurftig, New York, DaCapo Press, 1997

German Aircraft of the Second World War by J. R. Smith and Anthony L. Kay, Baltimore, Nautical & Aviation Publishing Co. of America, 1972

Germany by Terrence Prittie, New York, Time-Life Books, 1961

German Tanks at War by Bob Carruthers, London, Cassell & Co., 2000

German Uniforms of the Third Reich, 1933-45 by Brian Leigh Davis and Pierre Turner, New York, Arco Publishers, Inc., 1980

Guarding the Führer: Sepp Dietrich, Johann Rattenhuber, and the Protection of Adolf Hitler by Blaine Taylor, Missoula, MT, Pictorial Histories Publishing, Inc., 1993

Headgear of Hitler's Germany, Vol. 4 by William P.B.R. Saris et al, San Jose, CA, R. James Bender, 2005

The Historical Encyclopedia of World War II, New York, Facts on File, Inc., 1989

The History of the Fallschirm Pankerkorps (Parachute Armored Corps) Hermann Göring by Franz Kurowski, Winnipeg, Manitoba, Canada, J.J. Federowicz, 1995

Hitler's Military Headquarters: Organization, Structures, Security, and Personnel by Aaron L. Johnson, San Jose, CA, R. James Bender Publishing, 1999

Hitler's Secret Conversations, 1941-44, New York, Signet Books, 1953

Hitler: Speeches and Proclamations, 1932-45, Vols. 1-4 by Max Domarus, Wauconda, IL, Bolchazy-Carducci Publishers, 1990

Hitler's Table Talk, 1941-44, New York, Enigma Books, 2000

Hitler's War by David Irving, New York, Viking Press, 1977

Nazi Regalia by Jack Pia, New York, Ballantine Books, 1971

Nazism: A History in Documents and Eyewitness Accounts, 1919-45 by J. Noakes and G. Pridham, Editors, New York, Schocken Books, 1983

The NSDAP, edited by Alfred Salazar, Imperial Publications, 1990

NSKK/NSFK: Uniforms, Organization, and History by John R. Angolia and David Littlejohn, San Jose, CA, R. James Bender Publishing, 1994

Orders, Decorations, Medals, and Badges of the Third Reich by David Littlejohn and Col. C.M. Dodkins, San Jose, CA, R. James Bender Publishing, 1968

The Oxford Companion to World War II by General Editor I.C.B. Dear, Oxford and New York, Oxford University Press, 1995

Political Leaders of the NSDAP, edited by L. Milner, London, Almark Publications, 1972
Postcards of Hitler's Germany, Vol. 2, 1937-39 by R. James Bender, San Jose, CA, R. James Bender Publishing, 1998
Seduced by Hitler: The Choices of a Nation and the Ethics of Survival by Adam LeBor and Roger Boyes, Naperville, IL, Sourcebooks, Inc., 2001
Soldiers of Destruction: The SS Death's Head Division, 1933-45 by Charles W. Sydnor, Jr.; Princeton University Press, 1977
Third Reich Militaria by Robin Lumsden, London, Ian Allan Ltd., 1987
The Third Reich Almanac by James Taylor and Warren Shaw, New York, Pharos Books, 1987
Tiger I on the Western Front by Jean Restayn, Paris, Histoire & Collections, 2001
Uniforms and Badges of the Third Reich, Vol. II: *SA, NSKK, SS* by Rudolf Kahl, Kedichem, Holland, Military Collectors Service
The Underground Military Command Bunkers of Zossen, Germany by Hans George Kampe, Atglen, PA, Schiffer Military, 1996
War and Economy in the Third Reich by R.J. Overy, Oxford, UK, Clarendon Press, 1994
Who's Who in Nazi Germany by Robert Wistrich, New York, Bonanza Books, 1982

General Automobile Reference Works:

The Classic Car: The Ultimate Book About the World's Greatest Automobiles, edited by Beverly Rae Kimes, Classic Car Club of America, Inc., Stillwater, WI, Motorbooks International, 1990
The Complete Encyclopedia of Motorcars: 1885 to the Present, edited by G. N. Georgano, New York, E.P. Dutton and Co., Inc., 1968
Die Deutsche Cabrilolet/1945 bis Heute (The German Cabriolets/1945 to the Present) by Hans W. Mayer, Stüttgart, Motorbuch, 1985
Deutsche Autos/German Cars, 1920-45 by Werner Oswald, Stüttgart, Motorbuch Verlag, 1990
The Coachwork of Erdmann & Rossi, Berlin by Rupert Stuhlemmer, London, Dalton Watson, Ltd., 1979
Eyewitness Car by Richard Sutton, New York, DK Publishing, Inc., 2005
Historic Military Vehicles Directory by Bart Vanderveen, London, *After the Battle*, 1989
The Star and the Laurel: The Centennial History of Daimler, Mercedes, and Benz, 1886-1986 by Beverly Rae Kimes, Montvalle, NJ, Mercedes-Benz of North America, Inc., 1986
The Classic Mercedes-Benz by Phil Drackett, New York, Exeter Books, 1983
Great Marques: Mercedes-Benz by Roger Bell, Secaucus, NJ, Chartwell Books, Inc., 1989
Mercedes by Nigel Fryat, New York, Brompton Books Corps, 1991
Mercedes: The Complete History of the Marque by Graham Robson, London, Chevprime Limited, 1988
Great Marques of Germany, compiled and edited by Jonathan Wood, London, Octopus Books, 1985
Mercedes-Benz Personnenwagen (Personal Cars), 1886-1984 by Werner Oswald, Stüttgart, Motorbuch Verlag, 1985
Military Vehicles of World War II by John Church, New York, Crescent Books, 1982
Wheeled Vehicles of the Wehrmacht/Cars, Personnel Carriers, Trucks, Buses, Tractors, Motorcycles, Special Types edited by Chris Ellis, Bedfordshire, England, Avocet Books, 1988

Books About Volkswagen: The Beetle, the Kübelwagen, and the Schwimmwagen

Armament, Production and Forced Labor at Volkswagen by Klaus-Georg Siegfried, Federal Republic of Germany
Birth of the Beetle: The Development of the Volkswagen by Ferdinand Porsche by Chris Barber, Sparkford, UK, Haynes Publishing, 2003
Beetlemania by Kate McLeod, New York, Smithmark Publishers, 1999
Bug: The History of the Volkswagen, Bug: The Strange Mutations of the World's Most Famous Automobile by Phil Patton, New York, Simon & Schuster, 2002
Ersatzteiliste/Spar Parts List Typ 7 (166), Stadt des KdF-Wagens, April 1943
Fix Your Volkswagen: Volkswagen Owner's and Mechanic's Handbook of Repair and Maintenance by Larry Johnson, South Holland, IL, Goodheart-Willcox Co., Inc., 1974
Leichter Personenfraftwagen/Light Personal Cars K2s Typ 166, Berlin, May 12, 1942
The New Beetle by Matt DeLorenzo, Osceola, WI, MBI Publishing Co., 1998
The New VW Beetle: The Creation of a 21st Century Classic by Jonathan Wood, Ann Arbor, MI, Borders Press, 1998
Small Wonder: The Amazing Story of the Volkswagen by Walter Henry Nelson, Boston, Little, Brown and Co., 1965
The Volkswagen Beetle by Jonathan Wood, Haversfordwest, UK, Shire Publications Ltd.
Volkswagen Chronicle by Graham Robson and the auto editors of *Consumer Guide*, Lincolnwood, IL, Publications International, Ltd., 1996
Volkswagen and Its Workers During the Third Reich by Dr. Hans Mommsen, Volkswagenwerk, Federal Republic of Germany, 1996
Volkswagen KdF-Wagen, 1934-45 by Terry Shuler, Indianapolis, IN, Beeman Jorgensen, Inc., 1999
Volkswagen Military Vehicles of the Third Reich: An Illustrated History by Blaine Taylor, Cambridge, MA, DaCapo Press, 2004
Volkswagens of the Wehrmacht by Hans-Georg Mayer-Stein, Atglen, PA, Schiffer Publishing Ltd., 1994
2001 Volkswagen Media Information Kit, Volkswagen of America, Inc., Auburn Hills, MI
VW at War: Kübelwagen, Schwimmwagen, and Special Vehicles by Michael Sawodny, Atglen, PA, Schiffer Military History, 1991
VW at War Book Two: Development, Testing, Production by Dr. Bernd Wiersch, Atglen, PA, Schiffer Military History, 1992
VW Beetle at War by Dr. Hans-Georg Mayer, Atglen, PA, Schiffer Military History, 1992
VW Beetle by Clive Prew, New York, Mallard Press, 1990
VW Beetle by Keith Seume, Osceola, WI, Motorbooks International, 1997
Your Kdf-Wagen, Lakeville, MN, USM, Inc., 1993

First Person Accounts:

Hitler at My Side by LTG Hans Baur, Houston, TX, Eichler Publishing, Corp., 1986
The Memoirs of Field Marshal Keitel, New York, Cooper Square Press, 2001
Memoirs by Franz von Papen, New York, E.P. Dutton and Co., Inc., 1953
We at Porsche: The Autobiography of Dr. Ing. H.c. Ferry Porsche with John Bentley, Garden City, NY, Doubleday & Co., Inc., 1976

The Rommel Papers by Field Marshal Erwin Rommel, New York, Harcourt, Brace and Co., 1953
Berlin Diary by William L. Shirer, New York, Bonanza Books, 1984
Memoirs: Inside the Third Reich by Albert Speer, New York, The Macmillan Co., 1970
Spandau: The Secret Diaries by Albert Speer, New York, The Macmillan Co., 1976
Infiltration: How Heinrich Himmler Schemed to Build an SS Industrial Empire by Albert Speer, New York, The Macmillan Co., 1981

Biographies:
Göring by Roger Manvell and Heinrich Fraenkel, New York, Simon & Schuster, 1962
Göring: The "Iron Man" by R. J. Overy, London, Routledge and Kegan Paul, 1984
The Good Nazi: The Life and Lies of Albert Speer by Dan van der Vat, Boston, Houghton Mifflin Co., 1997
Hitler's Personal Pilot: The Life and Times of Hans Baur by C.G. Sweeting, Dulles, VA, Brassey's, Inc., 2000
Mussolini's Shadow: The Double Life of Count Galeazzo Ciano by Ray Moseley, New Haven, CT, Yale University Press, 1999

Other:
The 12-Year Reich: A Social History of Nazi Germany, 1933-45 by Richard Grunberger, New York; Holt, Rinehart, and Winston.

Museums, Archives, Libraries, and Collections:
The Anne S. K. Brown Military Collection, Peter Harrington, Curator, Brown University, Providence, RI
The Danzig Study Group, John H. Bloecher, Jr., Baltimore
The Eva Braun Hitler Albums, The US National Archives, College Park, MD
The Hermann Göring Albums, The Library of Congress, Washington, DC
The Heinrich Hoffmann Albums, The US National Archives, College Park, MD
The Joachim von Ribbentrop Albums, The US National Archives, College Park, MD
The Porsche Museum, Gmund, Carinthia, Austria
The Porsche Museum, Stüttgart, Federal Republic of Germany
The US Army Combat Art Collection, US Army Center of Military History, Renee Klish, Curator, Ft. Lesley J. McNair, Wash., DC
The US Army Signal Corps, The US National Archives, College Park, MD
National Capital Historic Sales, George Peterson, Springfield, VA
Volkswagen Museum, Wolfsburg, Federal Republic of Germany
Volkswagen of America Public Relations Department, Auburn, MI
The Roger Wychgram Collection. Aberdeen, MD

Magazine Articles:
"Adolf Hitler Dedicates the World's First Volkswagen Factory," *VW Trends,* Blaine Taylor, October 1992
"Beetles in Brown Shirts?" *History Today,* Michael Burleigh, November1992
"The Birth of the Beetle," *World War II Investigator,* Blaine Taylor, October 1988
"The Birth of the Volkswagen Beetle," *Car Collector,* Blaine Taylor, November 1987
"The Birth of the Volkswagen Beetle: A Little-Known Story," *Maryland Automotive Journal,* Blaine Taylor, February 1990
"Birth of the VW Beetle," *Bulb Horn,* Blaine Taylor, July-September 1986
"Hermann Göring Meets the Volkswagen," *VW Trends,* Blaine Taylor, July 1992
"Infamous Politician Begets Beloved Beetle," *Automotive News Centennial Celebration of the Car,* Blaine Taylor, Oct. 30, 1985
"Volkswagen 'Jeep' is Alive and Well in Mexico, Literally," *Motor Trend,* Steve Smith, March 1973
"The Four Battles for Kharkov," *After the Battle,* Karel Margry, 2001
"The KdF Wagen: Germany's Car for the Masses!" *VW Trends,* Robert Gilmore, February 1992
"VW Classics Toy Show," *VW Trends,* Robert Gilmore, October 1992
"Kubel and Schwimmwagen: It Happened Here," *After the Battle,* Kevin Brownlow and Andrew Mollo, 1966
"The People's Car," *Military Machines,* Blaine Taylor, December 2006
"Die Porsche Story," *Der Spiegel,* July 2009
"Porsche at War," *Military Machines,* Blaine Taylor, August 2007
"The Volkswagen Kübelwagen:Off-Road Vehicle of the Third Reich," *VW Trends* Staff and Blaine Taylor, March 1995
"VW Kübelwagen," *Military Machines,* Blaine Taylor, February 2007
"The VW Kübelwagen: An Illustrated History," Blaine Taylor, *VW Trends,* March 1995
"The Volkswagen Story," *After the Battle, 1976*
"VW Schwimmwagen," *Military Machines,* Blaine Taylor. April 2007
Volks World, October 2004

Newspaper Articles:
"Patient Offspring Runs Indonesia," *The Sun Journal, The Baltimore Sun,* Seth Mydans, July 24, 2001.